Talking Back to Emily Dickinson

Emily Dickinson

and Other Essays

TALKING BACK TO EMILY DICKINSON

and Other Essays

❧

William H. Pritchard

University of Massachusetts Press

AMHERST

Copyright © 1998 by William H. Pritchard
All rights reserved
Printed in the United States of America
LC 98-10322
ISBN 1-55849-138-4

Designed by Steve Dyer
Set in Adobe Minion
Printed and bound by Braun-Brumfield, Inc.

Library of Congress Cataloging-in-Publication Data
Pritchard, William H.
Talking back to Emily Dickinson, and other essays /
William H. Pritchard.
p.   cm.
Includes bibliographical references and index.
ISBN 1-55849-138-4 (alk. paper)
1. English literature—History and criticism.
2. American literature—History and criticism. I. Title.
PR99.P74   1998
820.9—dc21   98-10322
CIP

British Library Cataloguing in Publication data are available.

For *Warner Berthoff* and *Roger Sale*

who talked back to me

Contents

❧⸱❧

Acknowledgments

Except for "Writing Well Is the Best Revenge"—a survey of some fierce back-talkings by one writer to another—the essays are arranged chronologically by subject, from Shakespeare to the present. They include two previously unprinted talks: "Wordsworth's 'Resolution and Independence'" was given at Denis Donoghue's Henry James Seminar in Practical Criticism, New York University, December 1995; "Talking Back to Emily Dickinson" was given at the second annual conference of the Association of Literary Scholars and Critics, Boston, September 1996.

The bulk of these pieces were commissioned by and appeared in *The Hudson Review,* and I should like to thank its editors, Frederick Morgan and Paula Deitz, for their faithful and continuing support of my work.

As with a previous collection of essays and reviews, *Playing It by Ear,* Christopher Benfey gave me good advice on what and what not to include. Bruce Wilcox and Pamela Wilkinson are, in my experience, ideal editors.

Thanks to Susan Raymond for word processing and Julie Howland for proofreading, and to Amherst College for its support of this project.

Preface

ᰍᰍᰍ

O NE OF MY TEACHERS ONCE said that criticism, as well as speaking
back to the work of art, should try to do it one better. Presumptuous
as that sounds, it's not a bad way to think of the critic's burden to say
something new, rather than dutifully rehearse what the art in question has
already done very well. Each of the pieces in this collection attempts a fresh
look at a literary achievement through the lens of one reader reading—for
pleasure, imaginative extension of the self, moral instruction, professional
advancement, and (sometimes) money. At least some of these qualities and
effects used to be good names for what we presumably received from the
experience of literature. In Matthew Arnold's essays, for example, the stakes
were raised to the point where literature's high destiny became virtually
limitless: "More and more mankind will discover that we have to turn to
poetry to interpret life for us, to console us, to sustain us" ("The Study of
Poetry," 1880). Then inflation was discovered, Arnold was dismissed, and
the air went out of the balloon.

Anyone surveying the literary scene today, especially the criticism of literature, finds that the rules have changed drastically, with qualities that used to
pass as virtues now dismissed as the unfortunate legacy of Arnoldian "hu-
manism." The study of literature has become, we are told, a matter for professionals, practitioners of various academic "approaches" to the text that
have in mind something rather different from what used to be called appreciation. Though an unrepentant academic myself, I find my interests oddly

remote from those of many professional colleagues, especially younger ones. In his preface to *Lyrical Ballads*, Wordsworth declared that poetry was in its essence an homage to "the grand elementary principle of pleasure." One looks vainly in much current study of literature for any connection with that pleasure principle. It is as if an enthusiastic response to art were a species of bad form, or more likely, obsolete.

My corrective effort in these pieces is not, I hope, to nag a theme by way of insisting on my own virtuous procedures while condemning everyone else's. Many of the essays are wholly directed at celebrating an achievement—the literary criticism of Ford Madox Ford, Anthony Powell's *A Dance to the Music of Time*, the poetry of Robert Penn Warren—and have little or no polemical edge. They are "occasional" essays in that most of them take an occasion—often a new biography or the death of a writer—to revisit and revise a literary career. As with my earlier collection, *Playing It By Ear*, that is the only way I know how to play it, since some kind of "ear-reading" is essential to my apprehension of any imaginative writing, not just poetry. In the classroom I can't go for long without reading aloud some specimen of the writer at hand; so these critical essays attempt a similar practice, though without, except in the metaphorical sense, the aid of a performing voice. I imagine an audience of readers with their own thoughts and opinions who, more than once, will be provoked to disagreement with my accounts—in which case I invite them to talk back to me. Henry James famously remarked that art only lives "upon discussion . . . upon the exchange of views and the comparison of standpoints." My own discussions are aimed, in however small a way, to help art live.

A book whose title recommends "talking back" may threaten to flaunt the critic's personality and replace the art with something lesser. Referring to his own prose, Orwell speaks of the "struggle to efface one's personality" that should characterize any valuable criticism. And Randall Jarrell, in "The Age of Criticism," says memorably that

> a real critic has no one but himself to depend on. He can never forget that all he has to go by, finally, is his own response, the self that makes and is made up of such responses—and yet he must regard that self as no more than the instrument through which the work of art is seen, so that the work of art will seem everything to him and his own self nothing.

Yet only personalities as distinct and original as Orwell's and Jarrell's know what it means to want to escape from them. As critics they are inexhaustible partly because they fail to efface or negate the selves that animate each of their paragraphs.

There is of course more than one way of talking back to literature, for example, the way recommended by the poet Billy Collins, in his charming poem "The Norton Anthology of English Literature," where he makes a claim for what the activity of reading can do:

> Do you know that it is possible if you read a poem
> enough times, if you read it over and over again without stopping,
> that you can make the author begin to spin gently,
> even affectionately, in his grave?

Through quotation and admiring comment, the critic may try to do something like that. But there is also talking back as a form of aggressive engagement, not always gently and affectionately with the writer in question, whether William Blake or Charlotte Brontë, V. S. Naipaul or Doris Lessing. In the thirty years I've functioned as a working critic—much of that work done in the pages of *The Hudson Review*—I've tried, with equal attention to poetry, fiction, and criticism, to engage with literature in ways both appreciative and argumentative, aesthetic and judgmental. It may be that since so much of my criticism has been done in the reviewing mode, I'm less interested in "interpretation" than I should be. But too much interpretation of literature killeth rather than giveth life, and I seem to have adopted a different guiding principle, Robert Frost's, when at the end of his *Paris Review* interview he talks about writing as performance:

> It's just the same as when you feel a joke coming. You see somebody coming down the street that you're accustomed to abuse, and you feel it rising in you, something to say as you pass each other. Coming over him in the same way. . . . Something does it to you. It's him coming toward you that gives you the animus you know. When they want to know about inspiration, I tell them it's mostly animus.

Frost's connection between the humorous impulse and the impulse to talk back to literature, do it one better, seems to me profound. At any rate, I suspect it's the inspiration behind the present collection.

Talking Back to Emily Dickinson

Emily Dickinson

and Other Essays

Writing Well Is the Best Revenge

✺

WHEN, IN AUGUST 1929, the art critic Thomas Earp adversely criticized both D. H. Lawrence's introduction to a catalogue of his paintings, and the paintings themselves, Lawrence wrote and published the following poem:

> I heard a little chicken chirp:
> My name is Thomas, Thomas Earp!
> And I can neither paint nor write
> I only can set other people right.
>
> All people that can write or paint
> do tremble under my complaint.
> For I am a chicken, and I can chirp;
> and my name is Thomas, Thomas Earp.

How good a weapon is literature for settling scores with someone by making his person or art an object of ridicule? To what extent can we adequately account for a poem, story or novel by locating its origin in spiteful feeling, a determination on the author's part to celebrate—with humorous zest or steely-eyed contempt—the offenses of another?

Surely we have all felt the stirrings of such a retaliatory motive. After my first book was published in this country but not in England, I made bold to send a copy to an English critic interested in my subject. Immediately I

1

received back a neat postcard, graciously thanking me for the book and expressing anticipatory pleasure in sitting down to it. Three months later there appeared a fierce review in *The Spectator* in which the gracious critic took my work to task as a feeble specimen of academic incapacity—"timid," "donnish," "obtuse" were three of the adjectives applied to it. When I got through wincing and weeping (surely I was not obtuse, even if possibly donnish?) the thought of retaliation came to mind, some masterly reply loaded with irony and pity. But friends dissuaded me.

Good advice, yet of the sort not heeded by Alfred Tennyson when he encountered in *Blackwood's Magazine* John Wilson's review of his 1830 volume of poems. Writing under the name Christopher North, Wilson set out in the most patronizing manner to demonstrate that "Alfred," though undeniably a poet, was ridiculously overpraised and would only save himself by hearkening to Christopher North's criticism. Tennyson hearkened only enough to produce these stanzas:

> You did late review my lays,
>   Crusty Christopher;
> You did mingle blame and praise,
>   Rusty Christopher.
> When I learnt from whom it came,
> I forgave you all the blame,
>   Musty Christopher;
> I could *not* forgive the praise,
>   Fusty Christopher.

His friend Arthur Hallam pleaded with him not to include it in his next collection, but to no avail.

My candidate for the most brilliant piece of spitefulness in English poetry is Alexander Pope's portrait of Sporus in his "Epistle to Dr. Arbuthnot." In real life Sporus was an effeminate and profligate courtier, Lord Hervey, who combined with Lady Mary Wortley Montague (another antagonist) in publishing attacks on Pope. In the poem Pope's friend Arbuthnot gives him worldly advice about how the whole affair is not worth wasting his time on: "Satire or Sense alas! can Sporus feel? / Who breaks a Butterfly upon a Wheel?" But Pope, in the grip of an artistic necessity more imperious than merely the need to repay an insult, brushes the advice aside: "Yet let me flap this Bug with gilded wings, / This painted Child of Dirt that stinks and stings"; and proceeds through twenty-five lines of brilliant invention to excoriate Sporus/Hervey as an "Amphibious Thing!", a combination of "Froth" and "Venom." The wheel of Pope's verse is memorable not for the way it breaks a butterfly but for how it generates richness out of the negative emotions felt toward Hervey. It is the excess that makes the difference, turning a malicious payback of malice into a thing of beauty and a joy forever.

Nothing would be easier than to extend the list of satires, epigrams, and squibs tossed off by poets mocking or getting even with someone who has distressed them. But when we move to fiction, the relation between missile and target becomes less direct; indeed, the missile-target figure that more or less describes the bits of animus thrown off by Tennyson and Lawrence seems hardly useful. As the literary creation becomes lengthier and more leisured, what may have originated—at least in part—from the desire to pillory the offender becomes dispersed, complicated, and modified by other motives less unequivocal than pure spite or malice.

H. G. Wells's attack on Henry James in a little-read book of his titled *Boon* (1915) is remembered mainly for the stirring response it provoked in James. In a preface to *Boon* in his *Collected Works,* Wells spoke of it as "an outbreak of naughtiness," brought on by his boredom with "the pretentious solemnity of various literary artists and critics," among whom James was one. Wells objected to James's novels because they weren't "rough" enough. His characters were eviscerated, had no political opinions or lusts, didn't dream or go hungry or "perspire at poker." "He sets himself to pick the straws out of the hair of Life before he paints her," said Wells, adding in a rather sentimental formulation that "without the straws she is no longer the mad woman we love." The Jamesian novel is "like a church lit but without a congregation to distract you, with every light and line focused on the high altar. And on the altar, very reverently placed, intensely there, is a dead kitten, an egg-shell, a bit of string."

This is good work in the tradition of Mark Twain's essay on the literary offenses of James Fenimore Cooper, except that Wells and James were contemporaries, friends of sorts who, with some reservations, had praised each other's work. James took the "naughtiness" of *Boon* very hard; yet goaded by the attack, he responded with memorable sentences to Wells about why art mattered: "It is art that *makes* life, makes interest, makes importance, for our consideration and application of those things, and I know of no substitute whatever for the force and beauty of the process." They never wrote to each other again, and within a few months James was dead. Wells had got off his barbs just in time for the Master to reply with one final, large affirmation of a life's devotion.

ONE of the best modern attempts to destroy a writer by parodying his style and ideas is Hemingway's guying of Sherwood Anderson in *The Torrents of Spring,* his short novel published in 1926. This strange literary performance was in no sense a retaliation for some offense Anderson had committed against Hemingway. Indeed, Anderson had exerted his influence at Boni & Liveright—where he was a best-selling author—to help get Hemingway's book of stories *In Our Time* published the previous year. Such assistance did not deter Hemingway from striking at Anderson; in fact it may have sweetened the operation, given the spiteful childishness of Hemingway's moral character and the fact that he resented being compared to Anderson as a writer.

Whatever can be said for Anderson's merits as a novelist and story writer, however, cannot be said for *Dark Laughter,* his novel of 1925 that was the immediate occasion for Hemingway's attack. The satire of Anderson's primitivism is pretty broad. For example, Hemingway's thickheaded but "sensitive" hero, Yogi Johnson, falls in with some Indians and is taken to their clubhouse, with a splendid pool table and a committee room with autographed photographs of Chief Bender, Francis Parkman, D. H. Lawrence, Chief Meyers (those two chiefs being famous ballplayers), and a "full-length painting of Henry Wadsworth Longfellow" (doubtless in honor of "Hiawatha"). But the best parts of the parody can be appreciated only by readers familiar with the earnest tones and plodding rhythms of Anderson's sentences as, in *Dark Laughter,* they describe his hero's aspirations to be a writer: "One day he had gone with Bernice to a meat market—they were getting chops for dinner and he had noted the way an old fat meat-cutter in the place handled his tools. The sight had fascinated him and as he had stood in the place beside his wife, waiting his turn to be served, she began talking to him and he did not hear. What he was thinking about was the old meat-cutter, the deft quick hands of the old meat-cutter. They represented something to him. What was it?"

Hemingway's Yogi Johnson also has something on his mind, and it is conveyed to us through dogged repetition and artless questions when, as with Anderson's hero, a change of season brings troubled thoughts: "It was spring, there was no doubt of that now, and he did not want a woman. He had worried about it a lot lately. . . . He had gone to the Public Library and asked for a book the night before. He looked at the Librarian. He did not want her. . . . He passed a group of girls on their way home from High School. He looked carefully at all of them. He did not want a single one. Decidedly something was wrong. Was he going to pieces? Was this the end?"

Yet is this a parody of Anderson merely? In one of Hemingway's most interesting stories from *In Our Time*, "Soldier's Home," Harold Krebs returns from World War I to his small town in Oklahoma and spends his days looking at the girls, with mixed feelings: "He did not like them when he saw them in the Greek's ice cream parlor. He did not want them themselves really. They were too complicated. There was something else. Vaguely he wanted a girl but he did not want to have to work to get her. He would have liked to have a girl but he did not want to spend a long time getting her." And so on in this vein. It is not that the soldier, Krebs, is contemptible or a fool; rather, that Hemingway is turning sentences around him in odd, designedly awkward (or movingly simple?) ways, working toward a style. So the simple desire to score off Anderson becomes complicated, as Krebs, Anderson, Hemingway, the English sentence itself get mixed together in a result more interesting and hard to locate than a purely mean-minded one.

Sometimes we are both teased and disappointed by what looks to be a novelist's attempt to "get" someone, a public literary figure about whom we're curious. It is often assumed that in his much-acclaimed novel *Pictures from an Institution* (1954), Randall Jarrell set out to do in, among others, Harold Taylor and Mary McCarthy. Jarrell admitted that the identification of his character Dwight Robbins—the young president of a progressive small college named Benton—with Harold Taylor, the president of Sarah Lawrence, was inevitable, since, Jarrell said, there was only one young, curly-headed president of a progressive college. But he resisted the notion that Gertrude Johnson, Benton's novelist in residence, should be "confused with Mary McCarthy"—who had herself just published *The Groves of Academe*, which groves were associated with Bard College. When he sent a portion of the novel to *Partisan Review*, with which Mary McCarthy was affiliated, in hopes they would publish it, Philip Rahv demurred because of the resemblances between the novelist Gertrude and the novelist McCarthy. Jarrell replied that readers who knew Jean Stafford thought *she* was Gertrude.

But do sentences like the following ones about Gertrude's voice make one think of anybody? "The Southern past, the Southern present, the Southern future, concentrated into Gertrude's voice, became one of red clay pine barrens, of chain-gang camps, of housewives dressed in flour-sacks who stare all day dully down into dirty sinks. . . . Her voice was the voice of a small-town librarian pushing back from her forehead a strand of hair—a damp strand, that is . . . it was the voice of hominy, or turnip greens, of light-bread." What we have here and at other moments in the novel is not a person, certainly not Mary McCarthy or Jean Stafford, but rather Jarrell doing the Southern voice, improvising it inventively as he goes along. In fact, it would be only the slightest exaggeration to claim that there is nothing in the novel but Jarrell's voice—a brilliant and claustrophobic performance, rather than one in which real folk take their lumps. He was right when he said to Rahv about his heroine that Gertrude "is one of the principles of things—a naked one."

PROBABLY the liveliest and most intense example of a recent novelist's setting out, within the action of his book, to settle scores with an antagonist is Philip Roth's portrait of the critic Milton Appel in *The Anatomy Lesson*, the third book of his trilogy, *Zuckerman Bound*. That Milton Appel is meant to stand for Irving Howe is patently clear, not only through resemblances between their literary and personal lives but, more specifically, because in 1972 Mr. Howe published in *Commentary* a strong-worded attack on Mr. Roth's fiction, accusing him of vulgarity and of selling out to an "audience" rather than striving to reach true "readers." In physical and mental pain, the suffering hero of *The Anatomy Lesson*, Nathan Zuckerman, is quite simply furious with Appel's attack on his career ("that made Macduff's assault upon Macbeth look almost lackadaisical") and with a subsequent attempt on Appel's part to involve Zuckerman in writing an Op-Ed piece about Israel. In the novel, Zuckerman telephones Appel and abuses him but after hanging up feels worse than before. At which point he hops a plane to Chicago with the intention of applying to medical school. When the passenger next to him asks what line of business he's in, Zuckerman replies that he's in pornography, that he publishes a dirty magazine called *Lickety Split* and that his name is Milton Appel. ("A-p-p-e-l. Accent on the second syllable. Je m'appelle Appel.") There follows much more, none of it to Appel's credit.

On the face of it, such a blatant retaliation as Philip Roth's against Irving

Howe seems a bad idea, petty and vindictive in its nature. My own feeling is quite different, in that while admiring Irving Howe's writings, I also admire the twisted form in which, in Mr. Roth's novel, he emerges as Milton Appel, especially when in Zuckerman's fantasy he becomes the publisher of a very un-Howe-like magazine. There is something more than merely personal about this portrait of the critic as pornographer. Remember too that Zuckerman is well on his way to ending up in the hospital, after a very painful accident in which—of all bodily organs—his mouth is seriously injured.

In Philip Roth's bid at doing in an adversary and to a greater or lesser degree in the other instances of artistic savaging collected here, the missile is launched with the worst of intentions. Yet the target turns out to be not Sporus or Henry James or Sherwood Anderson or Irving Howe but rather some zone of aesthetic satisfaction in the reader, who is pleased to see mean- or bloody-mindedness, righteous indignation or irresponsible mischief, organize itself into stanza or speech or scene in a manner as irresistible as the following couplets:

> All people that can write or paint
> do tremble under my complaint.
> For I am a chicken and I can chirp;
> and my name is Thomas, Thomas Earp.

Nobody cares about Thomas Earp the art critic, but thanks to Lawrence's rhyme, his name lives on.

The New York Times Book Review, July 27, 1986
© 1986 by the New York Times Co.
Reprinted by permission.

That Shakespeherian Rag

❦

E VERY SO OFTEN a book comes along that, although less than a pleasure to read page by page, justifies itself as an important anatomy of
unhealthy practices in the stockyards of contemporary lit crit. The reason
Brian Vickers's formidable tome, which takes apart five "schools" of recent
Shakespeare criticism, is sometimes frustrating going has to do with its
scrupulousness as critique: in order for him to make the telling points
he makes against exponents of the different schools, he has to lay out
their approaches to the plays. This takes time and makes us wish occasionally we were reading *Henry V* or *The Winter's Tale* instead of being dragged
through what this New Historicist or that cultural materialist has to say
about them. Nevertheless, *Appropriating Shakespeare* is a salutary job of
sweeping up and marking as disposable a lot of stuff that's been choking the
life out of Shakespeare's art as it struggles to maintain itself in our Age of
Theory.

The schools Vickers names are five: Deconstruction, New Historicism,
Psychocriticism, Feminist, and (treated together in one chapter) Christian/
Marxist. He deals with them under an assumption which, most assuredly,
those sympathetic to any of the above movements will find hopelessly naive
and out of date: namely, that there was a time, not so many decades ago,

Appropriating Shakespeare: Contemporary Critical Quarrels, by Brian Vickers. New
Haven: Yale University Press, 1993.

8

when the criticism of Shakespeare was essentially "literary." In that climate the interested student could find a wide range of books and articles

> devoted primarily to interpreting the plays in a modern critical-analytical way, with varying emphases on their historical context. There were a few obviously political or ideological critics . . . but otherwise criticism was essentially literary, concerned with the plays' structure, language, moral values, theatrical history.

This has all changed as the fragmentation of literary studies into fiefdoms and bailiwicks has given us various competing groups determined to appropriate Shakespeare: "Each group has a specific ideology, a self-serving aim of proving the validity of their own approach by their readings of the text. Shakespeare's plays, for so long the primary focus of the critic's and scholar's attention, are now secondary, subordinated to the imperialism and self-advancement of the particular group." Fighting words, and Vickers may be too easy on Shakespeare critics predating the current appropriators—as if every previous book or essay on the dramatist manifested only disinterested concern for his work and was free of professional aggrandizings and self-advancings. Still, I'm convinced that he's mainly right, and that the loss, in these current schools, of "literary" motives and practices is a loss to the reading and teaching of Shakespeare (and not of Shakespeare only).

Vickers holds further that recent critics have aligned themselves all too easily with attitudes derived from what a friend of mine refers to as The French Liars of the late 1960s: Barthes, Foucault, Derrida, and Lacan. Vickers thinks it incumbent upon himself to give an account of the historical movement in which each flourished, so that readers can identify the ideas from which recent approaches derive; thus we get one chapter of 163 closely packed pages on "The Diminution of Language: Saussure to Derrida," and a second one in which Vickers runs through the work of the four theorists mentioned above. He argues that many of the assumptions and tenets by which language became diminished, suspect, wholly untrustworthy—assumptions inherited by the new schools of Shakespeare critics—derive from misinterpretations, on the part of the Parisian sages (or liars) of Saussure. I hope it's not just that mention of that name invariably causes my consciousness to glaze over, but I'm not convinced Vickers was wise to spend quite so much time in explicating the post-Saussurians. No doubt a specialist in any or all of these writers would argue with or reject Vickers's interpretations, though to a nonspecialist like myself they seemed sensible and fair-minded, if acerb. He points out the paradox that these thinkers don't—as does, say, Wittgenstein—invoke the "normal, everyday experience of speaking and understanding." Even though they knew about the untrustworthy slippages of the signifier, they continued "tirelessly publicizing their ideas, writing and speaking at great length, and thus showing an untiring faith in the powers of language to persuade, impose, deceive, confuse, convince. . . ." Their assertions, Vickers claims, "were mere assertions, not even theories about language," and these assertions did not derive from responsible analysis of forms of discourse (such analysis he finds, for example, in John Searle and Wendell Harris). He sums it up pungently and combatively by pointing to, in the French critics, "a metalanguage that displays coherence while claiming that the object language is incoherent." This for him "may stand as an ironic comment on the artificiality and futility of the whole tradition, which ought by now to be seen for what it is, a dead-end." To help us see that dead-end, Vickers journeys once more into the breach.

His book stands or falls not by its survey of the progenitors of what he calls Current Literary Theory, but by the convincingness of the cases he mounts against Shakespeare criticism actually produced by various practitioners. Since these cases amount to a detailed point by point arguing with particular critics, it's difficult for a reviewer—two places removed from the critic in question and three from the Shakespearean text—to give an adequate sense of Vickers's success. Yet at least the flavor of his criticism may be suggested. For example, he points out how often the targets of contemporary critics as well as their 1960s progenitors seem unreal—"straw men, opinions that have been manufactured only to be attacked." A strategy of this game is to divide things into two categories, the first of which (the bad, outmoded one) represents "some absurdly stupid or superficial point of view, to be mocked with withering scorn, and replaced by [the second], in all respects superior." In his discussion of deconstructive approaches to Shakespeare, he lights upon Terence Hawkes, an academic Brit with a penchant for "lively" writing and a wish to popularize and publicize Decon's procedures. Announcing that the implications of these procedures for the Shakespeare critic are "vast," Hawkes tells us we must abandon "Bradley's notion of reading poetry as a pathway to the final 'presence' of the author's mind," adding that "Bradley's sense of the capacity of the text to reveal 'character' is also doomed by it." Hawkes goes on to pontificate:

Precisely because of its tropes, its metaphors, its images, language cannot be reduced to a series of unified, graspable, "readable" and authorially validated meaning. *It certainly cannot accurately depict character* [Vickers's italics]. Texts are never accurate or finished or concluded. They are endlessly, like language itself, in free play. . . . As Hillis Miller puts it, all texts are unreadable, if by "readable" one means a single definitive interpretation.

Vickers's long commentary on this passage, only part of which I quote, begins as follows:

There we meet many of the familiar characteristics of deconstruction; the categorical assertions . . . the proliferation of inverted commas to mark suspect words or concepts [in another place he remarks that they're used like aftershave], the caricature of opposed critical practices in an attempt to legitimate its own.

He points out—as anyone would, encountering A. C. Bradley's name in this connection—that Bradley's great *Shakespearean Tragedy* was published in 1904 and is therefore a pretty ancient approach against which to prove Decon's superiority. Vickers doesn't say, though he knows it, that the language-focused Shakespeare criticism of this century's earlier decades— by, among others, F. R. Leavis, L. C. Knights, Cleanth Brooks and Maynard Mack—routinely used Bradley as a whipping boy in their attempt to redirect criticism away from Shakespeare's characters and onto his words. But these critics had the legitimate excuse that Bradley was then a force, somebody to argue with—as he is now no longer, although his book is still marvelous to read. As for assertions of Hawkes's like "It [Shakespeare's language] certainly cannot accurately depict character," Vickers italicizes but doesn't analyze the outrageousness of such a pronouncement. What is it outside of Shakespeare's words, one might ask, that can "accurately depict character"? Whoever would argue or has argued that the character of Hamlet or Lear is "accurately depicted"—or not accurately depicted, for that matter? As for the assurance of Decon's toastmaster, Hillis Miller, that there's no one "single definitive interpretation" of a Shakespeare play, it's a straw argument—who thought there was? For how many years has it been legitimate for any tyro in criticism to point out that (after all) there's more than one legitimate reading to make of a Shakespeare play (or of a novel or a lyric poem)? We hear it from college freshmen every day. Who do Terence Hawkes and Hillis Miller think they're kidding?

Vickers deals with the New Historicists almost wholly through the work of Stephen Greenblatt, particularly Greenblatt's essay on the *Henriad*, "Invisible Bullets." At the conclusion of his long analysis of Greenblatt's anti-monarchical line about the plays, Vickers accuses him of "a disregard for the integrity of the literary text; a bending of evidence, background and foreground, to suit one-sided interpretations; the foisting of modern cultural and political attitudes onto Renaissance texts." Although Vickers spends a good deal of time charging that Greenblatt distorts the historical anecdote with which, as usual, he begins his essay, the more serious distortion, it appears to me, is Greenblatt's assertion that Shakespeare's Henry plays are concerned with "the production and containment of subversion and disorder." Everything follows from this: the reform of Hal; the rejection of Falstaff; the victory over the French at Agincourt—and we are invited to cast a cold eye on such "containment," with its analogies to twentieth-century instances of state supremacy and the throttling of dissident individual factions. Vickers's point-by-point critique of Greenblatt's account of Prince Hal picks out of it characterizing devaluations like "the prince and principle of falsification"; "a counterfeit companion . . ."; "an anti-Midas"; "everything he touches turns to dross"; a "counterfeit coin." This unsympathetic reading is arrived at only by neglecting 95 percent of the text, says Vickers. But forget the percentage figure; the point is, in my judgment, that Greenblatt reads Shakespeare without ever evincing, as far as one can see, any pleasure in the text (to allude dangerously to another French Liar). He is so busy making his "case" against Hal and authority that he reads right through the magnificent poetry, converting it ruthlessly to "meanings" in the service of an argument. This sort of behavior is of course not confined to Stephen Greenblatt but is seen generally in the writings of most of the critics Vickers considers in his book. I shall return to the question of just what to do with the fact that Shakespeare is—and not just among other things—a poet.

Time and again in arguing with the different critical schools, Vickers makes effective war on "abstractionism." This practice consists—in the case of the Shakespeare criticism of a highly regarded philosopher, Stanley Cavell—of distorting the evident sense of a text in the direction of philosophical and psychoanalytical abstractions. An egregious example of this distortion is Cavell's (as always) tortuous dealings with *Othello*, where the philosopher claims that Cartesian skepticism is "in full existence" in Shakespeare's tragedies, then moves to the problem of how one can know the existence of another, then worries about what Othello did or didn't know about Desdemona's virginity when they married. Cavell's psychoanalytic attempt to provide Othello with a sexual trauma that determines his murder of Desdemona at the play's end, Vickers sees as distorting into abstractionism important overt meanings in the play—most notably Iago's elaborately successful plot to bring the catastrophe about. "Cavell's remarkable torturing of logic," Vickers argues, "pulls the play into a private nexus of interests, from philosophy to psychoanalysis, and finally to a spurious form of etymology." (At the end of the essay Cavell calls attention "to the hell and the demon staring out of the names of Othello and Desdemona.") "Competence," writes Vickers, "even distinction in philosophy is obviously no guarantee of sensitivity, tact, or inwardness with literary texts"; I would go further and say that distinction in philosophy is on the whole unlikely to go along with distinction in literary criticism, Mill or Santayana to the contrary.

Disregarding important elements of the play when they don't fit into the critical scheme you're attempting to impose on it, is what feminist critics also do with *Othello*—what Vickers calls "screening out Iago." Thus efforts by Carol Neely, and others from whose work Vickers illustrates, see the play in terms of attitudes of opposition between the sexes. Neely judges the play's females to be quite superior to the males—the men are in the main " 'murderous coxcombs' " (the words are Emilia's) while the women "are not murderous, and they are not foolishly idealistic or foolishly cynical as the men are." Vickers points out that only by screening out Iago in this way can Neely read the play in terms of gendered contrasts: "this whole superbly articulated claustrophilic, deeply painful plot structure is ignored by the feminist critic, reduced to its simplest components—'the men and the women'—and rearranged into two piles."[1]

---

1. Some of the most pious feminist critics are not, of course, female. Peter Erickson's *Rewriting Shakespeare, Rewriting Ourselves* (1991) has an admiring chapter on Adrienne Rich's treatment of the father-daughter situation as a "rewriting" of *King Lear* which shows us that because (in Erickson's words) Shakespeare "cannot give us Cordelia's point of view," he therefore "does not encompass everything, is not universal." And though most of Shakespeare's women aren't able to disrupt the patriarchal (or bad) social system of which they are part, Venus and Helena are able to challenge patri-

In his introductory paragraph to the chapter that takes up the Christians and the Marxists (I found this less lively than those preceding it), Vickers usefully sums up some of the ways of viewing Shakespearean characters he thinks are misconceived. All the schools except deconstruction—which reduces characters to "traces," "purely verbal effects"—accept the substantiality of characters within the play "but then force them into preconceived patterns":

> For the feminists it is essential that characters be seen as gendered, culturally superior or inferior, oppressor or oppressed. For the New Historicism the people in a play can be criticized for being in a dominant, exploitative relationship, or sympathized with as the victims of power, colonialism, or whatever. To the Freudians, they are individual case-studies, each manifesting one version or other of a limited, but endlessly recombinable repertoire of fantasies and neuroses. All these forms of criticism can be described as only partly literary, for they all ignore the primary experience of drama as a sequence of action which unfolds over time.

Your response to this formulation will be in line with your feelings about Vickers's book overall. If you think that the schools summed-up here are travestied beyond recognition, or if you think there's a narrowness in Vickers's conception of "literary" criticism, or if you think it naive to identify as "primary" any particular "experience of drama" and think the emphasis on sequential action is also naive, then you will dismiss *Appropriating Shakespeare*. By now my own bias should have become clear: that whatever particular errors or excesses are present in his arguments with particular critics and interpretations, Vickers is on to something very important, namely, the deflection of criticism (and not just in regard to Shakespeare) into abstracting and reductive "thematic" or ideological "readings."

Like Vickers, I judge these aggressive efforts to interpret Shakespeare to be insufficiently literary in that they don't tell us what it is like to read the plays. To illuminate that activity of reading, a critic would need, certainly, to consider the dramatic art as a sequence of action unfolding over time. But I would put the emphasis on something even prior to sequence, something I

---

archy—though, notes Erickson solemnly, "their assertiveness is by no means ideal in twentieth-century feminist terms." Poor Venus! Poor Shakespeare!

call, vaguely enough, Shakespeare's language—what has sometimes been referred to, though not so often anymore, as the "poetry" of the plays. This poetry is frequently, it will be agreed, of an extraordinary beauty and the reason why Shakespeare is admired, fetishized even; it is a great mistake, even at this late date in Western culture, to pay little attention to it, or to ignore it altogether in the interests of something presumably larger and more culturally significant. Or to try and liberate Shakespeare's characters from its grip: one misconceived approval of that attempt must do to illustrate a larger tendency in modern criticism. Discussing *Othello*, Richard Wheeler says with respect to the female characters that "it has taken the energies of feminist criticism to dislodge [Desdemona, Emilia, and Bianca] from the play's powerful rhetoric of both idealism and degradation."[2] In other words, criticism is praised for rescuing Shakespeare's characters from the richly disturbing poetry through which they are not just presented but created. A strange effort, surely.

Can it still be worthwhile to attempt something like a disinterested study of a Shakespearean drama, which would attempt to see the object as in itself it really is? Or, assuming that twentieth-century fin de siècle readers find Arnold's insistence about criticism hopelessly dated and an invitation to self-delusion merely, can there be an "interested" criticism that above all is interested in exploring that play's language, its poetry, not merely in order to move through it to themes or categories that would somehow explain it? As one who presumes, on occasion, to "teach" this or that play to a group of undergraduates, such interested criticism seems both possible and exhilarating. Where would one go for examples of the activity in books and essays? I think of Mark Van Doren's still useful *Shakespeare* (1939) and D. J. Enright's little-known gem *Shakespeare and the Students* (1970). Although Derek Traversi's books are prolix and sometimes plodding, they do try to keep us in touch with actual sequences of Shakespeare's verse. More recently two English critics, John Bayley (in *Shakespeare and Tragedy*, 1981) and Barbara Everett (in *Young Hamlet*, 1989), show that there can be value in

---

2. The quotation from Wheeler I found in a challenging essay by Richard Levin, "Feminist Thematics and Shakespearean Tragedy" (*PMLA* 103 [1988]: 125–38). See also the letter in response to this essay signed by twenty-four outraged feminist critics (also in *PMLA*) as well as Levin's letter in response to them. Levin's essays (see also "The Politics of Bardicide," *PMLA* 105 [1990]: 491–504) anticipate many of Vickers's arguments and should be looked up.

approaching the plays without a nameable "approach"—without becoming an appropriator who has paid his or her dues to a reigning school. (It seems difficult for American critics to operate independently of one or another of these schools, given the professionalized academy.) One of the ways of defending the practices of those writers criticized adversely by Brian Vickers in his book is to say that new approaches to Shakespeare were necessary because critics earlier in the century had more or less exhausted what there was to say about the language considered "in itself." This seems to me a shibboleth, and certainly not something that someone who claims to care about poetry should let pass. But you have to care enough about the poetry to want to see it for itself and not another thing (as Eliot used to say). With Shakespeare, there is still plenty more to see.

Hudson Review 47, no. 3 (Autumn 1994)

Burke's Great Melody

❧

Johnson: "Never believe extraordinary characters which you hear of people. Depend upon it, Sir, they are exaggerated. You do not see one man shoot a great deal higher than another." I mentioned Mr. Burke. *Johnson:* "Yes; Burke is an extraordinary man. His stream of mind is perpetual." . . . And once, when Johnson was ill, and unable to exert himself as much as usual without fatigue, Mr. Burke having been mentioned, he said "That fellow calls forth all my powers. Were I to see Burke now, it would kill me."

—James Boswell, *The Life of Samuel Johnson*

THIS MOMENT IN BOSWELL is among the most heartening ones for those who like to see great spirits appreciating one another, and Burke got a chance to reciprocate when, during Johnson's last illness, Burke in the company of others visited him. When at one point Burke apologized for the possible oppressiveness of this visit, Johnson replied that it was not so and that he would have to have been in a wretched state indeed " 'when your company would not be a delight to me.' Mr. Burke, in a tremulous voice, expressive of being very tenderly affected, replied, 'My dear Sir, you have always been too good to me.' Immediately afterwards he went away." At

The Great Melody: A Thematic Biography and Commented Anthology of Edmund Burke, by Conor Cruise O'Brien. Chicago: University of Chicago Press, 1992.

the end of Conor Cruise O'Brien's 700-page book on Mr. Burke, the reader is left marveling at the perpetual stream of mind to which he has been treated; and a reader like myself—one with no professional credentials in eighteenth-century English history and politics—finds all his powers drawn forth in the effort not to be overwhelmed by the superior ones of Burke. Insofar as one survives to tell the tale, it is a tribute to Mr. O'Brien's strong hand at the narrative helm.

Subtitled "A Thematic Biography and Commented Anthology of Edmund Burke," *The Great Melody* is exactly that, taking its main title from Yeats's oddly affecting poem, "The Seven Sages," in which are celebrated the spirits of Swift, Berkeley, Goldsmith, and Burke—"four great minds that hated Whiggery," as one of the sages claims, even though another replies that "Burke was a Whig." To which a further sage defines "Whiggery" as "A levelling, rancorous, rational sort of mind," insisting that, in those terms, Burke "hated" it. But he is celebrated positively in two subsequent lines:

> American colonies, Ireland, France and India
> Harried, and Burke's great melody against it.

It was brilliant of O'Brien to steal the great melody theme and make it the organizing principle for his thematic consideration of Burke's thought and writings with respect to these four areas of concern. We are to understand the melody in two aspects: first is "a profound inner harmony" that characterizes Burke's writing in which the melody is always "against it"—the "it" being, in O'Brien's term, "abuse of power." Second, there are those sequences and passages within the larger action of rhetoric and argument in which Burke's utterance "attains a glowing eloquence, unique in English literature and in the annals of oratory." O'Brien is scrupulous about pointing at—indeed, inviting us to listen to—the specific places where, in his judgment, the melody is at its most glowing. So that to read this book actively is to try out passages from the "commented anthology" on one's own ears in order to see what they register: this is how the book calls forth our powers.

In "The Tower," Yeats refers proudly to "the people of Burke and of Grattan," but O'Brien points out that in fact they were two distinct peoples, living in an adversarial relation to each other: Grattan's people being Anglo-Irish and Protestant; Burke's being Irish Catholic gentry. The Penal Laws in eighteenth-century Ireland by which the domination of the Protestants was enforced made for "a tense, equivocal and secretive" relation between Burke's family and his country. His father, Richard Burke, did conform to the established church; but his mother was a Catholic, and although Burke at age twelve went to a Quaker boarding school (run by Richard Shackleton, his admirable teacher), he previously had attended a Catholic "hedge" school while living with his mother's family in Cork. O'Brien's conviction, which deeply informs the pages of this book, is that Burke's equivocal relation to his Catholic heritage—even as he prepared himself, as a Protestant, for an English career—would inform his whole life, and not merely in his "guarded, cryptic, sometimes evasive" public statements and writings about Ireland. For the feelings he repressed about Ireland—partly by way of combating the attempt of his enemies to make him out a zealous Papist—were in fact expressed in his opposition to abuses of power in repressive institutions in India (the East India Company, Governor-General Warren Hastings) and in France (the Jacobins, the terrorists). Even though the "Great Melody" is seldom heard "against" intolerance in his native land, it gains force and eloquence in other contexts because of its underlying presence.

The other informing assumption—some would say obsession—of O'Brien's book is that something like a systematic belittling of Burke took place earlier in this century as a reaction to the Whig interpretation of history. Insofar as Burke was a hero to Macaulay and G. O. Trevelyan, just so far must his stature be reduced in the hands of Lewis Namier and his disciples. Much of O'Brien's Introduction is taken up with arguing that a generation of English undergraduates was infected with Namier's debunking of Burke—a debunking that took place mainly through Namier's ignoring or downplaying his significance as a mind and a politician. Although this Namierite reaction is pretty much over, O'Brien finds it surviving in L. G. Mitchell's introduction to volume 8 of the Clarendon Press edition of Burke's writings and speeches.[1] Mitchell's "assiduous intimations of Burke's

---

1. The Clarendon edition of *The Writings and Speeches of Edmund Burke:* Volume 8, *The French Revolution, 1790–1794,* ed. L. G. Mitchell (Oxford: Oxford University Press, Clarendon Press, 1991). O'Brien finds much more satisfactory Volume 9, *The Revolutionary War, 1794–1797 and Ireland,* ed. R. B. McDowell, (Oxford: Oxford University Press, Clarendon Press, 1991).

worthlessness" O'Brien sees as in the worst Namier tradition, so he raises his own melody against this abuse of the historian's power. In other words, *The Great Melody* is a fighting book and if you're convinced that Burke was anything less than a heroic figure it will provoke and irritate.

Predictably, reviews of the book have uncovered the reviewer's politics. In the *TLS* (Oct. 4, 1992), E. P. Thompson, the Marxist historian of the English working class, accuses O'Brien of employing his pen "as a shillelagh" in the hunting down of Burke's Namierite detractors. Thompson has praise for the sections of "enlightening commentary" that concern Burke's parliamentary work on behalf of the American colonies in their resistance to the Crown, also for the section on India and Burke's dogged pursuit of Warren Hastings and of the East India Company that had been energetically looting India's riches. But what Thompson cleverly and rather nastily calls "O'Burkian hyperbole" characterizes the book's attempt to emphasize at every possible moment Burke's Catholic associations and the depth, in his character, of the "Irish layer." Even more important—and for Thompson, detrimental to the book's truth—is its lack of appreciation of the French Revolution as anything but wholly destructive. O'Brien, Thompson feels, is too uncritical of Burke's conservative identification of liberties and rights with landed property. He reminds him that George III, after reading the *Reflections,* congratulated Burke on supporting "the cause of the Gentleman," not a gesture that a historian of the working class can tolerate.

The opposite position may be said to belong to Harvey C. Mansfield, professor of government at Harvard and longtime scholar of Burke (he has edited a selection of Burke's letters).[2] Mansfield finds it the case that truth and justice have finally been meted out to the man, and he provides a handy list of instances of political action in which Burke, while never in the position of a significant office-holding Whig politician, was nevertheless instrumental in getting important things accomplished and was in no sense the "lackey" Namier called him. Mansfield notes some of these contributions:

> On America, the decision to repeal the Stamp Act and George III's decision to end the American war. . . . on Ireland, the Catholic Relief Act of 1793 and the disaster of the Irish rebellion in 1798;

2. *Selected Letters of Edmund Burke,* ed. and with an introduction by Harvey C. Mansfield Jr. (Chicago: University of Chicago Press, 1984). Mansfield's review of O'Brien's book is in *The New Criterion* (Nov. 1992).

on India, Fox's East India Bill in 1783, establishing the principle of accountability in the proceedings against Warren Hastings; on France, a vindication of Burke's insights as responsible for his prophetic vision, and of Burke's side of his split with Fox, the creation of the Portland Whigs, the contest with Pitt over the "Regicide" peace, which was finally won by Burke.

There is much else, says Mansfield, and it all goes together as a whole.

As someone whose approach to Burke has been mainly "literary" (I first read anthology selections from his work in a course in eighteenth-century English writers given by Walter Jackson Bate—read him in the company of Johnson and Goldsmith, Cowper, Boswell, and Gibbon, rather than of political theorists), I realize that my appreciation of him may be warped in the direction of the aesthetic. Mansfield, in the Introduction to his selection of letters, writes that "Burke was a remarkable man because he was a remarkable thinker. One cannot confine his merit to his rhetoric and sum up his accomplishments as literary, while putting aside the substance of his thought as controversial or embarrassing. . . . His marvelous literary skills do not excuse us from taking him seriously, which requires taking his thought seriously as political philosophy." That seems cogent and worth keeping in mind. But perhaps it applies more to some parts of the writings than to others. From our current perspective, probably the least controversial area of Burke's melody is the American one, since people don't argue these days about the rightness or wrongness of the Stamp Act or whether conciliation with the colonies should have been the course for England to have followed. So we are the more free to admire, without thinking about it under the category of "thought" or "political philosophy," the following famous paragraph from "On Conciliation with America," quoted by O'Brien as an instance of Burke's great melody as it plays out the manner in which "the people of New England have of late carried on the whale fishery":

> Whilst we follow them among the tumbling mountains of ice, and behold them penetrating into the deepest frozen recesses of Hudson's Bay and Davis's Straits, whilst we are looking for them beneath the arctic circle, we hear that they have pierced into the opposite region of polar cold, that they are at the antipodes, and engaged under the frozen serpent of the south. Falkland Island, which seemed too remote and romantic an object for the grasp of

national ambition, is but a stage and resting-place in the progress of their victorious industry. Nor is the equinoctial heat more discouraging to them, than the accumulated winter of both the poles. We know that whilst some of them draw the line and strike the harpoon on the coast of Africa, others run the longitude, and pursue their gigantic game along the coast of Brazil. No sea but what is vexed by their fisheries. No climate that is not witness to their toils. Neither the perseverance of Holland, nor the activity of France, nor the dexterous and firm sagacity of English enterprise, ever carried this most perilous mode of hard industry to the extent to which it has been pushed by this recent people; a people who are still, as it were, but in the gristle, and not yet hardened into the bone of manhood. When I contemplate these things; when I know that the colonies in general owe little or nothing to any care of ours, and that they are not squeezed into this happy form by the constraints of watchful and suspicious government, but that, through a wise and salutary neglect, a generous nature has been suffered to take her own way to perfection; when I reflect upon these effects, when I see how profitable they have been to us, I feel all the pride of power sink, and all presumption in the wisdom of human contrivances melt and die away within me. My rigour relents. I pardon something to the spirit of liberty.

This is superbly orchestrated, carrying the reader-listener irresistibly along, eliciting admiration and agreement—although one doesn't so much "agree" with it as register and approve it. The best thing to do with such a feat of happy rhetoric is to read it again, perhaps memorize it. ("On Conciliation" was once required reading in American high school courses in rhetoric.) For that reason Burke's "marvelous literary skills" (in Harvey Mansfield's phrase) may make it more, rather than less, difficult to take his thought "seriously as political philosophy."

The India phase of Burke's great melody occupied the years 1783–1790 especially and Burke's remorseless pursuit of Warren Hastings has seemed to some observers excessive, as if he were as ruthless, in this single-minded endeavor, as Hastings himself. Here Burke worked beautifully in concert with Charles James Fox, with whom he would fatefully fall out over the French Revolution. But his speech on Fox's East India Bill (which substituted a Parliament-appointed commission responsible to Parliament, for the East India Company's board of directors responsible only to its proprietors), is among other things a wonderfully expressive portrait of India as a civilization:

> This multitude of men does not consist of an abject and barbarous populace; much less of gangs of savages, like the Guaranies and Chiquitos, who wander on the waste borders of the river of Amazons, or the Plate; but a people for ages civilized and cultivated; cultivated by all the arts of polished life, whilst we were yet in the woods. There, have been (and still the skeletons remain) princes once of great dignity, authority, and opulence. There, are to be found the chiefs of tribes and nations. There is to be found an antient and venerable priesthood, the depository of their laws, learning, and history, the guides of the people whilst living, and their consolation in death; a nobility of great antiquity and renown; a multitude of cities, not exceeded in population and trade by those of the first class in Europe; merchants and bankers, individual houses of whom have once vied in capital with the Bank of England; whose credit had often supported a tottering state, and preserved their governments in the midst of war and desolation; millions of ingenious manufacturers and mechanicks; millions of the most diligent, and not the least intelligent, tillers of the earth. Here are to be found almost all the religions professed by men, the Braminical, the Mussulmen, the Eastern and the Western Christians.

And on in this vein of expansively sympathetic portraiture. As with the passage about the American colonies, the melody, if one really listens to its cumulative repetitions and echoings, its massive leisurely summoning-up of what was once a great civilization, has the effect of commanding assent much more powerfully than were it presented to us, less rhetorically, as "objective" political ideas whose rightness we embrace with disinterestedness.[3]

That last word brings to mind Matthew Arnold who, in a dramatic

---

3. In his *History of English Prose Rhythm* (1912), George Saintsbury devotes a few pages to Burke, "scanning" sentences by marking them into the equivalent of poetic feet, with long and short stresses. He is concerned to describe "the juxtaposition of long sentences and short; of rising and falling clauses; . . . the vowel-sound of the paralleled word-groups" and so forth.

moment in "The Function of Criticism at the Present Time," cites a passage from Burke's 1791 "Thoughts on French Affairs" in which Burke claims to be done with the subject of the Revolution and even imagines the possibility that "this mighty current in human affairs" may be irresistible. Arnold found it—surprisingly, it must be said—"one of the finest things in English literature" and saluted "That return of Burke upon himself" as a prime example of living by ideas rather than within the language of party and personal inclination. But in Arnold's eagerness to make a dramatic point, he spoke as if these "Thoughts" ("among the last things Burke wrote") really came at the end of his career, when in fact they would be succeeded by the white-hot satirical energy of the four *Letters on a Regicide Peace.* There Burke returned to his excoriation of the Revolution and of any faltering on England's part in continuing to prosecute her war with France. Having broken with Fox and most Whigs over the Revolution,[4] and in alliance with Pitt and the Tories even though he knew Pitt was exploiting him for purposes of maintaining power, Burke became increasingly skeptical, even cynical, in his attitudes toward England—and, O'Brien maintains, toward the heritage of the Glorious Revolution of 1688. No longer do we have the "idealised view of the British Constitution" that made its final appearance in the lively "An Appeal from the New to the Old Whigs" (1791). By 1796, when *Letters on a Regicide Peace* began to appear, "The cloud-capped towers, the gorgeous palaces, which Burke had liked to evoke on appropriate occasions, are now dismantled, like Warren Hastings' Indian opera." From now on his references to the actual workings of British politics are bleak and often savagely sardonic.

Yet this "negative" animus makes *Letters on a Regicide Peace* more rather than less engaging in its polemical sweep. Now that Pitt was making overtures for peace with France, and had also, Burke felt, betrayed his friend Fitzwilliam and the Irish Catholics, he could feel "released from that self-imposed thralldom" (O'Brien's words) the alliance with Pitt had necessitated. The tragic death of his only son, Richard, in 1794 may have also

4. The *Parliamentary History* records the break with Fox in memorable terms: "Mr Fox rose to reply: but his mind was so much agitated, and his heart so much affected by what had fallen from Mr Burke, that it was some minutes before he could proceed. Tears trickled down his cheeks, and he strove in vain to give utterance to feelings that dignified and exalted his nature." Surely a great moment in the theater of politics.

contributed not only to Burke's desolation, but to his determination in the
Regicide Peace letters to let it all hang out, as if—like Frost's image of himself
as a poet—all he cared about was "what a hell of a good time" he had doing
it.[5] Consider a magnificently immoderate sentence like the following from
the first letter (actually the second in order of composition):

> The Republic of Regicide, with an annihilated revenue, with de-
> faced manufactures, with a ruined commerce, with an uncultivated
> and half-depopulated country, with a discontented, distressed, en-
> slaved, and famished people, passing, with a rapid, eccentric, incal-
> culable course, from the wildest anarchy to the sternest despotism,
> has actually conquered the finest parts of Europe, has distressed,
> disunited, deranged, and broke to pieces all the rest, and so sub-
> dued the minds of the rulers in every nation, that hardly any re-
> source presents itself to them, except that of entitling themselves to
> a contemptuous mercy by a display of their own imbecility and
> meanness.

Here, even more than in *Reflections*, Burke's hair-trigger pen is less concerned to analyze and diagnose than to confront—with its own verbal violence—the violent abuse of power exercised by France. We have moved away
from Arnoldian disinterestedness (if we were ever there, with Burke) into a
much more highly inflamed, excitingly unbalanced realm of display.

And indeed even early admirers of Burke like Arnold and John Morley
(who wrote the splendid entry on him in the eleventh edition of the *Britan-
nica*) pointed to excesses and inadequate understandings in his attitude
toward the Revolution. All the more likely then that an astute contemporary
political theorist like Alan Ryan of Princeton (see his important review of
The Great Melody in the *New York Review of Books,* Dec. 3, 1992) is struck by

---

5. Burke's son contracted tuberculosis of the trachea and died in a few days (ten days
previously to his illness he had been elected to Parliament). O'Brien writes:

> As he lay dying, he asked if it was raining. His father told him that the noise
> was the wind rustling through the trees. Richard then spoke his last words:
> three lines from Adam's morning hymn in Book V of *Paradise Lost*, a favourite
> passage of his father's:

> His praise ye winds, that from four Quarters blow,
> Breathe soft or loud; and wave your tops, ye Pines,
> With every Plant, in sign of Worship wave.

how, in his writings about the Revolution, Burke fails to be the "pluralistic liberal" O'Brien would have him be. Ryan finds it easy to resist what he takes to be Burke's, and by extension O'Brien's, wish that what happened to France could be undone: "the disputable point is whether, granted the violence and the chaos, but granted also the subsequent history of France— we can really wish that the Revolution had never happened." What Ryan, and, surely E. P. Thompson, is lamenting, is that O'Brien could have become so much of a counterrevolutionist as to side one-sidedly with Burke in his own counterrevolutionary activities. After Mary Wollstonecraft had read Burke's *Refections,* she wrote (in *A Vindication of the Rights of Man*) that "had you been a Frenchman, you would have been, in spite of your respect for rank and antiquity, a violent revolutionist. Your imagination would have taken fire." Yes, answers O'Brien, if Burke had been born in 1760 in a French village, we can imagine him as a revolutionary; but in fact he was born in Dublin in 1729. And in response to Thomas Paine's famous comment that Burke, in his fondness for the overthrown French royalty, "pities the plumage and forgets the dying bird," O'Brien notes how the comment has been used to "squelch sympathy with the victims of the Russian and Chinese revolutions." (A footnote mentions a further application of it, in 1977, to Northern Ireland, with the Protestant working class as the "plumage.")

My guess is that in order to write a book as passionate as *The Great Melody*, you must risk a certain amount of unbalance, becoming an advocate for your man in a way more dispassionate academic theorists like Alan Ryan have no cause to. As for Burke himself, if—as Arnold claimed—he and Swift were the two classics of English prose, it may be that it is no more necessary than with Swift to wish Burke had written differently than he had or attained more balance on certain issues, particularly on France. When Burke was dying in 1797, Charles James Fox attempted to have a final reconciling meeting with him. Burke's wife, Jane, wrote back to Fox, thanking him, but saying that it

> has cost Mr Burke the most heart-felt pain to obey the stern voice of his duty in rending asunder a long friendship, but that he deemed this sacrifice necessary; that his principles remain the same; and that in whatever of life yet remained to him, he conceives that he must live for others and not for himself. Mr Burke is convinced that the

principles which he has endeavoured to maintain are necessary to
the welfare and dignity of his country, and that these principles can
be enforced only by the general persuasion of his sincerity.

Who of us, in a similar situation, would not have embraced the opportunity
to be reconciled with a sometime ally and protégé? O'Brien explains that, in
his opinion, Burke didn't do it because the meeting would have signified
that differences of principle, in the last analysis, weren't all that important.
Instead he "wanted the political world to know that these principles are of
transcendent importance to him, and that Fox is still outside the pale, in
terms of these principles." Another way to put it was Yeats's in "Blood and
the Moon":

> And haughtier-headed Burke that proved the State a tree,
> That this unconquerable labyrinth of the birds, century after
> century,
> Cast but dead leaves to mathematical equality.

Hudson Review 46, no. 3 (Autumn 1993)

Responding to Blake

❦

TWENTY-FIVE YEARS AGO, with the war in Vietnam and turmoils on the home front, William Blake stood—at least among the more literarily inclined—for everything that was good and holy, to be enlisted in the struggle against oppression here and abroad. For example, in 1971, when Allen Ginsberg and Robert Duncan addressed a writing class at Kent State University a year after the killings there, Ginsberg sang Blake's "The School Boy" to the assembled students while accompanying himself on the harmonium. He and Duncan told the class that both school and war were prisons forced upon us by society and that there was a way to get out of those prisons. Would-be graffiti artists of the time, and there were plenty, found Blake an endless source of replenishment, from Everything that lives is holy, to The road of excess leads to the palace of wisdom, to Energy is eternal delight. At my own college a colleague offered a new, semester-long seminar in Blake's final prophetic book, *Jerusalem;* while at least one undergraduate, an almost totally inarticulate young man, was rumored to be deep into Blake and—like Ginsberg (who had his first vision of Blake in 1948 after "idly masturbating")—probably in direct communication with the master.

It's not clear what congruence, except in time, the heroicizing of Blake on a popular, antiestablishment front bore to the critical scholarship the academy had been devoting to him, especially since the Second World War. That

Blake: A Biography, by Peter Ackroyd. New York: Alfred A. Knopf, 1996.

period (1946–1970) saw, among other contributions, Mark Schorer's ambitious attempt to place Blake historically and intellectually, and David Erdman's extensive research into the popular and historical circumstances in which his art developed. There were many books about the shorter poems, perhaps most notably by Robert Gleckner, E. D. Hirsch, Hazard Adams, and Stanley Gardner. Most dauntingly, there were the interpretive attempts to make more available the prophetic books as objects of reading and study—notably Northrop Frye's *Fearful Symmetry* (1947) and Harold Bloom's *Blake's Apocalypse* (1963). Frye's massively original study of Blake's symbolism and his relation to earlier English poets, particularly Spenser and Milton, is still an astonishing achievement in literary scholarship. (Its opening sentence—"This book offers an explanation of Blake's thought and a commentary on his poetry"—is one of the great deadpan statements of modest purpose.) Bloom's "study in poetic argument," as he subtitles his book, traces such argument with special reference to "the major poems"— to *The Four Zoas, Milton,* and *Jerusalem.* Though a much less witty writer than Frye, Bloom agreed with him that the poems are "major" Blake and not just in length. "This is poetry of the highest order," he says about *Jerusalem,* "because every syllable in it bears the almost intolerable pressure of an inward torment that the poet is not content to express as such but insists on transvaluing into a universality of artistic process." (The critic himself clearly aspires to "major" status.) Now as the century nears its close, there is no visible abatement in the Blake industry, with his graphic designs, politics, religion, sexuality, and mythical proclivities all receiving intensive treatment.

When the news came through that the English novelist Peter Ackroyd had been paid an enormous sum by a publisher (Sinclair-Stevenson) to write biographies of Dickens and Blake, it seemed the right time for a new, comprehensively informed biography of Blake (Alexander Gilchrist's biography of him was published in 1861; Mona Wilson's in 1927). In many ways Ackroyd, consummately professional and fluid writer that he is, does not disappoint. He sets down the events of Blake's life in a more than sympathetic spirit; his reconstruction of Blake's London couldn't be better. (In his own novels and in the Dickens book, Ackroyd has already shown how thoroughly inward he is with London.) Blake's techniques and art-historical aspects are minutely described. As I shall go on to suggest, the treatment of the poems is not as full or satisfactory, although Ackroyd's admiration for them is patent. Yet overall the book felt like a bit of a trudge—though much more compact than the Dickens biography—and at its end I wondered just what, in fact, I had learned of new importance about Blake. It was good to pretend to have "the life" gathered up, as it were, into this handsome, lavishly illustrated volume; yet, exactly what need does it serve? Should people read a biography of Blake? Shouldn't they rather be trying to read the poems?

One can't deny the force of Ackroyd's sustained commitment to describing in detail Blake's procedures and methods as a draftsman, an engraver, and a producer of "relief etchings" in which copper plate is painted rather than engraved. These descriptions are highly informed, but in fact, as someone unfamiliar with the techniques and materials of graphic production, I am a sucker for anyone who sounds as if he knows whereof he speaks. Consider these sentences in partial description of the way Blake worked on copper plate as if it were a sketch pad:

> His first step was to cut out plates from a large sheet of copper, using a hammer and chisel, and to prepare the surface for his labours upon it. Then he made out a rough design with white or red chalk and, with that as his guide, he used a camel-hair brush to paint the words and images upon the plate with a mixture of salad oil and candle-grease. This mixture resisted the aqua fortis (of vinegar, salt armoniack, baysart and vert de griz purchased from the local druggist) which bit into the surrounding plate for three or four hours. . . . After that time the words and images stood up, and stood out, as part of one coherent design.

There are further references, in the paragraph on quills, to a "conventional printer's ball of cloth," to "burnt walnut oil," "burnt linseed oil," "Whata-man paper," "colour pigment," and "carpenter's glue." Ackroyd really relishes, so it feels, these descriptions, as he does the particularities of the engraving workshop Blake was apprenticed to for seven years under James Basire. There he worked twelve hours a day, six days a week, surrounded by "iron pots for the boiling of the oil, pans for warming the copper plates, tallow candles, racks of needles and gravers, fine linen cloths to strain the varnish, vessels for mixing the aqua fortis . . . old rags, pumice stones, feathers." Yet the effect of such particularity, in one sense admirable for the way it brings us in close to Blake's compositional techniques, is also—at least to this uninitiated reader—baffling: the more I'm told about how Blake went about his graphic procedures, the more I'm convinced of their inaccessibility to me.

Ackroyd notes that while Blake was the poet of eternity he was also the poet of late eighteenth-century London, and there are memorable vignettes in the biography of chimney sweepers, of the Gordon "No Popery" riots, of a London "built in the shadows of money and power." Blake's art, Ackroyd claims reasonably enough, is an art "entranced by the scenic and spectacular in a city that is filled with those great London forms, spectacle and melodrama," with the "energy and variety" that he (a "Cockney visionary," Ackroyd calls him) brilliantly perceived. So the biography is itself a kind of spectacle, given body and color by the scores of plates (both black-and-white and colored) that diversify and animate the text. Ackroyd tends to emphasize Blake's differences from rather than his similarities to members of the radical artistic-political circles he knew—Henry Fuseli, Mary Wollstonecraft, Tom Paine, Joseph Priestley, William Godwin, and so on. He notes that Blake has been called many things, such as "a Shakespearean populist, a Platonist, an anarchist, a Christian reactionary, or a quietist"; but he is less interested in classifying Blake than in insisting on his uniqueness as a prophet of the imagination, as an artist. Readers who want more searching argument about exactly what kind of radical Blake was will go elsewhere: most recently to E. P. Thompson's *Witness against the Beast* (1993) or Michael Ferber's *The Social Vision of William Blake* (1985).

HAVING said this much about the biography, I will turn to Blake's poetry, in particular to some claims made about it by critics from this century. My interest is centered on the shorter poems: the early *Poetical Sketches,* the *Songs of Innocence and Experience,* and the poems from the Rossetti and Pickering manuscripts. This interest has grown out of my attempts—as a nonspecialist teacher of English Romantic poets—to see what can be said about the Blake who is often thrown in with Wordsworth, Keats, Shelley, and who is harder to teach than any of them. By "hard" I don't mean just that the prophetic books are forbidding—which they are, even after Frye and Bloom—but that Blake's shorter poems present a unique challenge to criticism. In this respect, Ackroyd's book gives little help, although there is a revealing moment when, prepared to discuss *The Marriage of Heaven and Hell,* he speculates that Blake "might not have wanted to come too close to himself, in case he did not care for what he found there"; therefore that "he felt the pressing need to express himself and yet at the same time to frame doubts about the nature of that expression by making it ambiguous, satirical or impersonal." This is properly conjectural, but the adjectives point to a central aspect of the poems as well as accounting for the wide interpretative divergences that surround them.

The name of neither T. S. Eliot nor F. R. Leavis appears in Ackroyd's bibliography, yet—though not "Blakeans"—their remarks about the poet are full of useful insight. Eliot's short essay, published in *The Sacred Wood,* is an oddly fascinated response to a poet one might think Eliot would have been wary of. And so he was, at least to the extent that he called Blake's honesty "terrifying," while claiming that his best work had "the unpleasantness of great poetry." Although Eliot seldom descended to particulars and certainly failed to back up his claims, he had strong praise for the Blake of *Poetical Sketches* and *Songs* along with strong reservations about the prophecies insofar as they had fallen under the domination of Blake's "ideas." In depreciating those ideas, Eliot set himself against Yeatsian reverence toward Blake's symbolic philosophy and against later critics like Middleton Murry who (in Murry's words) set out to "elucidate [Blake's] doctrine." (Frye and Bloom, for all their emphasis on individual poems, would also be mainly concerned with elucidating that doctrine.)

In his occasional pronouncements about Blake, Leavis was also wary of the "doctrine," even as (in "Justifying One's Valuation of Blake," 1972) he argued in the strongest terms for Blake's greatness as a poet. Leavis was uneasy with Eliot's emphasis on Blake's "technique" (although, as Eliot himself said, one can't say where technique begins or where it ends), and he saw Blake as a man of genius who, in the eighteenth century, altered expression. Like Eliot, Leavis admired things in the early *Poetical Sketches* such as "My silks and fine array," "To the Muses," "Memory, hither come," and "Mad Song." But when Leavis comes up against an actual Blake poem, even one of his own choosing, he has trouble knowing what to do with it. His appendix in *Revaluation* (1936) on "Hear the Voice of the Bard," from *Songs of Experience,* is, to say the least, confusing. In "Justifying One's Valuation of Blake" he tells us that "The Tyger" "exhibits marked complexity," that it can't be paraphrased, that it makes an "immediately compelling imaginative impact," but that it conveys no "protest"; rather it "constates." I sympathize with Leavis in walking carefully round such a strange and formidable poem as "The Tyger," but find more immediately useful, as an indicator of why Blake is hard to read, a remark Leavis made some years previously in "Literature and Society" *(The Common Pursuit,* 1948). There he referred to the "peculiar kind of difficulty that [Blake's] work offers to the critic," and called it "the difficulty one so often has in deciding what kind of thing it is one has before one." As illustration, Leavis quotes the eight-line epilogue to *For the Sexes: The Gates of Paradise* (one of Blake's illuminated printings) titled "To The Accuser who is The God of This World":

> Truly My Satan thou art but a Dunce
> And dost not know the Garment from the Man
> Every Harlot was a virgin once
> Nor canst thou ever change Kate into Nan
>
> Tho thou art Worshipd by the Names Divine
> Of Jesus & Jehovah: thou art still
> The Son of Morn in weary Night's decline
> The lost Travellers Dream under the Hill

I am quoting, as Leavis couldn't, from the Erdman-Bloom *Complete Poetry and Prose of William Blake* (1988), whose capitalizings and lack of punctuation (except for that unhelpful colon in the second stanza) make the "kind of thing" this poem is even more weird. Leavis says it has "curiously striking qualities" and clearly comes from "a remarkable poet" but that it also shows "lack of self-sufficiency as a poem." This seems, in its ambiguity, the right way to recognize Blake's oddity, his insidious success at making us memorize his poems when we don't understand them. (Since I can't understand it, I can at least memorize it.)

But Leavis's most notorious, and probably his earliest, reference to Blake comes as the final sentence-paragraph of his essay "The Irony of Swift." After measuring Swift and finding him wanting ("He is distinguished by the intensity of his feelings, not by insight into them"), he delivers the coup de grâce: "We shall not find Swift remarkable for intelligence if we think of Blake." An infuriating thing to say, by way of departing from an essay, but it was extremely perceptive of Leavis to link together these two ironists from the beginning and the end of the eighteenth century. Still, it strikes me as strange to think of Blake, as Leavis prompts us to, as distinguished for intelligence because he possessed insight into his feelings—as Swift didn't into his. Keats and Byron, to some extent Wordsworth, might be judged to have possessed and expressed "insight" into their feelings: but Blake? In his wholly unapologetic performances in verse and prose, Blake was too busy knowing the world, its institutions and inhabitants, to have the time to develop insight into his "feelings." "One of the ghastly, obscene knowers," D. H. Lawrence called him (who, as himself a know-it-all, should know). It is the affiliations, rather than the differences between Blake and Swift, which become more credible when we consider the following, extremely rich formulation in Frye's *Fearful Symmetry*—he is speaking of Blake's early satire "An Island in the Moon," but the formulation extends to much of Blake's work: "One may wonder," Frye writes, "whether Blake's sense of the grotesque, of broad caricature and ribald parody, was really a minor quality . . . whether satire was not his real medium, whether in the long run he was not of the race of Rabelais and Apuleius, a metaphysical satirist inclined to fantasy rather than symbolism." This seems to me the single best thing ever said about Blake's poetry, but its implications turn me away from rather than toward the later prophetic works where the fantasy tries to be truth and where the satirist loses his cool.

Satire, ambiguity, fantasy rather than symbolism—if these are truly the elements of *The Songs of Innocence and Experience* (the earlier *Poetical Sketches* are more uniform in tone), then how can the critic best serve them? Perhaps by not interpreting and elucidating too confidently, by not pronouncing too finally on the "kind of thing" the individual poem is. I have in mind, as instances of all-too-confident elucidation, Harold Bloom's accounts in *The Visionary Company* and in *Blake's Apocalypse,* and will demonstrate my point by quoting—from the latter book—his analysis of "Holy Thursday," one of the *Songs of Innocence:*

> 'Twas on a Holy Thursday, their innocent faces clean,
>   The children walking two & two in red & blue & green,
>   Grey-headed beadles walk'd before, with wands as white as snow,
>   Till into the high dome of Paul's they like Thames' waters flow.
>
> O what a multitude they seem'd, these flowers of London town!
>   Seated in companies they sit with radiance all their own.
>   The hum of multitudes was there, but multitudes of lambs,
>   Thousands of little boys & girls raising their innocent hands.

Now like a mighty wind they raise to heaven the voice of song,
Or like harmonious thunderings the seats of Heaven among.
Beneath them sit the aged men, wise guardians of the poor;
Then cherish pity, lest you drive an angel from Your door.

Bloom writes as follows about the poem:

> On Ascension Day the charity children are led into St. Paul's to celebrate the charity of God, that loving pity of which human charity is intended as a direct reflection. The voice of this song is not a child's, but rather of a self-deceived onlooker, impressed by a palpable vision of Innocence, moved by these flowers of London town. The flowing metre is gently idyllic, and the singer gives us two stanzas of Innocent sight, followed by the triumphant sound of Innocence raising its voice to Heaven.
>
> The ambiguity of tone of Blake's songs is never more evident than here, and yet never more difficult to evidence. One can point of course to several disturbing details. The children's faces have been scrubbed clean, and are innocent, in a debased sense—because they ought to appear brutalized, which they are, and yet do not. The children are regimented; they walk two by two, and the beadles' wands are both badges of office and undoubtedly instruments of discipline in a savage British scholastic tradition. The children are dressed in the colors of life; the beadles are greyheaded and carry white as a death emblem. It is the fortieth day after Easter Sunday, forty days after Christ's ascension into Heaven, yet the children, his Lambs, still linger unwillingly in the wilderness of the exploiting society. Though they flow like Thames' waters, this is not a mark of their freedom but of the binding of the Thames, which is already the "chartered" river of the poem "London" in *Songs of Experience.*

There is more to Bloom's interpretation, but perhaps this is enough to suggest the great distance of such interpretation from what I call "responding to Blake." Bloom claims to find "ambiguity of tone" in this, and in other of Blake's songs: yet what is most evident in his own commentary is its utter lack of ambiguity, as he tells us what the poem really means. The children "are innocent, in a debased sense"; the beadles' wands are "undoubtedly instruments in a savage British scholastic tradition"; the children "linger unwillingly" in "the wilderness of the exploiting society"; the waters of the Thames are identical to the "chartered" Thames of "London"; most important, the narrator of the poem is a "self-deceived onlooker"—whereas the critic-interpreter is wholly undeceived, has taken (presumably) the precise measure of things.

In fact, aside from a quick reference to "flowing metre" as "gently idyllic," Bloom seems uninterested in listening to "Holy Thursday," is indeed quite impervious to its climactic and thrilling moment when

> Now like a mighty wind they raise to heaven the voice of song,
> Or like harmonious thunderings the seats of Heaven among.

Here is where, if any place, "ambiguity" asserts itself, as Blake sweepingly makes claims for the power of the children's voices, their "innocent hands," their "multitude" as a "multitude of lambs." To "understand" all this as the self-deceiving reflections of an inadequate speaker actually makes the poem a good deal less strange and less disturbing than it is without such a convenient fiction. And it makes Blake's satire less wild, more precisely controlled, than at least this reader feels it to be. "Holy Thursday" first appeared in Blake's "An Island in the Moon," where—in a completely unprepared-for moment—it is sung by a character named "Obtuse Angle." (Other characters proceed to sing other Blake songs.) In "An Island in the Moon" the contrast was between the silly-satiric prose context and the sudden exciting break into song; in *Songs of Innocence,* "Holy Thursday" incorporates satire and lyric side by side, even simultaneously, in such a way as to defeat the reader who tries to make clear sense out of it, even as we find ourselves singing along with the verse.

This sort of satire (ambiguity is no better a word for it) animates the best of Blake's songs, as well as *The Marriage of Heaven and Hell,* surely the most brilliant and wickedly humorous of the prophecies.[1] It bears out Richard Poirier's quite daring suggestion, in his *Poetry and Pragmatism,* that, for those who like to "vocalize" their reading—who pay attention to the sounds

---

1. Perhaps the best, and not well-known, account of Blake's fiercely satirical propensities in the *Songs* is found in Thomas R. Edwards's *Imagination and Power: A Study of Poetry on Public Themes* (New York: Oxford University Press, 1971), 141–59.

and rhythms of Blake's verse—"The meaning of the piece of writing . . . is in the perceived difficulty of securing one." In those terms, the trouble with the later prophetic books is that their difficulty, experienced in overlong, often arid, stretches of Blakean fourteeners, presents itself as something to be figured out afterwards: elucidated, rather than held in the mind and ear. One thinks of the dull stretches of Pound's *Cantos* that may yield to explication but not to imaginative experience; and indeed Pound put Blake in the Hell of Canto 16: "And the running form, naked, Blake, / Shouting, whirling his arms, the swift limbs, / Howling against the evil, / His eyes rolling." Like Pound, Blake wanted to know everything, and eventually persuaded himself that he did.

One of Blake's oddest and most memorable poems is a ballad from the Pickering Manuscript hardly anyone talks about (Ackroyd makes no mention of it). Titled "William Bond," it begins with a stanza that only Blake— or perhaps some pop lyricist—could have contrived:

> I wonder whether the Girls are mad
> And I wonder whether they mean to kill
> And I wonder if William Bond will die
> For assuredly he is very ill

The poem relates how William went to church one morning attended by three Fairies, but the Fairies were driven away by Angels of Providence, and William returned home in Misery, in "a Black Black Cloud," took to his bed, attended by the Angels of Providence and by his sweetheart Mary Greene and his sister Jane. Mary asks William whether there is "another" he loves better than her, and William admits to it—"For thou art melancholy Pale . . . But she is ruddy and bright as day"—at which point Mary falls down in a faint. The poem then concludes:

> When Mary woke and found her Laid
> On the Right hand of her William dear
> On the Right hand of his loved Bed
> And saw her William Bond so near
>
> The Fairies that fled from William Bond
> Danced around her Shining Head
> They danced over the Pillow white
> And the Angels of Providence left the Bed

I thought Love lived in the hot sun shine
But O he lives in the Moony light
I thought to find Love in the heat of day
But sweet Love is the Comforter of Night

Seek Love in the Pity of others Woe
In the gentle relief of anothers care
In the darkness of night & the winters snow
In the naked & outcast Seek Love there

As with "Truly my Satan," the difficulty is in deciding the kind of thing one has before one, a difficulty not quite solved by calling it a ballad. It helps to recall Northrop Frye—satire, ambiguity, fantasy rather than symbolism—and helps even more to experience the wonderful discovery made by whoever speaks those last two stanzas, the "I" that might be William Bond or William Blake or maybe just some lucky onlooker, like you or me, but with the audacity to end a poem with three stresses, "Seek Love there."

Hudson Review 49, no. 3 (Autumn 1996)

Wordsworth's
"Resolution and Independence"

❧ ❧ ❧

N EW CRITICISM TOLD US to seek out, describe, and admire a poem's organic unity; if upon due study such unity wasn't to be found, so much the worse for the poem. The teacher who introduced me to Wordsworth, Reuben Brower, didn't talk about organic unity (his key term instead was imaginative design), but he liked to teach poems that held together with no loose ends or fallings off—no embarrassing bits. So the Wordsworth on which he lavished his close reading, encouraging students to do likewise, were fairly short and compactly organized poems: "A slumber did my spirit seal"; "To a Butterfly," "The Solitary Reaper," sonnets like the Westminster Bridge one, "Surprised by Joy," and "Mutability." I think it appropriate then that I never encountered "Resolution and Independence" until, as a fast-fading graduate student in philosophy, I sat in on an undergraduate class of Lionel Trilling's at Columbia. A very different sort of reader from Brower, Trilling made much of the poem, most of which has faded from memory. But he was interested in it for its ideas about poetry and being a poet, rather than for its coherence and aesthetic value.

From the outset, readers of "Resolution and Independence" have been unsure just how or whether it "goes together" and how much difference such going together makes to the poem's achievement. In a remark often quoted from *Biographia Literaria*, where Coleridge took up the characteristic defects of his friend's poetry, he put "inconstancy of the style" at the top of the list. This inconstancy consisted in Wordsworth's seemingly thoughtless mixture of "noble" and ignoble lines or stanzas within the same poem, and Coleridge quoted as ignoble a stanza Wordsworth later omitted (though for some reason now restored in the recent Oxford selection edited by his biographer Stephen Gill), and three others (XVIII, XIX, XX), the middle one of which fitted ill with the two good ones that surrounded it.

For the next hundred and more years, nobody paid much attention to "Resolution and Independence." Arnold included it in his selection from Wordsworth, but didn't mention it in his introductory essay on the poet. Only within the last few decades have critics dedicated themselves to proving Coleridge wrong, or rather, proving that seeming inconstancy of style is really a subtle instance of the poem's dialectic (I take the word from an essay by Anthony Conran). Still, Coleridge said the real right thing that any reader of "Resolution and Independence" is sure to be struck by: that visionary-sublime Wordsworth jostles with humble-rustic-language-of-real-men Wordsworth so as to make for a strange combination, a strange poem.

Its 140 lines are too long to quote in their entirety, but you know the story, I trust: the poet, out in nature on a magnificent morning, falls unaccountably into depression, thinks large gloomy thoughts about the fate of poets and his own previous life, then encounters a solitary by whose agency he is eventually rescued from despair, into affirmation. Wordsworth's editor in the Riverside edition, Jack Stillinger, puts it this way: "The main point of the poem . . . is the apt admonishment of the speaker's romanticizing on the misery and despondency traditionally suffered by poets. The leechgatherer's troubles are much more real than those of the mighty Poets, but instead of ending in madness he cheerfully perseveres, and the speaker, when he is finally able to take in the old man's story, could have laughed myself to scorn at the contrast." Well, if that's the "point" of "Resolution and Independence," I'm not much interested in it, certainly not moved by it.

Not that Wordsworth himself didn't think it exactly the point when in a letter to Sara Hutchinson, written shortly after he had sent her the first version and considered her insufficiently impressed by the Leech-gatherer, he insisted that the figure had rescued him from "dejection and despair." He told Sara Hutchinson, who had complained that the old man's speech was "tedious," that "everything is tedious when one does not read with the feelings of the Author" and went on in his insufferable Wordsworthian way further to put Sara in her humble place: "It is in the character of the old man to tell his story in a manner which an *impatient* reader necessarily feels as tedious. But Good God! Such a figure, in such a place, a pious self-respecting, miserably infirm . . . Old Man telling such a tale!" (Nevertheless, Wordsworth in revising the poem reduced the Leech-gatherer's direct discourse to a single assertion in the penultimate stanza.) But I think we must be as resistant as Sara to such importunings, since their implication is to render the poetry of little account compared to the marvelous truth to life it presumably, transparently, conveys.

Let us pause over some aspects of that poetry and attempt to suggest its curious and unforgettable life, even as that life emerges out of a verse that is sometimes—to say the least—less than memorable, awkward, embarrassing. The stanza, rime royal with the final line an alexandrine, is unusual for Wordsworth and has an ancestor in "An Excellent Ballad of Charitie," a poem by the eighteenth-century poet Thomas Chatterton, who appears in stanza 7. Other predecessors—without the closing alexandrine—are Chaucer in his *Troilus* and some of the Canterbury Tales, Spenser in "Four Hymns" and Shakespeare in "The Rape of Lucrece." By the early seventeenth century the stanza was all but dead as a useful literary form, so Wordsworth's resuscitation of it, perhaps thinking it especially appropriate for a "quaint" narrative, is consciously old-fashioned, but useful for description and digression, activities in which the narrator of "Resolution and Independence" engages.

It is convenient to divide the poem in three, with the first seven stanzas setting forth the speaker-poet's (call him Wordsworth's) plight, beginning memorably with "There was a roaring in the wind all night." That roar will soon translate into an inner turmoil as Wordsworth, despite the splendid weather following the night's storm—or maybe because of it—finds himself (or found himself, since with stanza 3 we move surprisingly into the past) out of harmony with the natural scene. (A similar disharmony, though for a different reason, is set forth in the opening stanzas of the Immortality ode, composed during the same period as "Resolution.") At any rate, nobody to my knowledge has ever questioned the thrilling directness of these opening stanzas:

> There was a roaring in the wind all night;
> The rain came heavily and fell in floods;
> But now the sun is rising calm and bright;

The birds are singing in the distant woods;
Over his own sweet voice the Stock-dove broods;
The Jay makes answer as the Magpie chatters;
And all the air is filled with pleasant noise of waters.

All things that love the sun are out of doors;
The sky rejoices in the morning's birth;
The grass is bright with rain-drops—on the moors
The hare is running races in her mirth;
And with her feet she from the plashy earth
Raises a mist; that, glittering in the sun,
Runs with her all the way, wherever she doth run.

I was a Traveller then upon the moor;
I saw the hare that raced about with joy;
I heard the woods and distant waters roar;
Or heard them not, as happy as a boy:
The pleasant season did my heart employ:
My old remembrances went from me wholly;
And all the ways of men, so vain and melancholy.

But as it sometimes chanceth, from the might
Of joy in minds that can no further go,
As high as we have mounted in delight
In our dejection do we sink as low;
To me that morning did it happen so;
And fears and fancies thick upon me came;
Dim sadness—and blind thoughts, I knew not, nor could name.

I heard the skylark warbling in the sky;
And I bethought me of the playful hare:
Even such a happy Child of earth am I;
Even as these blissful creatures do I fare;
Far from the world I walk, and from all care;
But there may come another day to me—
Solitude, pain of heart, distress, and poverty.

My whole life I have lived in pleasant thought,
As if life's business were a summer mood;

As if all needful things would come unsought
To genial faith, still rich in genial good;
But how can He expect that others should
Build for him, sow for him, and at his call
Love him, who for himself will take no heed at all?

I thought of Chatterton, the marvellous Boy,
The sleepless Soul that perished in his pride;
Of Him who walked in glory and in joy
Following his plough, along the mountain-side;
By our own spirits are we deified:
We Poets in our youth begin in gladness;
But thereof come in the end despondency and madness.

How much the power of these opening stanzas was enhanced by my first hearing them read out by the voice of Lionel Trilling I can't say; I suspect much. But the splendid directness of observation and registration; the delicacy with which the natural scene is presented in the declarative succession of sentences in the first three stanzas; and the fact that, for Wordsworth, such troubled and untranquil self-presentation is not a usual thing for him—these imbue the poem with audible intensity. The intensity is summed up and made into a moral shape by the two wonderful utterances that we also might not expect to hear from Wordsworth: one about dejection, the other about the fate of poets.

"As high as we have mounted in delight / In our dejection do we sink as low" is the best celebration and critique of the romantic spirit I know of, and I have quoted it to myself so many times over the years that I've managed almost wholly to extirpate that spirit in my own life. That the dejection which overtakes Wordsworth is sudden, too deep for words ("Dim sadness—and blind thoughts, I knew not, nor could name"—a fine use of the extra foot to enact confusion) and unknowable, is, as an idea, a way of looking at the mind just plain more interesting than being told the poet's heart dances with the daffodils or even that nature is the guardian of his heart and soul of all his moral being. The other formulation, concluding stanza 7, which begins with thoughts of "Chatterton, the marvellous Boy," says that "We Poets in our youth begin in gladness / But thereof come in the end despondency and madness." The same inevitability that governs the relation between delight and dejection presides over the fate of poets: it is *because* their "genial spirits"—their genius—is so pronounced, and singled out for special treatment, that what they get in time, in the end, will be equally, painfully, extreme. In Robert Lowell's poem to Delmore Schwartz, Lowell has Schwartz, probably wilfully, misquote the line as "We poets in our youth begin in sadness." Whether or not Schwartz thought it rightly described his own life, the formulation sentimentalizes and simplifies Wordsworth's hard saying.

How does the poem resolve or mitigate this hard saying? Or does it? In the Intimations ode, Wordsworth asked himself a leading question "Whither is fled the visionary gleam?" and spent most of the poem insisting that the gleam was both essentially irrecoverable and, through imagination, recoverable. In our poem, resolution of and independence from the sadness and blind thoughts about life's inevitable miseries, especially for poets, is presumably effected by the miraculous appearance on the scene of an old man. Or say rather that with stanza 8 the scene completely changes—no chattering jays and magpies, no warbling skylark or playful hare, but only "a pool bare to the eye of heaven," a "lonely place" in which a capital Man is standing "unawares." Beginning with Wordsworth himself, readers have admired the comparison of the man to a huge stone, to a huge stone that's like a sea-beast, and Wordsworth singled out stanza 9 as an instance of "the conferring, the abstracting, the modifying powers of imagination." Like other solitaires who appear out of nowhere and somehow admonish Wordsworth as boy, as man, as poet, the Leech-gatherer is at or beyond some limit of human existence. He must be described in the negative ("not all alive nor dead, / Nor all asleep") since mere positives would misstate and mislead; he is "bent double"; and of course he is unmoving, motionless as a cloud: "That heareth not the loud winds when they call; / And moveth all together, if it move at all." He is integral, the essence of integrity.

To be sure, there is one moment in the stanzas introducing him that, rather than conjuring up strangeness, difference, nonhuman "natural" integrity, just seems clunkish. I, at least, can only accept the alexandrine in stanza 8, ending by rhyming "unawares" with "hairs," in the spirit of saying something like, well that's Wordsworth, you know, while trying out the line, impiously, in the accents of W. C. Fields: "The oldest man he seemed that ever wore grey hairs." As a rhymer, Wordsworth is not of the first rank (Pope, Keats, Bryon, Yeats) and here the attempt to quantify, a bit, the man's age, rather than compare him to something inanimate, seems bathetic. No matter: Wordsworth, the traveller, in taking "a stranger's privilege" and remarking that "This morning gives us promise of a glorious day," is reasonable enough; maybe even leech-gatherers don't mind talking about the weather. But what particular words can this stone-sea-beast-cloud be given to speak? Wisely, Wordsworth the poet hopes we'll accept that the man's answer was "gentle," his speech "courteous." Emboldened, our narrator tries again, asking the man what he does for a living and remarking that "This is a lonesome place for one like you." No wonder the Leech-gatherer responds first with "a flash of mild surprise" to this suggestion that the place, lonesome enough for anybody, is especially so for the old man. "Just who does he think I am," we might imagine the Leech-gatherer thinking to himself, "that he can use *lonesome* as the sort of human adjective I could agree to? For old *ordinary* men, yes, certainly lonesome—but for me, the oldest man it seemed that ever wore grey hairs, wholly appropriate."

Wordsworth, the traveller, seems to recognize this specialness in stanza 14 when, by emphasizing both the feebleness and solemnity of the man's words (which of course we don't hear), he places them "above the reach of ordinary men." We can't help thinking here of the preface to *Lyrical Ballads* in its insistence that the language "really used by men"—those men in humble and rustic life—is more simplified, purified, permanent, and philosophical than the language poets often use. Yet in what seems to me perhaps the worst two lines in the poem, the poet attempts, in stanza 14, to particularize this amazing speech as the sort of thing "grave Livers do in Scotland use," informing us, as if we wanted to know, that such livers are "Religious men, who give to God and man their dues."

Stanzas 15 and 16 juxtapose further homely details of the old man's employment, with Wordsworth's insistence on the visionary, admonitory meaning of this creature sent from somewhere to give him human strength. Then, in stanza 17 everything comes back in thrillingly summarizing lines:

> My former thoughts returned; the fear that kills
> And hope that is unwilling to be fed;
> Cold, pain, and labour, and all fleshly ills
> And mighty Poets in their misery dead.
> —Perplexed, and longing to be comforted,
> My question eagerly did I renew,
> "How is it that you live and what is it you do?"

The powerfully moving rhetoric of the first four lines makes the question, a reiterated one, rather more drastic and unanswerable than in its previous form, "What occupation do you there pursue?" Indeed I would deliver it in exaggerated mode beyond any social decorum, as befits an address to a man met with in a dream: "How is it that you *live,* and what is it you *do?*" How is it that you "live" at all, or "do" anything? We may, I think, sympathize with the Leech-gatherer at this point as he entertains the Romantic equivalent of our current "What can I tell you?" And the genius of Lewis Carroll's parody in *Through the Looking-Glass* fixed on this moment in Wordsworth's poem:

> I shook him well from side to side,
>   Until his face was blue:
> 'Come, tell me how you live,' I cried
>   And what is it you do!

(Carroll's aged man replies that he hunts for haddocks' eyes and makes them into waistcoat buttons.)

As previously remarked, Coleridge, perhaps fearing the possibilities for parody presented by the next stanza, deplored it as incongruous with the ones that precede and follow it. I like to take the Leech-gatherer's smile here as the politesse someone from outer space might summon up to address a mere earthling; indeed the man from somewhere else for the first time deigns to let himself be quoted directly. Surely his reply ("Yet still I persevere and find them where I may") didn't tell Wordsworth, the traveller, anything he hadn't already heard. Or did it? The final two stanzas claim that, somehow, it did:

> While he was talking thus, the lonely place,
> The old Man's shape, and speech—all troubled me:
> In my mind's eye I seemed to see him pace
> About the weary moors continually,
> Wandering about alone and silently.
> While I these thoughts within myself pursued,
> He, having made a pause, the same discourse renewed.
>
> And soon with this he other matter blended,
> Cheerfully uttered, with demeanour kind,
> But stately in the main; and when he ended,
> I could have laughed myself to scorn to find

In that decrepit Man so firm a mind.
"God," said I, "be my help and stay secure;
I'll think of the Leech-gatherer on the lonely moor!"

It's not clear how the troubled poet of stanza 19—troubled by his image of the old Man wandering about, continually, silently alone—is within a few lines brought to the presumably ringing affirmation to God which concludes the poem. Most bogus, I think, is the pretense that the Leech-gatherer went on, with cheerful utterance, to blend other "matter" into his discourse. What on earth could such matter have been, uttered by the essence of the monolithic? Various critical accounts have been given of what happens finally: the poet has shifted from the nightmare world of metaphor and myth to the solid world of good sense; or he has moved forward from the world of fact to the world of vision; or he has arrived at some middle ground; or he rests in comforting (or is it disquieting?) simultaneity. W. W. Robson, one of the best critics of the poem, says that in accepting the Leech-gatherer the poet has recognized "others' independence of one's own fantasies." I don't find myself voting for any of these "meanings" as the right one; nor can I believe that the hopeful Wordsworthian voice that insists "I'll think of the Leech-gatherer on the lonely moor" can banish, for more than half an instant, the other Wordsworth who knows about hopes and fears, about "cold, pain, and labour, and all fleshly ills / And mighty Poets in their misery dead." Nothing cancels out anything else in "Resolution and Independence"; it's all there, all not to be reconciled, certainly not the disparate voices. But the poem is the better for such disparity.

Byron in His Letters

❦

L IVING IN RAVENNA in 1819, Byron wrote Count Giuseppe Albor-
ghetti a polite letter which concluded with assurances about the
count's literary style: "I congratulate you . . . on your English—I am *not* 'the
greatest poet' &c. as you are pleased to say—and if I were you need not be
afraid as you have written very good English prose—a better thing when
well done than poetry at any time." An extraordinary thing to say, especially
because he sounds as if he believes it. And Byron would be amused at the
chorus of praise his own prose has received over the last nine years in which
Leslie Marchand's edition of the letters and journals has appeared. Claims
for him as one of the greatest letter writers have been made; *Newsweek* has
saluted the "sinewy, funny, electrifying" nature of these "emergency bul-
letins"; the Modern Language Association has awarded them a prize for
being "the fullest portrayal of [his] complex nature." Having previously
encountered Byron through his letters only in small doses, I must admit to

Byron's Letters and Journals, ed. Leslie A. Marchand. 12 vols. Cambridge: Harvard University Press, Belknap Press, 1973–82. Volume 1, *"In My Hot Youth"*: *1798—1810;* Volume
2, *"Famous in My Time"*: *1810–1812;* Volume 3, *"Alas! The Love of Women"*: *1813–1814;*
Volume 4, *"Wedlock's the Devil"*: *1814–1815;* Volume 5, *"So Late into the Night"*: *1816–1817;*
Volume 6, *"The Flesh Is Frail"*: *1818–1819;* Volume 7, *"Between Two Worlds"*: *1820;* Volume
8, *"Born for Opposition"*: *1821;* Volume 9, *"In the Wind's Eye"*: *1821–1822;* Volume 10, *"A
Heart for Every Fate"*: *1822–1823;* Volume 11, *"For Freedom's Battle"*: *1823–1824;* Volume 12,
"The Trouble of an Index."

mixed feelings about the whole affair, since I can't imagine who, except the Byron scholar, would want to sit down and read through all three thousand letters. If one doesn't want to spend much of the summer at it, the four-hundred-page Everyman's selection is still the place to go to hear Byron reveal himself over the course of a life, though one will be misled by this earlier selection. For example, in reading the last letter Byron wrote to Tom Moore it might be assumed that he really signed it "Ever and affectionately yours," when in fact Byron, annoyed by the tone of Moore's recent letter to him, actually wrote "ever and truly yrs," which was a cut below his usual warmth, and Moore affectionately doctored it up so as not to lose face with his public. But enough plaudits have been handed Marchand's beautifully engineered editorial operation to make it unnecessary for a non-Byron scholar like me to add mine; I should like instead to share my sense of the letters as expressions of the masterful personality of their author.

In a memorable stanza from "Stanzas from the Grand Chartreuse," Matthew Arnold cried out despairingly

> What helps it now, that Byron bore,
> With haughty scorn which mock'd the smart,
> Through Europe to the Aetolian shore
> The pageant of his bleeding heart?
> That thousands counted every groan,
> And Europe made his woe her own?

and had previously, in his "Memorial Verses," opined that "He taught us little; but our soul / Had *felt* him like the thunder's roll." But the overwhelming portion of Byron's letters reveals something quite different from either a bleeding heart or the sound like thunder rolling; it is rather the cool, resourceful, absolutely secure voice of the confirmed skeptic that speaks. Reviewing the earliest volumes of the edition (*Listener*, 27 September 1973) Christopher Ricks tellingly located the essence of Byron in his use of the word "but"—"In short, I deny nothing but doubt everything"—and his greatness to lie "in his various insistence upon the word and upon the thousand ways in which it is urgently apt." As Ricks nicely puts it, "But me no buts? But Byron seeks to but himself no end of buts." At that point Marchand's third volume hadn't appeared, but Ricks would have had a good time with the following sequence from a Byron escapade which began in September 1813 when he went down to Aston Hall in Rotherham to stay with a rather silly friend, James Wedderburn Webster, and his bride, Lady Frances:

> The place is very well & quiet & the children only scream in a low voice—so that I am not much disturbed & shall stay a few days in tolerable repose.—W[ebster] don't want sense nor good nature but both are occasionally obscured by his suspicions & absurdities of all descriptions he is passionately fond of having his wife admired— & all the time jealous to jaundice of every thing & every body—I have hit upon the medium of praising her to him perpetually behind her back—& never looking at her before his face—as for her I believe she is disposed to be very faithful—& I don't think any one now here is inclined to put her to the test.

But . . . a couple of weeks later something has happened:

> In these last few days I have had a good deal of conversation with an amiable person . . . well—these things are dull in detail—take it once—I have made love—& if I am to believe mere *words* (for there we have hitherto stopped) it is returned.—I must tell you the place of declaration however—a billiard room!—I did not as C [Caroline Lamb] says "kneel in the middle of the room" but like Corporal Trim to the Nun "I made a speech."

Years later Byron referred to *Don Juan* as "a poetical *Tristram Shandy*," and here he was acting out his material in advance to Lady Melbourne, his main confidante in affairs of the heart. As he thinks about Wedderburn Webster's vanity, his chasing after other women and boasting about it, Byron finds that, really, Webster is to blame for the flirtation between himself and Lady Frances: "He must not be surprised if others admire that which he knows not how to value . . . Oons! who is this strange monopolist?" And as he may have remembered from writing it to Lady Melbourne a year previously about another woman, "She is very fond of her husband, which is all the better, as thus, if a woman is attached to her husband how much more will she naturally like one who is *not* her husband."

By November Lady Frances was writing intimately to Byron and he was delightedly sharing the correspondence with Lady Melbourne. Although the affair, it appears, was not consummated ("a fervent, but inconclusive passage," Peter Quennell has dubbed it), it hardly matters, since he had taken it to a high comic literary plane of pure, even disinterested contemplation. He is amused by "the simplicity of her cunning" and how she vindicates her "treachery" to Webster:

> Again she desires me to write to him *kindly*—for—she believes he cares for nobody but me! besides she will then hear of when she can't from me.—Is not all this a comedy?— . . . it has enlivened my ethical studies on the human mind beyond 50 volumes—how admirably we accommodate our reasons to our wishes!— — —She concludes by denominating that respectable man *"Argus"* a very irreverent appellation—if we can both hold out till Spring—perhaps he may have occasion for his Optics.—After all—"it is to deceive un Marito" does not this expression convey to you the strangest mixture of right & wrong?—a really guilty person could not have used it—or rather they would *but* in different words find she has not the *but* and that makes much difference—if you consider it—the experienced would have said it is *"only* deceiving *him"*—thinking of themselves she makes a *merit* of it on his account & mine.

One couldn't ask for a more brilliant and concentrated example of Byron's vigorous detachment—vigorous because one feels him warming to the analysis as it proceeds, hardly able to believe what, through his own words, he is bringing forth from Lady Frances. It anticipates nothing so much as the diligent ease of *Don Juan* at its best when it seems the opposite of anything made up in advance. The improvisatory elegance of this prose, its sparkle and high intelligence (surely the word is justified), are wonderful, especially when we remember that at the time Byron wrote it he was turning out (in the intervals of dressing for dinner, or undressing after a night out) things like "The Bride of Abydos" and "The Corsair," poems that not even T. S. Eliot's praise of their ingenuity in story-telling has made me read all the way through.

"Mad—bad—and dangerous to know," said Lady Caroline Lamb about him, in a feat of self-definition. But who can read, without wholly admiring it, the beginning and postscript from this letter to a woman (Henrietta D'Ussières) who persisted in writing the newly famous poet and eventually received a reply:

Excepting your compliments (which are only excusable because you don't know me) you write like a clever woman for which reason I hope you *look* as unlike one as possible—I never knew but one of your country—Me. de Stael—[who had said Byron was "totally insensible to *la belle passion*"]—and she is as frightful as a precipice.—As it seems impracticable my visiting you—cannot you contrive to visit me? telling me the time previously that I may be in ye. way—and if this same interview leads to the "leap into the Serpentine" you mention—we can take the jump together—and shall be very good company—for I swim like a Duck—(one of the few things I can do well) and you say that your Sire taught you the same useful acquirement.

The postscript contains this: " 'Surprized' oh! no!—I am surprized at nothing—except at your taking so much trouble about one who is not worth it." Compare the overall friendly spirit of this (they never got together, in or out of the Serpentine) with Evelyn Waugh's equally splendid but rather less mannerly letter to the husband of a woman who had the nerve to write to him (Waugh told the husband he should restrain his wife from writing to strange men).

Of course Byron's reference to swimming, in the above paragraph, was in no way lightly made. We remember, and he informs his correspondents often in the early letters, that he swam the Hellespont (like a duck, doubtless) from Sestos to Abydos. As for making love, "It is true from early habit, one must make love mechanically as one swims, I was once very fond of both, but now as I never swim unless I tumble into the water, I don't make love till almost obliged" (this was only 1812, when he'd barely gotten started!). And to an English critic, reported by Byron's publisher John Murray to have objected to the mixture of humor and seriousness in *Don Juan* by stating that "We are never scorched and drenched at the same time," he replied

Blessings on his experience! . . . Did he never spill a dish of tea over his testicles in handing a cup to his charmer, to the great shame of his nankeen breeches? Did he never swim in the sea at Noonday with the Sun in his eyes and on his head, which all the foam of Ocean could not cool? . . . Did he never inject for a Gonorrhea? Or

make water through an ulcerated Urethra? Was he ever in a Turkish
bath, that marble paradise of sherbet and sodomy?

This is undeniably the voice of experience. After all, he had years ago (1810)
written home from a frigate in the Dardanelles, off Abydos, that "I see not
much difference between ourselves & the Turks, save that we have foreskins
and they have none, that they have long dresses and we short, and that we
talk much and they little.—In England the vices in fashion are whoring and
drinking, in Turkey, Sodomy & smoking, we prefer a girl and a bottle, they a
pipe and pathic." There is something intensely life-giving and totally sane
about these blends of feeling which scorch and drench us at the same time,
as the comic spirit is wont to do. One thinks, to the later writer's disadvan-
tage, of D. H. Lawrence's solemnities about how different from us were
those natives south of the border—but then, Lawrence never got to Turkey.

Byron claimed that he reveled in contraries and self-contradiction. At
one point in 1813, when he was keeping the journal he sporadically kept
(these journals are of unfailing interest), he rather loudly welcomed the
spirit of contradiction: "If I am sincere with myself (but I fear one lies more
to one's self than to any one else), every page should confute, refute, and
utterly abjure its predecessor." In fact, to a reader it feels more of a piece
than that, though with plenty of variety in the poses he tries on to suit his
inner weather. There is the man who knows all about women and affairs of
the heart, and who knows why Lady Melbourne has remained his friend: "If
she had been a few years younger, what a fool she would have made of me,
had she thought it worth her while,—and I should have lost a valuable and
most agreeable friend. Mem. a mistress never is nor can be a friend. While
you agree, you are lovers; and, when it is over, any thing but friends"—a
truth, I believe, which hasn't lost its freshness a century and a half later.
There is the lover who tells his mistress in words what a bundle of marvelous contradictions she is: "I have always thought you the cleverest most
agreeable, absurd, amiable, perplexing, dangerous fascinating little thing
that lives now or ought to have lived 2000 years ago," he wrote Caroline
Lamb in April 1812. Six months later, it was a new ball game: "correct yr.
vanity which is ridiculous & proverbial, exert yr. Caprices on your new
conquests & leave me in peace, yrs. Byron." A mistress never is nor can be
a friend.

Or there is the literary critic who sees through everything, including Shakespeare: "[His] name, you may depend on it, stands absurdly too high and will go down. He took all his plots from old novels, and threw their stories into a dramatic shape . . . That he threw over whatever he did write some flashes of genius, nobody can deny: but this was all." So speaks the most un-Shakespearian user of language among the major English nineteenth-century poets, content to write off the master as merely a genius with words who was seriously deficient in executive skill. (Though Byron was not above quoting Coriolanus more than once—"There is a world elsewhere"—as he acted out the hero preparing to exile himself.) There is the satisfied lecher boasting a bit of his own executive skill with maidens of the south and telling his pal Hobhouse about what an agreeable life it is in hospitable Venice, if you can just manage to meet the right people:

> I asked Rizzo to introduce me—who declined . . . so I found a way by means of Soranzo another Venetian noble and friend of mine and have fucked her twice a day for the last six—today is the seventh—but no Sabbath day—for we meet at Midnight at her Milliner's—She is the prettiest Bacchante in the world—& a piece to perish in. . . . I have a world of other harlotry—besides an offer of the daughter of the Arlechino of St. Luke's theatre— so that my hands are full— —whatever my Seminal vessels may be—With regard to Arpalice Teruceli (the Madcap above mentioned)—recollect there is no *liaison* only *fuff-fuff* and passades—& fair fucking.

(Mr. Marchand has not provided a footnote on *"fuff-fuff,"* so we can assume he knows what it is, though I have had to use my imagination.) There's absolutely no doubt about it, Byron treated women as sexual objects rather than persons, and the annoying thing is he seems to have had pretty good luck with it, especially in Venice:

> You may suppose that in *two years*—with a large establishment—horses—houses—box at the opera—Gondola—journeys—women—and Charity—(for I have not laid out all upon my pleasures—but have bought occasionally a shillings-worth of Salvation) villas in the country—another carriage & horses purchased for the country—books bought &c. &c.—in short every thing I wanted—&

more than I ought to have wanted—that the sum of five thousand pounds sterling is no great deal—particularly when I tell you that more than half was laid out on the Sex—to be sure I have had plenty for the money—that's certain—I think at least two hundred of one sort or another—perhaps more—for I have not lately kept the recount.

No great deal, indeed no big deal, and one sympathizes with the difficulties of keeping count after the two hundred level is reached. What else can you do if your wife leaves you ("the Princess of Parallelograms" Byron more than once called Annabella Milbanke) but keep going somehow, in another country. There was certainly a world elsewhere. Tennyson, by contrast, after he went out into the woods and wrote "Byron is dead," decided it would be wisest to stay at home and keep house with Emily Sellwood.

The quoting of choice bits from these letters and journals, as I have been doing, may give the impression that reading them is one continuous pleasure; that however would be far from the case. I cannot begin to suggest the boredom induced by too many letters to Lady Melbourne complaining about Caroline Lamb, or the endless ones protesting Lady Byron's conduct in leaving him. From first to last the letters dealing with matters financial—most of them eventually written to Douglas Kinnaird, about the sale of Newstead Abbey or Rochdale, or the convenience of having more cash—are a trial. There is a great moment in the "London" cantos of *Don Juan* when Byron disputes the truth of a line from his idol, Sir Walter Scott—"Love rules the Camp, the Court, the Grove"—by doubting that Love so rules:

> But if Love don't, *Cash* does, and Cash alone:
> Cash rules the Grove, and fells it too besides;
> Without cash, camps were thin, and courts were none;
> Without cash, Malthus tells you—"take no brides."

But I could not maintain the necessary interest in Byron's cash problems, as rendered in prose. There are also a great many letters making changes in poems he's submitted, only of interest to the Byron scholar. The letters (given both in the Italian and in translation) to his long-term last love, the countess Teresa Guccioli, seemed to me a monotonously high profession of noble motives and feelings, humorless and yawn-provoking. And though it may just have been your reviewer running down, I found the late letters, particularly the ones written from Greece during the final adventure, not up to the standards set by Byron at his best.

The letters concerning other writers, however, are fine indeed. Byron's tributes to Scott are handsome throughout, from his early ranking of that poet at the apex of a triangle, to his late, passionate defense of him to Stendhal. Speaking of a decision to use the heroic couplet for one of his own poems, he confesses that "Scott alone (he will excuse the Mr. 'we do not say Mr. Caesar'), Scott alone of the present generation has hitherto completely triumphed over the fatal facility of octosyllabic verse—and this is not the least victory of his varied and mighty genius." Although he put Southey-Wordsworth-Coleridge near the base of his poetry triangle, just above "The Many," he also said about Wordsworth (while doubting that *The Excursion* could be fine as a whole) that "there can be no doubt of his powers to do about any thing." He patronized Keats unfailingly ("such writing is a sort of mental masturbation— he is always f—gg—g his *Imagination.*—I don't mean that he is *indecent* but vigorously soliciting his own ideas into a state which is neither poetry nor any thing else but a Bedlam vision produced by raw pork and opium." (Discuss, with reference to "Ode on Melancholy.") But his response to Keats's death was decent: "I am very sorry for it—though I think he took the wrong line as a poet," even though he didn't really believe the poet could have been done to death by the savage review of *Endymion*. He recalls an early savage review of himself by Jeffrey: "Instead of bursting a blood-vessel—I drank three bottles of claret—and began an answer." Along with the rapture he always directed at Pope, there is a nice appreciation of the greatness of the "Sporus" passage from the Arbuthnot epistle.

He is equally interesting about his own poetry. Of the many excellent nineteenth-century criticisms later to be made of it (those by Jeffrey, Hazlitt, Carlyle, and Ruskin should be specially consulted) Swinburne's comparison of Byron's two long poems is outstanding:

> Much of the poet's earlier work is or seems unconsciously dishonest; [*Don Juan*] if not always or wholly unaffected, is as honest as the sunlight, as frank as the sea-wind. Here, and here alone the student of his work may recognise and enjoy the ebb and flow of actual life. . . . Here for the first time the style of Byron is beyond all praise or blame; a style at once swift and supple, light and strong,

various and radiant. Between *Childe Harold* and *Don Juan* the same difference exists which a swimmer feels between lake-water and sea-water; the one is fluent, yielding, invariable; the other has in it a life and pulse, a sting and a swell, which touch and excite the nerves like fire or like music.

What would Byron have thought of Swinburne's late tour de force "A Swimmer's Dream"? He surely would have approved the latter's distinction between the two long poems, since he himself wrote to Murray in 1820 that "a very pretty Italian lady" had complimented him on *Juan,* but also remarked upon its "drawbacks": "I answered that 'what she had said was true—but that I suspected it would live longer than Childe Harold.'—'Ah (but said she) I would *rather have the fame of Childe Harold for three years than an immortality of Don Juan!'* The truth is that it is *too true*—and the women hate every thing which strips off the tinsel of *Sentiment*—& they are right— or it would rob them of their weapons." And he was right; *Don Juan* has lasted, while *Childe Harold,* except for some of its "action" scenes, as of Waterloo in the third canto, is a series of frozen postures which lack the "life and pulse, a sting and a swell" Swinburne felt in the later poem. Byron had started out in *Don Juan* meaning to be "a little quietly facetious upon everything"; he believed, rightly about his own work at least, that "poetry is *generally* good—only by fits & starts—& you are lucky to get a sparkle here & there you might as well want a Midnight *all stars*—as rhyme all perfect." So if but "one half of the two new Cantos be good in your opinion" he wrote to his publisher, "What the devil would you have more"? No more, is I think our answer; *Don Juan* is a wonderful poem to read all the way through (as I have finally done, after avoiding the middle cantos for years) or to read aloud from with a class at the end of a semester of high seriousness in Wordsworth, Shelley and Keats. The very best parts of the poem come at its beginning (the first three cantos) and toward the end with the London cantos. There the pure performance of the words sometimes dazzles, as in the marvelous "thieves language" stanza, which Eliot admired, about Juan killing the highwayman:

> He from the world had cut off a great man,
>   Who in his time had made heroic bustle.
> Who in a row like Tom could lead the van,
>   Booze in the ken, or at the spellken hustle?

> Who queer a flat? Who (spite of Bow-street's ban)
>   On the high toby-spice so flash the muzzle?
> Who on a lark, with black eyed Sal (his blowing)
> So prime, so swell, so nutty, and so knowing?

(That last line especially brings tears of joy to the eyes.) But Eliot pointed out that Byron also had a real subject in those late cantos. When he wrote near the end of his life "that there is no society so intrinsically (though hypocritically) *intrigante* and profligate as English high life," he knew whereof he spoke. Yet the overall effect of the satire is more genial than that, and even in places sympathetic. Anything so solemn as "condemnation" just wasn't possible, given the necessary rhyming of the famous stanza.

"I should never have thought myself good for anything if I had not been detested by the English," he wrote Douglas Kinnaird, and concluded a paragraph with the promise, "But Courage! I'll work them." He did, although a few places held out, like Westminster Abbey where (believe it or not) he had to wait until 1969 before they honored him with a plaque. But a better honor was the poem he wrote and entered as the last words in his final journal, and which editor Marchand prints at the front of the concluding volume of letters: "On This Day I Complete My Thirty-Sixth Year," written at Missolonghi, 22 January 1824. It begins with the lover's complaint:

> 'Tis time this heart should be unmoved,
>   Since others it hath ceased to move:
> Yet though I cannot be beloved,
>   Still let me love!

then moves from despair at his days having fallen "in the yellow leaf," to one last self-arousal:

> Awake (not Greece—she is awake!)
>   Awake, my Spirit! think through whom
> Thy life-blood tracks its parent lake
>   And then strike home!
>
> Tread those reviving passions down
>   Unworthy Manhood—unto thee
> Indifferent should the smile or frown
>   Of Beauty be.

If thou regret'st thy Youth, *why live?*
   The land of honourable Death
Is here:—up to the Field, and give
   Away thy Breath!

Seek out—less often sought than found—
   A Soldier's Grave, for thee the best;
Then look around, and choose thy Ground,
   And take thy Rest.

He didn't find a Soldier's Grave; instead came a convulsion, leeches at his temples, endless bleeding by a parcel of doctors, until his breath was finally given away. But Life contradicts Art, just as he expected the pages of his journal to contradict each other. And this late little poem, which contradicts everything his Romantic contemporaries were showing about what could be done with language, is a fine one nonetheless. Of such surprises is the essential Byron, and this edition lets us see him plain.

Hudson Review 34, no. 4 (Winter 1982)

My Brontë Problem—and Yours?

❧

FOR AT LEAST the past two decades I have read very little by or about the Brontë sisters, have left their novels off course syllabi that regularly included Jane Austen and George Eliot, have even—when in England—continued to avoid a pilgrimage to Haworth and environs. The publication of Juliet Barker's massive compound biography of the family—for once, "magisterial" is an understatement—roused me from my dogmatic slumbers, as it became time to render some account of how much I'd been missing. Accordingly, over the past few months, I've reread *Jane Eyre* and *Wuthering Heights*, finally completed *Villette*, skimmed Charlotte's *The Professor*, got bogged down in her *Shirley*, dipped, briefly, into Anne's *The Tenant of Wildfell Hall*. Not enough to pass muster as a knowledgeable critic of the sisters' art, but enough to aid my navigation of Barker's biography, as well as a recent one on Charlotte Brontë by Lyndall Gordon. This report on my experience is offered with the tentativeness of one who wonders whether his own difficulties in responding to the Brontës' novels with admiring pleasure—the way I respond to those of Austen and Eliot—are any more than another mark against my character as a critic and a human being. Richard Aldington wrote a book about D. H. Lawrence titled *D. H. Lawrence, Portrait of a Genius . . . But.* Pluralizing the ascription and apply-

The Brontës, by Juliet Barker. New York: St. Martin's Press, 1995. *Charlotte Brontë: A Passionate Life,* by Lyndall Gordon. New York: W. W. Norton & Co., 1995.

ing it to the genius of Charlotte and Emily Brontë, I would still want to underline *but.*

There are no buts about Juliet Barker's wholly confident, indeed mind-boggling, history of the family, from the Reverend Patrick Brontë's entry under the gateway of St. John's College, Cambridge in 1802 (he had originated in a thatched two-room peasant cabin in the parish of Drumbally-roney in Ireland), to an evocation, on the book's final page, of the hundreds of thousands of Brontë enthusiasts who come yearly to tread the ground where "some of the greatest novels in the English language" were written. The biography's 800 plus pages of text is followed by a further 150 pages of notes, in extremely small typeface, providing the kind of minute documentation that only the serious Brontë scholar or fanatical fan could care about. A single instance of Barker's assertion and documentation of her endless parade of facts, facts, facts is the following clarification of something not all of us were wondering about, the exact coloring of Anne Brontë's hair. Charlotte's friend and correspondent Ellen Nussey, in one of the first descriptions of the family on record, wrote that Anne's hair "was a very pretty light brown and in falling curls" but Barker quickly sets her straight, noting that "Anne's hair was actually darker than Ellen remembered: a little plait, cut off and carefully preserved by Patrick on 22 May 1833, suggests that it had deepened to a rich brown with a hint of auburn, though it remained fairer than her sisters." This correction of Ellen Nussey's memory is occasion for the seventh chapter's eighty-ninth footnote, which reads as follows if you care to turn to p. 874: "Plait of AB hair, with PB autograph note, 22 May 1833: MS BS 171, BPM. Anne's hair had been fair as a baby, when Sarah Garrs cut off a lock in 1824: see above, p. 134." In other words, one has the feeling that Barker did not make it up out of whole cloth and that Ellen Nussey made a slight mistake. But something like a slight depression, attendant on the little item, descended on this reader.

It is surely admirable for a biographer to be relentless in pursuit of the Truth, but an important part of Barker's operation is her relentless trashing of Mrs. Gaskell, whose *Life of Charlotte Brontë* appeared two years after the subject's death, and has since become a classic, endlessly reprinted. Barker calls Elizabeth Gaskell's book a "wonderfully evocative picture," but her own biography seems to be animated by taking one smack after another at Gaskell's unreliability. Some of the smacks are harmless enough: Mrs. Gaskell's description of a Yorkshire landscape as "desolate and wild, great tracts of bleak land" comes out of her living on "the softer side of the Pennines" and so never being attracted to the wilder Yorkshire landscape; so she "disdained" the open moorland around the village of Thornton. Gaskell's amusing story about how a predecessor of Patrick Brontë's was persecuted by his congregation is "completely untrue, as are her sensational stories about Patrick's 'eccentricities.'" In assuming, because of all those written pages in the Brontës' juvenilia (the Angria and Gondal sagas), that the children's interests were sedentary and intellectual, Mrs. Gaskell falls into a "trap"; whereas statistics on liquor sales at Haworth pubs belie "the picture of drunkenness" found in her pages. Even though Patrick tried hard to prevent Charlotte's marrying his curate, Arthur Bell Nichols, Gaskell's negative opinion of the father's heavy hand is described as "poisoned" by gossip, and Gaskell confused the Brontës' life and work by making their lives "an excuse for their works." Even on Barker's final page Gaskell is still there, as the new biographer concedes, magnanimously, "For all her faults, Mrs. Gaskell at least ensured that the lives of the Brontës would be . . . perennially fascinating." There is a mean-mindedness about all this that stuck in my craw, especially since I would rather read Mrs. Gaskell than her relentless corrector.

Juliet Barker obviously subscribes to the belief that if you get in all the facts and get them right, and if your subject—the Brontë Family Fortunes—is interesting enough, then all you have to do is keep on writing without worrying overmuch about the quality of individual sentences. So she gives us in detail the dress code at Cowan Bridge School (Charlotte would make the school into Jane Eyre's Lowood), or a full-fledged treatment of the ecclesiastical controversies and difficulties in Patrick's parish, or a fully detailed topography/geography of—it sometimes feels like—every village in Yorkshire. The same thoroughness goes when the places are imaginary ones, like those of the Angria and Gondal sagas the young people concocted on winter nights at the parsonage. We are told, at truly mesmerizing lengths, the plots of these different stories—no matter that they are extremely tedious, at least to one not in on the writing of them. (One of the salutary remarks in Lyndall Gordon's life of Charlotte is Gordon's admission that these juvenilia are "no less boring" for their being "so voluminous.")

In the course of all this information-conveying, Barker writes sentences that made me shake my head in disbelief, as this in reference to Charlotte's and Emily's employment at Roe Head School (where Emily lasted only a short time): "If Charlotte felt the need for privacy, how much more must

Emily have done so when she had to share even her bed with one of her fellow pupils?" Yes, how much more. There is an odd—if/then—sequence about Charlotte's refusal of a marriage proposal by Ellen Nussey's brother: "If the character of St. John Rivers [in *Jane Eyre*] is also drawn from that of Henry Nussey, then Charlotte was indeed wise not to marry him." Sometimes these very strange young women are presented in such garden-variety terms that the result sounds ludicrous: "Though Charlotte was clearly an awkward person to deal with, she had much to put up with in her role as governess." Assuredly so, but calling her "awkward to deal with" is equivalent to opining, as a student did recently in my presence, that Emily Dickinson was "lonely, wasn't she?" When Branwell Brontë, about to set out for a new job in the morning, overindulges himself in "a riotous drinking session" the night before, Barker finds it "instructive" that this relatively sheltered young man "could indulge in . . . the occasional binge just like any other young man of his age." Why is it instructive? And why are we treated to the instruction that Branwell "probably exaggerated the amount he had drunk as he is unlikely to have wished to travel the last tortuous twenty miles of the mountainous southern Lakeland road between Kendal and Ulverston in a stagecoach with a hangover"? Tell that to anyone who has persisted in tying one on even as tomorrow's important prospect loomed. As this long book nears its completion, the writer seems fatigued, to the point of just grabbing for the nearest cliché: "Had it not been for the increasingly difficult and unhappy situation at Haworth, Charlotte could well have rested on her laurels and got on with her life." Resting on your laurels is pretty bad, but only on the soap opera I watch do characters try to get on with their lives. When Charlotte decides to marry the curate, despite her father's objections, we are told that she "would fight tooth and nail for the right to a chance of happiness." Mrs. Gaskell—always the target for patronizing—is described as "her romantic heart all acquiver with sympathy for the thwarted lovers," and as "all agog" about her own part in the outcome. Such writing cheapens, rather than explores experience.

At any rate, no one will ever need to do this sort of job on the Brontës again. Meanwhile, from a perspective more literary and more critical, Lyndall Gordon—who has written sensitively about T. S. Eliot and Virginia Woolf—has given us an excellent biographical study of Charlotte. Unlike Barker, Gordon pays handsome tribute to Mrs. Gaskell's book—"the rare conjunction of a moving and eloquent storyteller with a great subject of whom she had first-hand knowledge." Gordon's book is subtitled "A Passionate Life" and its emphasis throughout is on Charlotte Brontë's search for a voice adequate to express the fiery spirit within. More than one contemporary of Charlotte's resorted to the fire metaphor. George Eliot, as well as George Henry Lewes, found it in the novels ("What passion, what fire within her," said Eliot) and Thackeray, who made the mistake of introducing Charlotte—at the party he gave for her at his Kensington home in 1849—as Currer Bell, was told off by C.B. in no uncertain terms: "I believe there are books being published by a person named Currer Bell, but the person you address is Miss Brontë—and I see no connection between the two." At that dinner party, she refused to be drawn out by the other guests, eventually retiring to the dimmest corner of the study, not even deigning to speak with Jane Carlyle. Of course the Brontës never set up as ideal guests for a good social evening. During their sojourn in Brussels, when Charlotte and Emily were invited to the British embassy by a clergyman and his wife, Emily confined herself to the "occasional monosyllable" while "Charlotte's habit was to wheel round in chair so as almost to conceal her face from the person who addressed her." At any rate, Thackeray refused to put up with it: "There's a fire and fury raging in that little woman, a rage scorching her heart which doesn't suit me," said he, and one can see his point, indefatigable clubman that he was.

But Thackeray strongly admired *Jane Eyre*, admitting that it interested him so much he lost (or gained) a whole day in reading it, even as his printers were waiting for copy. And the feeling was mutual, since Charlotte admired Thackeray more than any other contemporary fictionist and dedicated the second edition of *Jane Eyre* to him. But after Thackeray's dinner party their relationship cooled. Barker is eager to blame Thackeray—at least as much as Charlotte—for inviting guests who were "society women, mere dabblers in the world of literature" and whose "interests and lives had nothing in common with her own." But the Carlyles were there, as was the poet Adelaide Proctor, along with a female novelist or two: how bad could it have been? Where indeed could poor Thackeray have found guests whose lives had something in common with Charlotte's own? Surely a tall order. At any rate the fire raging within the little woman didn't burn itself out, and Thackeray backed off, calling *Villette*, when it was published, "a plaguy book" whose heroine he didn't like (though he called the novel "clever"). My own hunch on the evidence of these biographies is that Charlotte was in a fair way to being an impossible person, certainly in the social arena, whether earlier in Brussels or at the time of her fame in London.

Perhaps the best formulation of why she had to be "impossible" and couldn't be chums with Thackeray for long is made by Lyndall Gordon in her discussion of the painful end of correspondence between Brontë and M. Heger, the Brussels schoolmaster under whose powerful influence she fell. Monsieur eventually put an end to that correspondence, devastating Charlotte. In one of her poems she wrote

> Devoid of charm, how could I hope
> My unasked love would e'er return?
> What hope, what influence lit the flame
> I still feel inly, deeply burn?

Gordon wants to "unlock desire from sexuality" and to see desire rather as "a longing for something as yet unformulated, which is other, and more, than what is available." She speaks tellingly of "Charlotte's particular desire for a voice in whose presence her own might rise." That "voice"—or the longing for it—was, Gordon says, her life, and remained so until near the end of it when she married the curate Arthur Nichols, stopped writing, and, having become pregnant, died three weeks before her thirty-ninth birthday.[1]

More than Barker, Gordon makes us care about and admire the unstoppable will in this fiery soul and the cruelly unfair way in which it burnt itself out so soon after entering into the new life of marriage. I am a good deal more doubtful about how useful or newly convincing are the fairly full treatments she gives to Charlotte Brontë's novels. There is of course no reason to demand that a biographer provide fresh critical insight into the art of her subject, but it's always a nice bonus when it happens. (Juliet Barker doesn't pretend to be a literary critic and limits her commentary on the novels to factual matters, reception, and reviews and the like.) But Lyndall Gordon is a sensitive reader and, as demonstrated in her analysis of Charlotte's character, a good psychologist. I was somewhat disappointed then, as a reader always looking for a new way to think about *Jane Eyre*, not

---

1. Barker reports that the attendant surgeon called this progressive wasting disease "Phthisis." Gordon speculates that it may have been Addison's disease, but was more likely a deadly infection of the digestive tract. (Charlotte could have caught it from her recently deceased servant, Tabby.) At any rate, her pregnancy doesn't seem to have been the cause of her death.

to find her analysis repaying. My main problem with her way of talking about the novel—which is to see the book as a "progression" by which the heroine moves through various barriers and oppressions to a married equality with the "new" Mr. Rochester—is that the discussion is conducted too much in terms of what "Jane" must do to get where she wants to be. For example:

> The pioneer of a new Progress must break through the encrusta-
> tions of language, lover's and religious cant, to see, or *see* in the
> sense of revelation, the destructive self-interest of persons in posi-
> tions of power. As Christian once did battle with Obstinate or
> the Giant Despair, so Jane must outface the deceptive faces of
> nineteenth-century Benevolence.

And on, in this manner, as if Jane were somehow independent of her creator and as if all these "breakthroughs" can only be seen in an admirably positive light, since we are sympathetically attuned to the condition of women in nineteenth-century England.

Gordon thinks she has a more enlightened way to understand *Jane Eyre* than earlier critics, remarking that back there "in the mid-twentieth cen-tury" it was common to read the novel as an expression of gender antago-nisms and to point to Rochester's physical blindness as "emasculation." But her own way of conceiving Rochester may be at least as simplistic: "He is the educable man. Though blinded in the fire that destroys his wife, he can learn to 'see' his true mate who is not to be his grateful dependent but his equal." She announces, without, it seems to me, enough of an ironic sense, that "Jane Eyre will not settle for anything beyond or less than a trans-formed Rochester." To which one might reply: I'll say! Gordon seems un-concerned with or unaware of the violent energy that accompanies our heroine's rise from inferiority to superiority—superiority over everything and everybody. No half measures can be brooked by the novelist, who is also the first-person narrator lifted up into triumph. As G. Armour Craig said (back in the mid-twentieth century in an essay I've never seen answered), "The movement of this novel is literally transcendence with a vengeance"; society, other people, the world outside the mind are reduced neatly to one mind's desires. Craig concludes his essay with a brilliant formulation: "The power of the 'I' of this novel is secret, undisclosable, absolute. There are no terms to explain its dominance, because no terms can appear which are not under its dominance."[2] There is a sense in which, among other things, *Jane Eyre* is a kind of metaphysical joke, accomplished by the novelist's sleight-of-hand. This isn't to say that the novel is any less readable, compulsively so, than generations of readers have found it to be; but it may speak to Leslie Stephen's question in his essay on Charlotte Brontë in *Hours in a Library;* "Why is the charm so powerful and why is it so limited?"

The charm is likely more powerful for female than for male readers of *Jane Eyre* and of Brontë's other novels, especially her last one, *Villette*. Composed when she was periodically depressed, all her siblings dead, the Reverend Patrick to be looked after, it's no wonder that she produced her gloomiest and some would say deepest piece of fiction. Strong claims have been made for *Villette*, in recent years, to be in fact Charlotte's great work, more densely explorative of the female imagination and voice than even *Jane Eyre*. Q. D. Leavis's passionate account of the novel as embodying the final expression of the impulses that made her a novelist, a work "almost preternatural in its power," is an account one must take seriously (as one takes anything Leavis wrote). Sandra Gilbert and Susan Gubar give it a long chapter in *The Madwoman in the Attic*, terming it "perhaps the most moving and terrifying account of female deprivation ever written." Strong claims, but no stronger than Matthew Arnold's response to it in an 1853 letter to Clough: "Miss Brontë has written a hideous undelightful convoluted constricted novel . . . one of the most utterly disagreeable books I ever read" (an opinion only confirmed by his seeing the physical Charlotte as entirely "a fire without aliment"). Of course no one reveres Arnold as a critic of fiction, or perhaps of women, but—as I slowly, tortuously made my way through *Villette*—the word "undelightful" or something like it came more than once to mind.

How much does this have to do with intransigent males like me and Matthew Arnold and Thackeray being unable and unequipped to sense the greatness of a fierce work? My only appeal is to the reader who, while impressed by the symbolic organization of *Villette* (Leavis is good on how the England-Brussels cultures are played off against each other) and the undeniable inwardness Brontë expresses through her heroine, Lucy Snowe, still runs up against something rebarbative in the actual writing of the book.

2. G. Armour Craig, "The Unpoetic Compromise," in *Self and Society in the English Novel*, ed. Mark Schorer (New York: Columbia University Press, 1956).

Q. D. Leavis insists, without qualification, that Brontë is "a great prose-writer," but her analysis of *Villette* is conducted in almost total indepen-dence of its particular sentences and paragraphs. I mean the sort of writing that happens when, fairly late in the book, M. Paul Emanuel—the school-master figure who stands in for the real life M. Heger—suggests to Lucy that at the next public examination she improvise a composition in French. This prospect throws our heroine into a tizzy:

> I knew what the result of such an experiment would be. I, to whom nature had denied the impromptu faculty; who, in public, was by nature a cypher; whose time of mental activity, even when alone, was not under the meridean sun; who needed the fresh silence of morning, or the recluse peace of evening, to win from the Creative Impulse one evidence of his presence, one proof of his force: I, with whom that Impulse was the most intractable, the most capricious, the most maddening of masters (him before me always excepted)—a deity which sometimes, under circumstances, apparently propitious, would not speak when questioned, would not hear when appealed to, would not, when sought, be found; but would stand, all cold, all indurated, all granite, a dark Baal with carven lips and blank eyeballs. . . .

I could go on—Lucy Snowe certainly does—but submit that "a great prose-writer" is not the right name for the author of these sentences, and that they are not untypical of much in *Villette* about whose prose Arnold's word "constricted" is a mild characterization.

My Brontë problem probably comes to no more—no less—than that: that too often, in her final novel especially, the surface of Charlotte Brontë's prose impedes rather than encourages the kinds of satisfactions I regularly get from Austen, Dickens, Trollope, the Thackeray of *Vanity Fair,* George Eliot, Henry James, Hardy. It's clear from the number of recent consider-ations of *Villette,* that its appeal is that of a "deep" text, whose properties and strategies may be rewardingly probed—and the academy is busy at such probing. With that other deep text, *Wuthering Heights,* proliferating critical commentary has been an important part of its continuing life: indeed Frank Kermode treats it as, by virtue of number and plurality of interpretations it has received, a classic text. But however "problematic" Emily Brontë's novel has been felt to be (and I for one have no "interpretation" of it to offer) no one ever suggested that, page by page, paragraph by paragraph, it was not dazzlingly readable. The mode may be high theatrical, as in the arias sung by Heathcliff and Cathy; or delicate-poetical observations about natural life on the moors; or realistic (rich detail of specification and localization); or knockabout violence with a farcical component—Lockwood doused with ice water to cure his bloody nose or Heathcliff covering Edgar Linton with a tureen of hot applesauce. I don't know how often it's been remarked that there's a likely connection between the variety of these styles and literary modes in *Wuthering Heights,* and its absence of a central commentator—in first or third person—who can be felt to emanate from Emily Brontë. In other words, for all the heated "passion" in its pages, *Wuthering Heights* has the quality of impersonality, even of coldness, that makes for something beyond what Charlotte's fierce but always *interested* spirit managed to achieve.

Hudson Review 49, no. 2 (Summer 1996)

Reading Hawthorne

❦

I n 1879 Anthony Trollope published a little-known essay, "The Genius of Nathaniel Hawthorne," in which he described that genius—so much the opposite of his own. Since Hawthorne had previously praised Trollope in an oft-quoted letter as a writer whose works were "solid and substantial, written on the strength of beef and through the inspiration of ale," it was unlikely that, in return, Trollope could be truly disinterested. Still, his characterization of Hawthorne strikes the essential note, as he speaks of "that weird, mysterious, thrilling charm" permeating Hawthorne's work. No one, Trollope says justly, will feel himself immediately ennobled "for having read one of my novels." Hawthorne, on the other

The essential Hawthorne is now handsomely available in two volumes from The Library of America: *Tales and Sketches,* ed. Roy Harvey Pearce. New York: Viking Press, 1982, and *Novels,* ed. Millicent Bell. New York: Viking Press, 1983. The following critical and biographical studies are briefly treated or referred to in my essay: Richard Brodhead, *The School of Hawthorne* (New York: Oxford University Press, 1986); Samuel Coale, *In Hawthorne's Shadow: American Romance from Melville to Mailer* (Lexington: University of Kentucky Press, 1985); G. R. Thompson, *The Art of Authorial Presence: Hawthorne's Provincial Tales* (Durham, N.C.: Duke University Press, 1993); Sacvan Bercovitch, *The Office of the Scarlet Letter* (Baltimore: Johns Hopkins University Press, 1991); Richard Millington, *Practicing Romance: Narrative Form and Cultural Engagement in Hawthorne's Fiction* (Princeton: Princeton University Press, 1992); Edwin Haviland Miller, *Salem Is My Dwelling Place: A Life of Nathaniel Hawthorne* (Iowa City: University of Iowa Press, 1991).

hand, by plunging us into melancholy enables us to catch "something of the sublimity of the transcendent, something of the mystery of the unfathomable." Indeed the effect of his work is all but to persuade us that, like that work, we too "might live to be sublime, and revel in mingled light and mystery." Hawthorne's was a mind powerful and active, also as "lop-sided" as any mind could be; his charm and appeal as a writer were inseparable from such un-Trollopian lopsidedness.

The convergence of Trollope and Hawthorne, the genuine admiration of each for the other's quite different novelistic operation, is one of the more heartening facts of literary history. The question is whether, more than a century later, Hawthorne can be read, is in fact read (as is Trollope most assuredly) with the pleasure and sense of gratification that attends our engagement with a living writer. In his extremely interesting and useful study of Hawthorne's continuing presence in American literature, Richard Brodhead points out that, along with Emerson, Hawthorne has always been there, has from the outset and continuously been a canonical classical presence, in fact—and unlike even Emerson—"the only major American author never to have been underestimated." Yet even as we acknowledge this cultural fact something about it seems less than fully convincing. Let us ask ourselves (again with Trollope in mind as a comparative standard) how often we or anyone we know pick up Hawthorne's novels and tales out of nothing more than the itch to reread, to re-experience the thrill of fictional discovery, to rehearse again the delights of compositional mastery. When was the last time anyone except a professional student of American literature attempted *The House of the Seven Gables* or *The Blithedale Romance* or *The Marble Faun*, or even *The Scarlet Letter* for no better reason than the pleasure of the text? Is it that Hawthorne's reputation is of a comparably deadly kind to that of the Ben Jonson about whom T. S. Eliot wrote so acutely in 1919: "To be universally accepted; to be damned by the praise that quenches all desire to read the book; to be afflicted by the imputation of the virtues which excite the least pleasure; and to be read only by historians and antiquaries—this is the most perfect conspiracy of approval." Thus Eliot, setting out to rescue Jonson from his seeming fate as a frozen unread classic. Hawthorne's classic status seems to be similarly hedged round with ironies and unease.

Criticism of Hawthorne pretty much begins with Henry James's brilliant monograph, published the same year as Trollope's essay and one of the most rereadable books ever written. Brodhead shows carefully what any reader of James's biography can see; that the Master gives with one hand only to take away with the other; that every positive claim he makes for Hawthorne's virtue and importance is qualified by an insistence on the impoverishment, the restriction, the unworldliness and unsophistication of that artist. Hawthorne's writing is notable for its "charm" and that charm lies in its "purity and spontaneity and naturalness of fancy"; it is almost as if a remark James makes about "Night Sketches," to the effect that it is "So light, so slight, so tenderly trivial" as to be "about nothing at all," were true—by extension—of the work generally. James found Hawthorne's mind characterized by, as it were, an absence of mind insofar as serious ideas went. Hawthorne has no "appreciable philosophy at all—no general views that were in the least uncomfortable." Indeed his mind "had no development that it is of especial importance to look into." Unlike Melville, who called Hawthorne a seer into "the blackness of darkness," James is unimpressed by the depth of his sense of sin; or it is an intellectual sense purely, not a moral or theological one, and it exists merely for artistic and literary purposes.[1] He pays tribute to Hawthorne's imagination, which did have a development, James says, but one that seems unconnected to the use of language. It is as if the charm of his predecessor's writing were too evanescent or delicate or (in Trollope's word) sublime to be described with any reference to Hawthorne's sentences.

I am scarcely faulting James for not close reading his artist, but suggesting rather that Hawthorne is a writer whose individual sentences, paragraphs, pages don't invite the kind of strenuous analytical response on criticism's part that (say) is demanded by *Moby Dick* or *The Wings of the Dove*. Hawthorne wouldn't have minded this in the least, since he wrote to an editor in 1851 that he never strove after "beauty" in his prose, never attempted to make it anything else than plain: "The greatest possible merit of style is, of course, to make the words absolutely disappear into the thought." Here Trollope would have agreed with him absolutely. The difference, so far as criticism of each writer goes, is that there is plenty to talk

---

1. But on another occasion Melville was less certain about the issue: "Whether Hawthorne has simply availed himself of this mystical blackness as a means to the wondrous effects he makes it to produce in his lights and shades; or whether there really lurks in him, perhaps unknown to himself, a touch of Puritanic gloom, —this, I cannot altogether tell."

about in terms of story, character, social reference in Trollope's thick, well-rounded fiction. For the lopsided Hawthorne, by contrast, if you decide not to make the style a subject of consideration, you may not find, much of the time, any satisfying place to rest in character, story, or social reference. Where you will be led instead is to ideas, to the deep structures and psychic resonances that have, in fact, fascinated so many of his modern critics.[2]

The "critical problem" concerning Hawthorne then goes something like this: he is an American classic to whom are indebted not just—as Brodhead shows—James and Howells and Faulkner (Brodhead connects *Light in August* to *The House of the Seven Gables*) but, as Samuel Coale has argued, all manner of contemporary fictionists from McCullers and O'Connor and Styron on through Cheever and Updike, John Gardner, Joyce Carol Oates, and Joan Didion. But his classical status has oddly little to do with readers, young or old, eagerly perusing him. He is kept alive rather by a steady outpouring of books and articles from the academy of which one of the most recent by G. R. Thompson has this to say about Hawthorne's perhaps most popular story in the eyes of nineteenth-century readers, "The Gentle Boy":

> Psychopathology of culture: narrative pattern and frame function: Paralleling the narrative commentary at the end, the tale is preceded by a historical introduction that sets a cultural context requiring a double reading for full understanding. From a narratival perspective of exterior and interior narrative framing and commentary and non-commentary the pattern of the narrator's intrusion into and withdrawal from the tale looks like this:

There follows a breakdown into the various "frames." Surely this is sound enough but does seem a rather brutal instance of how commentary has absolutely severed itself from being of interest to anyone not exclusively professional. From considering literature in terms such as Wordsworth considered poetry—as an homage to "the grand elementary principle of pleasure"—we are to analyze it rather in terms of "narratival perspective" and "frame function."

---

2. Although Frederick Crews would now qualify some of the approaches in his psychological reading of Hawthorne (*The Sins of the Fathers: Hawthorne's Psychological Themes* [New York: Oxford University Press, 1966]), it remains the boldest, most exciting interpretive study of Hawthorne's fiction.

To some extent, of course, literary criticism will necessarily fail to do justice to the immediate pleasure, sentence by sentence, that falls to an absorbed reader of any imaginative artist. But Hawthorne presents special problems for someone trying to give a faithful account of what it's like to read him. Two recent (and expert) studies of him, by Sacvan Bercovitch and Richard Millington, testify nonetheless to the distance between their sophisticated interpretive accounts and what I've been speaking of, loosely, as the pleasures of a text. Bercovitch learnedly and vigorously takes it upon himself to investigate and delineate the "cultural work" done by *The Scarlet Letter* and its "far-reaching implications about the symbolic structure of the American ideology." Millington's subtitle emphasizes the "cultural engagement" of Hawthorne's work as a romancer; his account of *The House of the Seven Gables,* for example, is designed to show it as a work of "extraordinary sophistication in its account of the culture it addresses and of extraordinary ambition in its attempt to reshape that culture." His book is the best account of Hawthorne as a romancer that I know of. Still when we put down these critical books and return merely to reading the novels in question, it takes some substantial effort to move from the immaculate surface of Hawthorne's prose to the deep cultural and symbolic resonances it has been found to possess.

My own tendency is to adopt Eliot's strategy in dealing with that other frozen unread classic, Ben Jonson. Eliot proposed that as a dramatic writer Jonson was no less a poet than Shakespeare but that unlike Shakespeare's, his poetry was "of the surface." It had to be grasped and appreciated in its details and in their relation to one another; it did not, typically, provide us with the profundities and spiritual stirrings that Shakespeare provided us and that lesser Jacobean dramatists like Beaumont and Fletcher attempted to provide. Admittedly, nothing seems more remote from Hawthorne's mistiness and moodiness than the large, bold, vigorous activity of Jonsonian verse in *Volpone* and *The Alchemist.* Yet as Q. D. Leavis insisted in her ambitious argument for Hawthorne's greatness ("Hawthorne as Poet"), he was a writer whose work demands the kind of concentrated attention we give to real poems. The question is, supposing that Hawthorne's poetry is of the surface, just where to direct such attention: how deep should close reading go?

Leavis reprimanded James for patronizing Hawthorne's work by calling it charming, and she was concerned to admire it rather as the symbolic art of a dramatic poet who had taken Shakespeare as his mode. This seems to me too much to claim for Hawthorne since—after James and Proust—his symbolic powers, even in impressive tales like "My Kinsman, Major Molineux" or "Young Goodman Brown" or "Roger Malvin's Burial" (always singled out as examples of Hawthorne's best), are relatively minor. Nor—after Chekhov and Kafka and Virginia Woolf—do his insights as a revealing psychologist astonish us. There is always that air of quaintness, of oddity—of the strange, the out-of-the-way—that pervades the very texture of his prose; we never forget that we are *reading* something. For me at least this situation is often highly pleasurable, indeed delightful, and it's a pleasure, a delight that stubbornly resists translation into the terms of social or moral or psychological value.

Take the following instance from *The House of the Seven Gables,* a book Q. D. Leavis is very severe about ("quite uninteresting, illogical in conception and frequently trivial in execution") but which seems to me at least arguably the most varied and interesting of Hawthorne's longer works. In Chapter 11, "The Arched Window," Clifford Pyncheon is suddenly and irresistibly seized by the impulse to blow soap-bubbles, something he and his sister Hepzibah used to do when they were young. He proceeds to act on the impulse:

Behold him, with his gray hair, and a wan, unreal smile over his countenance, where still hovered a beautiful grace, which his worst enemy must have acknowledged to be spiritual and immortal, since it had survived so long! Behold him, scattering airy spheres abroad, from the window into the street! Little, impalpable worlds, were those soap-bubbles, with the big world depicted, its hues bright as imagination, on the nothing of their surface. It was curious to see how the passers-by regarded those brilliant fantasies as they came floating down and made the dull atmosphere imaginative about them. Some stopped to gaze, and perhaps carried a pleasant recollection of the bubbles, onward, as far as the street-corner; some looked angrily upward, as if poor Clifford wronged them, by setting an image of beauty afloat so near their dusty pathway. A great many put out their fingers or their walking-sticks, to touch withal, and were perversely gratified, no doubt, when the bubble, with all its pictured earth and sky scene, vanished as if it had never been.

Finally one bubble floats down and bursts against the nose of dignified Judge Pyncheon who calls up to his cousin "What! Still blowing soap-bubbles!" In the most recent biography of Hawthorne (a labor of love, well executed but why do we need another biography of Hawthorne?), Edwin Haviland Miller finds this, rightly, "a delightful and subtle scene" but then takes away its subtlety and delight by converting it into meaning: "Literally Clifford's bubble collides with Pyncheon's, or art and beauty assault materialism and ugliness. Psychologically . . . [the soap-bubble] is his means of attacking his betrayer and emasculator. . . . Once again the Judge's sexual power is attacked when the bubble bursts on that symbolic phallus, the nose." Wouldn't it be better to say that this is *writing*, an art that—like the bubbles—is an art of surface? The sentences hover right on the edge of the cloying, the over-exclamatory, the "cute"; but with the "Little, impalpable worlds" sentence Hawthorne's imagination begins to animate the world as those bubbles float down. Surely he is writing about himself here, about his life as an artist and the kinds of creation he attempts. Can we respect and admire the soap-bubbles without hastening their demise by ramming into them?

"O you man without a handle," Henry James Sr. is supposed to have exclaimed to Emerson. My reading of Hawthorne over the past couple of months, done in a more or less amateurish spirit, while dipping into the vast critical literature that has accumulated about him, convinces me that he too is a man without a handle. Instead of moving closer to his "secret," persuading myself that I've begun to assimilate him, get a handle on him, the opposite has happened. As far as I can see, his commentators—from James and Melville and D. H. Lawrence, to Yvor Winters, F. O. Matthiessen and Harold Bloom—have called *The Scarlet Letter* a masterpiece, while conspicuously failing to provide terms for a critical appraisal that would convince a reader such was the case. Presuming that a reader needed convincing, of course. But can this work of genius (assuredly) be taken in and admired in ways at least analogous to the ways we admire *Emma* or *Middlemarch* or *Sons and Lovers*? If, as Winters claimed, it is "pure allegory" isn't that a mark against it? (James said, with some justice, that allegory never seemed to him "a first rate literary form.") As for the tales, after all that has been written about the fineness of "Young Goodman Brown," is it a literary experience obviously superior to the visual analogue in *Rosemary's Baby* or *Invasion of the Body Snatchers* or *The Stepford Wives*, modern cinematic efforts to show a protagonist struggling to avoid joining a community of evil? Is there, page by page and paragraph by paragraph, a verbal life and intensity comparable to one of James's or Hemingway's or Flannery O'Connor's short fictions? The answer to these questions, I hasten to add, is not obviously "no," but it doesn't seem to me obviously "yes" either. A lot of the time, while reading Hawthorne, we're not just sure how significant is the experience we're having.

Unlike the greatest writers, Hawthorne almost never, maybe never, touches the heart. He's as incapable of tragedy as Trollope, and perhaps that has something to do with their affinity for each other. He can be appreciated historically for his insights into and his role in creating, as Bercovitch calls it, American ideology. But as far as the tales go, those like "The Maypole of Merry Mount" or "Endicott and the Red Cross" or "The Grey Champion," though they can justly be called successful attempts (the only ones, James said) at historical fiction, have beyond that no stronger claim on our attention or affections. Allegorical tales like "The Minister's Black Veil," "The Prophetic Pictures," "The Birth-Mark," "Egotism; or, the Bosom-Serpent," "Earth's Holocaust," and "The Christmas Banquet" have their strengths, are impressively done but don't, at least for me, grow richer and more various upon rereading. Even relatively expansive efforts like "Rappaccini's Daughter" and "Ethan Brand" feel essentially claustrophobic, lacking in the free creative play found in the highest art. Hawthorne never let a story run away with him, but kept his characters as closely under his thumb as Nabokov did. Do we really *care* about any of these simulated lives? Shouldn't we, sometimes, just a little? To my judgment he is at his best in two of the very shortest tales—"Wives of the Dead" and "Wakefield"—where the imaginative treatment is most bizarre and undidactic; also appealing are the ones in which he's outrageously "humorous" and tall-taleish—as in "Mr. Higginbotham's Catastrophe" and "Peter Goldthwaite's Treasure" (and, in its way, "My Kinsman, Major Molineux"). Some of the sketches, like "Our Visit to Niagara," "Chippings with a Chisel," and "Snow-Flakes," have their mild but distinct satisfactions.

"This is the real charm of Hawthorne's writing—this purity and spontaneity and naturalness of fancy"—I realize I'm doing little more than echoing James's impressionistic terms for expressing what he found valuable and enduring in Hawthorne. But I would account for much of what's good about *The House of the Seven Gables* in similar terms. Whether it all goes together in a dramatically compelling way (I don't think it does), there's no denying how indelibly it renders—again, in James's words—"the impression of a summer afternoon in an elm-shadowed New England town." He succeeded, said Mark Van Doren in what is still the best introduction to Hawthorne (*Nathaniel Hawthorne*, 1949), "by lavishing all of his gift upon a picture." Surely he is our American master of the picturesque, and it is invariably a picturesque laced with humor. This can be illustrated by three or four pages in *The Blithedale Romance* for which I'd gladly trade the rest of that irritating book. In those pages the impossible hero, Miles Coverdale, goes to a saloon to meet Old Moodie so he can find out more about Priscilla (herself an impossible heroine). But first Hawthorne has Coverdale light a cigar and speculate on the "boozy kind of pleasure in the customary life that was going forward." (Hawthorne almost always has a good word to say for taverns and for the activity of what's here called "tippling.") We view various pictures on the walls—of a beefsteak, of cheeses, of revelers "drinking their wine out of fantastic long-stemmed glasses; quaffing joyously, quaffing forever with inaudible laughter and song; while the champagne bubbled immortally against their moustaches, or the purple tide of Burgundy ran inexhaustibly down their throats." Then we view the two bartenders, one of them a magnificent concocter of "gin-cocktails," and are introduced to the "staunch old soakers" who fill the saloon. When eventually Hawthorne gets back to unfolding his romance, things become much less lively and intelligent. And surely *The Marble Faun* is most alive not when its preposterous figures are spouting deep thoughts about art and death, but when Hawthorne gives us the Piazza del Popolo, or walks us along the Pincian or the Borghese Gardens.

His finest achievement in humorous picturesque poetry of the surface, and a book that should be known much more than it is, is *Our Old Home* (1863), the fruit of his years spent in England at the United States Consulate in Liverpool. Its introductory chapter, "Consular Experiences," ranks with the Custom House introductory to *The Scarlet Letter* and his preface to *Mosses from an Old Manse*, as Hawthorne's finest efforts in the informal reflective mode, dense with comic seasoning. There are wonderful portraits of life at Leamington Spa, Warwick Castle, Old Boston, the haunts of Liverpool's poor, and (in "A London Suburb") his own garden, where, after praising the English garden for all the facilities it offered "for repose and enjoyment"—its arbors and garden-seats, its flowers, and all the "exuberance of English verdure," which he admits is superior to that of his native land—he concludes a paragraph with this very Hawthornesque observation:

> Loyally anxious for the credit of my own country, it gratified me to observe what trouble and pains the English gardeners are fain to throw away in producing a few sour plums and abortive pears and apples—as, for example, in this very garden, where a row of unhappy trees were spread out perfectly flat against a brick wall, looking as if impaled alive, or crucified, with a cruel and unattainable purpose of compelling them to produce rich fruit by torture. For my part, I never ate an English fruit, raised in the open air, that could compare in flavor with a Yankee turnip.

This is exquisite and funny, but it also sustains Mark Van Doren's strong tribute to Hawthorne's genius: "He was so alone, so aloof, because he found so few around him whose seriousness equaled his; and by seriousness he meant the real thing, a thing consistent with irony and love, a thing indeed for which comedy might be as suitable an expression as tragedy." A good deal more suitable, I'd say, for it's in his pervasive and sometimes perverse comedy that the genius shows itself most distinctly. The narrator of one of his late unfinished tales, "Septimius Felton," surely spoke for Hawthorne when he opined that "old age is something like the feeling as if you had a cold for the rest of your life." It's this note of chill drollery that's there even in *The Scarlet Letter,* which permeates the Italian notebooks and the American ones, and which makes Hawthorne at his best—that is, at his most readable—as flavorful as a Yankee turnip, if you like that sort of thing.

Hudson Review 46, no. 4 (Winter 1994)

Nineteenth-Century American Poetry

❦

T HE LIBRARY OF AMERICA has already given us many books to be
grateful for, but now they have outdone themselves with two volumes of Henry James's travel writings (complete with the Pennell illustrations) and—even more ambitiously, since the editorial task has been monu-
mental—a two-volume anthology of nineteenth-century American poetry,
edited by John Hollander. Not only is Hollander an accomplished poet
whose knowledge of prosody is unmatched (see his witty and useful guide
to English verse, *Rhyme's Reason*), but he knows as much poetry as anyone
in England or America—"knows" in the sense that he has the poems going
round in his head. Imagine the scope of this undertaking: given roughly two
thousand pages of room, the editor is faced with deciding whom to include,
how much of X or Y to print, and what proportion of space to allot the
major figures. (And who *are* the major nineteenth-century American poets
anyway?) By way of embracing a large democratic vista, Hollander gives us
one hundred pages of American Indian poetry and another seventy-five of
folk songs and spirituals. Each volume contains notes to the poems and
extensive biographical sketches of the poets. (Hollander wrote the notes but
farmed out the sketches.) We have here a labor of some years.

American Poetry: The Nineteenth Century, ed. John Hollander. Volume 1, *Philip Freneau
to Walt Whitman;* Volume 2: *Herman Melville to Trumbull Stickney, American Indian
Poetry, Folk Songs and Spirituals.* New York: Library of America, 1993.

The undertaking with which Hollander's may be compared is Edmund Clarence Stedman's *An American Anthology,* published in 1900. I bring up Stedman, rather than the Oxford books of American verse edited by F. O. Matthiessen (1950) and Richard Ellmann (1976), because his anthology—except for some poets who wrote at the end of the eighteenth century—is exclusively nineteenth-century in its selections. Unlike Hollander, Stedman (also a poet himself and represented in the new anthology by one poem, his "Prelude to *An American Anthology*") prefaced his book with a long critical review of the nation's poets in which he looked forward to "poesy's return to dignity and favor." (He could scarcely have imagined the sort of "return" that such poets as Frost, Stevens, Pound, and Eliot were about to effect.) Stedman printed the work of nearly 500 poets; Hollander prints 142 poets along with the anonymous spirituals and Indian poetry. Stedman printed more poems—about 2,000, and the double-columned pages of his Cambridge edition are cluttered, unlike Library of America's readable pages—but Hollander makes more distinctions among his poets. Generous space is allotted to those he sees as most significant: Whitman (more than 200 pages); Dickinson, Emerson, Melville, and Longfellow (between 80 and 95 each); smaller but still substantial allotments to Whittier, Bryant, and Poe. You can tell who weighs more than whom.

I presume that, among readers over the age of fifty at least, I am not alone in enjoying an ambiguous and unsatisfactory relation to our classic poetry heritage. In elementary school English classes we were presented with—often asked to memorize—examples of that heritage, from Bryant's "Thanatopsis" and "To a Waterfowl" through Whittier's "Barbara Frietchie," Holmes's "The Chambered Nautilus," Lowell's prelude to "The Vision of Sir Launfal," and Longfellow's "The Village Blacksmith" (I chose to memorize "The Skeleton in Armour" instead). These Fireside Poets are now largely condescended to and wholly avoided by professors of American literature on the grounds of their alleged tameness and privileged status as establishment white males (the two conditions are presumed to go together). We also read—in Johnson City, New York, that is—Poe's "The Bells" and "The Raven," Edwin Markham's "The Man with the Hoe," and sugary bits from James Whitcomb Riley ("Little Orphant Annie's come to our house to stay") and Eugene Field ("The gingham dog and the calico cat"). No Melville and, except perhaps for "Concord Hymn," no Emerson; Whitman's "O Captain! My Captain!" only, and a poem or two of Dickinson's in the old smoothed-out versions of her texts. To me, and probably to most of my teachers, these American poems were equated with *poetry;* we read few or no English authors until high school when Scott, Shakespeare, and George Eliot made obligatory appearances, though not as poets. So when, in college and graduate school, I was introduced to a whole different order of figures, from Donne to Keats to Yeats, it was easy to forget about the Firesiders and equate our nineteenth-century poetry with Dickinson and Whitman—two "impossible" artists making their impact out of verse procedures contrary to the going ones.

Now that the impulses of feminism and gay studies have further secured the place of Dickinson and Whitman as virtually the only classic American poets who make it into the classroom, what does a leisurely trip through Hollander's immense museum yield to an interested reader, rather than a professional taxonomist or spotter of trends? First, and maybe last, that there is in these two thousand pages an intolerable deal of what Frost called "poetical" verse—which may best be pronounced *poy-tree. Poy-tree* is what you know you're in for when Richard Watson Gilder, one of the countless three-pronged names that mark our literary heritage, begins a sonnet with the question "What is a sonnet?" You can already predict the poetical an-swer " 'T'is the pearly shell / That murmurs of the far-off murmuring sea; / A precious jewel carved most curiously." Quite so, alas, and alas as well that Gilder has added one more to the much-too-large pile of sonnets that almost convince us it's an impossible form in which to say anything seriously.

An overplus of uplift, then, and a prevailing eagerness to point a moral and adorn the tale ("Then, in most poetic wise, / I began to moralize," writes Joseph Rodman Drake in "The Mocking Bird") go hand in glove with humorlessness. Thus we're all the more delighted to discover that Americans even back then could be wittily sophisticated in verse. New to me, and extremely satisfying in this vein, was "The Wants of Man" by our sixth president, John Quincy Adams (his grandson Henry's "Buddha and Brahma" does not fare so well). Whittier's "The Haschisch" sparkles as does his excellent "Maud Muller" (so does Bret Harte's sequel to the latter, "Mrs. Judge Jenkins"); Holmes's "The Deacon's Masterpiece" ("The Wonderful 'One-Hoss Shay'") in its swing and idiom retains some of the pleasure it gave me when I read it in ninth grade. Phoebe Cary, whom I'd never read, is represented by some amusing parodies of predecessors like Poe ("Samuel Brown" displacing "Annabel Lee") and Tennyson, whose "Locksley Hall" becomes "Granny's House," about the sad plight of a young woman from the city:

> Where one winter fell my father,
>   slipping off a keg of lard,
> I was left a trampled orphan,
>   and my case was pretty hard,
> Or to burst all links of habit,
>   and to wander far and fleet,
> Or from farm-house unto farm-house
>   till I found my Uncle Pete.

If my excessive appreciation of such humorous poems and moments was the result of an overdose of *poy-tree* when young, something similar happened in the encounter with half-forgotten gems like "Woodman, spare that tree!" or "Over the river, and through the wood, / To grandfather's house we go," or "I never saw a purple cow," or "A capital ship for an ocean trip," or "Curfew shall not ring tonight" (I identify these mainly by famous lines rather than their proper titles). Not to mention "We three kings of Orient are," the final two words always heard in my youth as "Orientar."

But what to say about the poets who, in Hollander's judgment, weigh most? In order of chronology they are Bryant, Emerson, Longfellow, Whittier, Poe, Whitman, Melville, and Dickinson—how large would they bulk in some putative anthology of world poets, or even in one that also includes their nineteenth-century English cousins? My possibly severe or misguided judgment is that they would not bulk large. To indulge in some sweeping pronouncements: Bryant, Whittier, and Longfellow are distinguished men of letters (the biographical sketch of Bryant is particularly amazing for the scope of his attainments) and attractive minor poets. Bryant gives us admirable, sometimes beautiful, blank verse, unexceptionable sentiments, and no interesting ideas; the first half of Whittier's "Snow-Bound" is a regionalist gem, and several of his poems are nice examples of a species Kingsley Amis calls the "Reciter," to be declaimed aloud. Longfellow, though his longer works are probably dead, wrote exquisite lyrics such as "The Fire of Drift-wood," "Snow-Flakes," "Aftermath" (all included here) and "Hawthorne," "The Village Churchyard in Cambridge," and "My Books" (which might have been included). Emerson in "Concord Hymn," "Two Rivers," "Uriel," "The Rhodora," and "The Snow-Storm" is beyond praise. But most of his poetry is windy, incoherent (or "profound") and prosodically ungraceful. Melville—strangest of all American writers, I am convinced—has stirring lines and a very few poems that hang together convincingly. Poe is a sport.

That leaves Whitman and Dickinson, whose power to move us is commensurate with their power to offend, or at least annoy. Whitman does this through, yes, his barbaric yawp that never stops yawping. The wonderful case Randall Jarrell made for him in a famous essay is achieved, of course, by quoting marvelous bits like "I am the man, I suffered, I was there" (Jarrell's essay, in *Poetry and the Age,* is titled "Some Lines from Whitman") and abusing readers who overlook those bits. But surely, most of the time, Whitman should be resisted, even mocked, by an active reader who won't be easily taken over. Reading him in bulk makes one feel again how many marvelous stretches of musical verse there are and how they're almost always stretches rather than full poems. And Dickinson? Isn't it time at least to suggest the possibility that her quatrains involve enormous built-in limitations; that often the ubiquitous dashes get in the way as much as they enhance the voice's power; that, as Philip Larkin remarked, too many of the poems issue in "a teased-out and breathless obscurity"? This is but a surly way of saying that, rather than assuming (as it is assumed these days) the greatness of Whitman and Dickinson, we must, as individual readers, actively distinguish the particular poems and sequences in which we can win through to a sense of that greatness.

Finally, a few prizes should be handed out. Best undervalued poem: "Gloucester Moors" by William Vaughn Moody ("Who has given to me this sweet, / And given my brother dust to eat? / And when will his wage come in?"). Novelist whom we didn't know was such a promising poet: William Dean Howells. Worst single poem: "Avalon" by Thomas Holley Chivers ("The worms are feeding on thy lily-lips, / My milk-white Dove!"). Most attractive minor-minor American poet: Edward Rowland Sill (1841–1887). Two most distinctive poems left out of this anthology: one, for its bathos, Eugene Field's "Little Boy Blue" ("The little toy dog is covered with dust"); two, for its sublimity, this by Emily Dickinson:

A Death blow is a Life blow to Some
Who till they died, did not alive become,—
Who had they lived, had died, but when
They died, Vitality begun.

Medal for outstanding service to the republic of letters for producing these volumes: John Hollander.

American Scholar 63 (1994)

Talking Back to Emily Dickinson

❧

T HE BOLD TITLE HAS a personal reference, since in decades of reading and teaching English and American poetry, I've largely managed to avoid talking back to, indeed talking *about,* Emily Dickinson. My occasional attempt to engage one of her poems in class hasn't been markedly successful; visits to the Homestead in Amherst, with some curious out-of-towner in tow, never yielded much; not even the just-effected presence of a piece of sculpture in a little park near the Homestead (in which she is presumed to be in "colloquy" with Robert Frost, another piece of Amherst sculpture facing her) could propel me into serious reading of her. Only the invitation to speak to this audience was strong enough to launch me on a three-month crash course in the poems and some of what has been written about them. Any interest these remarks have must come, then, from a non-Dickinsonian, even a nonbeliever's immersion in a bewildering body of verse.

Bewildering, in that the more I read her and about her, the more uncertain I become about questions of value, of just how much—as F. R. Leavis used to say—the achievement "weighs" and what kind of achievement it is anyway. More than a hundred years ago, W. D. Howells began his review of the Todd-Higginson first selection by referring to "the strange *Poems of Emily Dickinson.*" A century later, in his Dickinson chapter in *The Western Canon,* Harold Bloom has recourse to the same word—"as strange as Dante or Milton"—he also drags in the fashionable "uncanniness"—then asserts that strangeness is the prime requirement for entry into the canon. In opening the door for Dickinson, Bloom praises her "extraordinarily cognitive power," her display, again and again, of "tough writing and hard thinking" that puts her in league with Dante, Milton, and William Blake. Bloom's student Camille Paglia is equally enthusiastic about her in the fifty pages that, with a flourish, conclude *Sexual Personae*: for Paglia, Dickinson is Amherst's Madame de Sade, a denatured vampire whose masculine, sadistic poetic speech and brutal metaphors unite her with Blake and Spenser in "helping 'pagan' Coleridge defeat Protestant Wordsworth." For Paglia, not only does nature betray the heart that loves her, nature does so with wonderfully satisfying violence: "Wham! Chop! Faster than a speeding spear, the Dickinson ear demolishes a hapless heart, which is like a piece of liver hewn by the cook's cleaver." (This in relation to the final stanza of poem #1764—"An ear can break a human heart / As quickly as a spear, / We wish the ear had not a heart / So dangerously near"—an utterance that seems to this reader something less than a wham-chop operation.)

Of course neither Bloom nor Paglia ever understated anything, their mode of literary commentary being heated, strident, excessive, and sometimes very entertaining. Still, it's possible that Dickinson's is the kind of poetry one can say almost anything about without being arrested and hauled into court. It is extremely hospitable, that is, to hearings, readings, interpretations, valuations that are quite at odds with one another. To some extent this is true of any poet, but a lot more so of Dickinson than, say, of Ben Jonson, or William Cowper, or Byron, or Philip Larkin—poets with whom, to my knowledge, she has never been compared. This up-for-grabs quality has importantly to do with my Dickinson problem, if perhaps not yours, the problem of explaining why I've had trouble "talking back to Dickinson" or—in the words of a recent book title—why I have "the trouble with genius."

Let me begin not with some patently problematic poem to which critical response has been uncertain, but with one universally admired. "Because I Could Not Stop for Death" first appeared in the Higginson-Todd selection of 1890, was written about by the New Critics Allen Tate and Yvor Winters and by many since. I have no fresh reading of the poem to offer, nor would I suggest it is any less powerful than generations of readers have found it to be. Yet a clear account of it, of its value, is not easy to provide:

Because I could not stop for Death—
He kindly stopped for me—
The Carriage held but just Ourselves—
And Immortality.

We slowly drove—He knew no haste
And I had put away
My labor and my leisure too,
For His Civility—

We passed the School, where Children strove
At Recess—in the Ring—
We passed the Fields of Gazing Grain—
We passed the Setting Sun—

Or rather—He passed Us—
The Dews drew quivering and chill—
For only Gossamer, my Gown—
My Tippet—only Tulle—

We paused before a House that seemed
A Swelling of the Ground—
The Roof was scarcely visible—
The Cornice—in the Ground—

Since then—'tis Centuries—and yet
Feels shorter than the Day
I first surmised the Horses' Heads
Were toward Eternity—

#712

Todd and Higginson changed the opening of stanza 3 to "We passed the school where children played / Their lessons scarcely done" (so as to rhyme with "sun"); they omitted the fourth stanza, made the Cornice of the penultimate stanza a "mound" (so as to avoid the Ground / Ground rhyme), and rewrote "and yet / Feels shorter" in the final stanza to "but each / Feels shorter."

An early reviewer in the *Boston Evening Transcript* was in no doubt about what the poem meant nor that he admired it: "Clearly, Death is here regarded . . . as a benignant and friendly being; the poet was not allowed voluntarily to seek him out, so he kindly waited for her and introduced her to Immortality, where a thousand years are as one day." This reviewer was the first of many to admire the personified "gazing grain," and he recommended learning the poem by heart. Tate's pioneering essay of 1932 was even more certain of its high value: "One of the most perfect poems in English"; "one of the greatest in the English language." Tate admired its images as they were fused into a central idea, also the "subtly interfused erotic motive" and the way the terror of death "is made ironically to serve the end of Immortality." He said the poem presented, but didn't resolve, a typical Christian theme: "There is no solution of the problem; there can be only a presentation of it in the full context of intellect and feeling." A few years later Winters also found it a "beautiful poem" whose subject was "the daily realization of the immanence of death." He thought however that its final statement was "not offered seriously" and that insofar as it attempted to experience "the death to come," it was "fraudulent." But as a presentation of the life being left behind, the poem was "wholly successful."

More recent critics have found it says a number of different things: Clark Griffith discovers "psychological ambivalence" and declares that when "Dickinson thinks about her own death she can not honestly make up her mind about what her feelings and attitudes are." Sharon Cameron finds a "dialectic in which the self comes to terms with its impulse for fusion and identic relationship, and with the loss attendant upon realizing that such fusion is truly illusory." Vivian Pollak says that it "enacts the death of her quest motif" and that Dickinson is suggesting that "life contains many such deaths." Cynthia Griffin Wolff finds in it a victory, "the poet's victory over time and mortality." Judith Farr is convinced that when Dickinson arrives at her grave, she "also realizes she has been buried for many years" (For Farr, the "Ground/Ground" rhyme shows Dickinson's complete assurance that the grave is "an airless vacuum, out of Nature") and finds the dash at the poem's end a declaration that "unending immortality has been achieved," that the poem "is thus her supreme assertion of the continuance of the self or soul." Jane Eberwein is convinced, on the contrary, that not Dickinson but "the speaker mistakes Death for a human suitor," and that by the poem's end the deluded woman has ended up "with eternity as an inadequate substitute for either Immortality or Mortality."

These statements by Dickinson scholars about what happens in "Because

I Could Not Stop for Death" are set forth with a minimum of qualification and uncertainty. For all the aggressive reading they display, they have little to say about what, in other poets, would engage us—matters of tone, of verse movement, of compelling imagery. (The field of "Gazing Grain" is admired, but what of the Gossamer Gown and "Tippet—only Tulle," which sounds a bit to these ears like the Belle of Amherst?) Some have found it amusing that Dickinson's poems in common meter like "Because I Could Not Stop" can be sung to the tune of "The Yellow Rose of Texas" (I have heard it performed by a chorus). Should an account of it engage the question of how or whether Dickinson's rhythms subtly play off against the metrical grid? How should the drama in the poem—if indeed it is a "dramatic" lyric—be described, and in what sort of tone should it be delivered? (Randall Jarrell once described the opening address as something like "We have a nice hotel room. The girl, myself, and the Sphinx.") Rather than talk back to Dickinson's poem, critics tend to talk *for* her by bringing out, usually at length, what it is she's implying, not just stating, in the poem. The Russian poet Marina Tsvetaeva once called the short lyric poem "a catastrophe. It's hardly begun when it's already come to be ended. The cruelest self-torture." Critics of Dickinson's short poems seem to be in the business of prolonging, by drawing them out into coherent statements that bear only obliquely on the poem as experienced.

One further response to "Because I Could Not Stop" and, by extension, to a significant part of Dickinson's poetry. This was Philip Larkin's, when with reference to "the Day" of her surmise in the poem's final stanza, Larkin wondered whether it was the day Dickinson realized that "love was not for her, but only death." He quickly dismisses his query as useless, saying that she was determined to keep hidden the nature of her preoccupations, "that her inspiration derived in part from keeping it hidden," and that the price she paid "was that of appearing to posterity as perpetually unfinished and wilfully eccentric." Then, in a formulation that has stayed with me, Larkin says that "too often the poem expires in a teased-out and breathless obscurity."

Larkin was talking back to Dickinson out of his own practice as a poet who took the greatest pains to avoid obscurity, breathless or not, and who did so partly through a technique of extended specification and delicately nuanced tone. I shall return to his charge, indirectly, later on but consider now another famous Dickinson poem, perhaps her best-known one about the soul. Are we clear what happens in it and do we need to be?

The Soul selects her own Society—
Then—shuts the Door—
To her divine Majority—
Present no more—

Unmoved—she notes the Chariots—pausing—
At her low Gate—
Unmoved—an Emperor be kneeling
Upon her Mat—

I've known her—from an ample nation—
Choose One—
Then—close the Valves of her attention—
Like Stone—

#303

In early editions it was titled "The Exclusion" and reviewers cited its first stanza as an example of Dickinson's "reticent" or "nun-like" behavior. Recent commentary concurs to some extent, as Eberwein says in a flash of understatement, "Evidently, Dickinson found most people unrewarding." Griffith in a similar vein decides that "she worships only at an inward shrine" and effects "a spiritualization of the total self." Charles Anderson, on the one hand, finds various possibilities for the "One" chosen, speculating that it "may be muse rather than lover." On the other hand, "as suggested by the capitalization," the "One" may be God. (But should one try to make *anything* out of Dickinson's capitalization?) Wolff, however, finds her rejecting the deity and choosing "One other with herself," a choice, she claims, that is signaled by the final line, "a two-word spondee." Shira Wolowsky decides that the "One" chosen might, like Emerson's or Whitman's "still include all," although this "One" seems to be "just herself." There's a question, then, of just how exclusive is this exclusion; I see no definitive way to answer the question.

A traditional way of trying to answer it—at least since I. A. Richards and the New Critics—was to direct us to matters of tone and voice, the relation of speaker to listener. When Archibald MacLeish came to Amherst's bicentennial in 1960 to speak about "Emily" (as he called her) he put all his eggs in the tonal basket: "It is the tone rather than the words that one remembers afterwards." And what were the main characteristics of that tone? It was a "wholly spontaneous" one in which "Something is being *said*." Moreover, what is being said, or spoken, speaks to *you*—there is an intensely direct relation between poet and reader. MacLeish quoted bits from poems to illustrate this "spontaneous" immediate tone, but—perhaps wisely—did not attempt to describe or characterize what, in the individual instance, it sounded like: after all, if the Tone was "wholly spontaneous," why should any particular description of it be useful or accurate?

What *is* there to say about the tone of the first stanza: "The Soul selects her own Society—/ Then—shuts the Door—/ To her divine Majority—/ Present no more—"? Can it be called declarative and annunciative? Or should it be contrasted with the relative confidentiality and informality of "I've known her—from an ample nation—/Choose One"? In the chapter titled "Tone" from *T. S. Eliot and Prejudice,* Christopher Ricks offers the following: "Tone has been called the expression on the face of the words; you may know exactly whose face your eyes are meeting but may still need reassurance as to just what expression is on that face." I need more than reassurance as to just what expression is on the face of Dickinson's words at the climactic moments of "Because I Could Not Stop" and "The Soul Se-lects"; and though exceptions can be produced ("How dreary to be some-body / How Public—like a Frog"), her poems in the main don't invite the sort of rhetorical tonal analysis we give to Donne or Keats or Frost or Eliza-beth Bishop. Attempts to present Dickinson as a "dramatic" poet might consider the extent to which the drama is dependent on, or somehow takes place without, strong tonal indications. "Never if you can help it," wrote Frost in a letter, "write down a sentence in which the voice will not know how to posture *specially.*" My sense is that there are plenty of those sen-tences in Dickinson's poetry. Punctuation is sometimes a help in determin-ing tone, but the dashes in this over-dashed poem don't help, indeed make the tone harder to specify. (Of course, by way of justifying the dashes, there is Wendy Martin in the *Columbia Literary History of the United States:* Dickinson's "dashes signal an urgent immediacy that undercuts the pos-sibility of an absolute cultural hegemony. Her phrases referring simulta-neously backward and forward permit the reader to make connections and create the ambiguity necessary to create new modes of perception." Clear on that, are we? And the capitalizations?)

Another, somewhat less talked-about one of her soul poems may tell us something about the nature of the Dickinson performance:

Of all the Souls that stand create—
I have elected—One—
When Sense from Spirit—files away—
And Subterfuge—is done—
When that which is—and that which was—
Apart—intrinsic—stand—
And this brief Drama in the flesh
Is shifted—like a Sand—
When Figures show their royal Front—
And Mists—are carved away,
Behold the Atom—I preferred—
To all the lists of Clay!

#664

Commentators are pretty much agreed that this is a salute to "the invisible spirit," to an immortality "purified of all but created soul," although one of them says rather wistfully that "the reader finds no promise of beholding this fascinating atom until eternity brings its revelations," so that "speculation naturally ensues." But the nature of this, and other Dickinson performances, is such as to not make me want to speculate at all. I recall a graduate school classmate, standing next to his kitchen refrigerator, reciting "Of All the Souls" aloud from memory and asking me if I didn't think it a wonderful poem. I said I did, and I still do—especially that fine line in which the dashes are perfectly justified—"Apart—intrinsic—stand". A great poem to "perform" in the sense that I discharge it, execute it, begin and end it with a flourish. But if Dickinson the poet is satisfyingly on display, the performance is not such as to make me care about the character—the "I" of the poem. Indeed I'm not much interested in her, have no yearning to behold the "Atom" she prefers, am not much taken up with what used to be called "the dramatic situation." For there's little drama here, little variety of interest in the tone that shows forth the expression on the speaker's face—in fact I don't know *what* she looks like. For all the poem's images—of sand and mists, filing and carving—there is something unignorably *abstract* about the proceedings. David Porter says, justly, that in reading her we are often "caught in the bright but indefinite lights of a highly figural style." Bright lights the highly figural style of "Of All the Souls" most certainly gives off; maybe "indefinite" too, insofar as, while I'm more than satisfied in reading it aloud, I'm not further tempted to explore its definiteness, its definities.

In her recent, accomplished book *The Passion of Emily Dickinson,* Judith Farr, before launching a case for the overwhelming importance, to the poems, of Dickinson's love for her sister-in-law, Sue Gilbert Dickinson, disposes of critics like me who would attempt to stay, for better or worse, with the words on the page. Farr concedes that, yes of course, one *could* regard the poems as "études in poetic . . . form" merely, but that such a "severely formalistic" procedure "seems a solipsistic avoidance and even unhelpful in studying an art that is so clearly post-romantic." It is a "fantasy," she continues, to think that great artists write without directly experiencing "what is called 'life.'" And the life Dickinson lived, the people she cared about, influenced the language she made poems out of. What Farr doesn't consider, in her sharp opposition between solipsistic formalists and healthy post-Romantics who believe in "life," is the extent to which Dickinson experienced "what is called 'life'"—how directly, or indirectly, it entered her poetry. Compared to poems by post-Romantic contemporaries, most of whom she admired—Tennyson's *In Memoriam,* Browning's "By the Fireside," Elizabeth Barrett Browning's sonnets, Christina Rossetti's poem to her brother, "By Way of Remembrance," or Arnold's "Stanzas from the Grand Chartreuse," Dickinson's poems typically don't set up lines of easy commerce between themselves and life. "Depersonalization," as Eliot infamously praised it in his "Tradition" essay, is more appropriate to characterize her poems than theirs. Just exactly what experience, what people, went into the forming of "My Life had stood—a Loaded Gun"?

I don't think of my procedures as a reader of Dickinson's poetry as "severely formalistic" and I have introduced various critical readings and explanations of three anthology favorites by way of suggesting there may be another way of reading her than one that works mainly at getting the right interpretation of an individual poem. When I teach her in an introductory course, about to begin next week, I shall at all costs avoid laying out strenuous readings demonstrating how one or another poem of hers is the product of genius. Rather I hope the students will get well-lost in her, as I have done this summer. David Porter says that after reading her work "other poetry seems hesitant and slack in comparison." While not in favor of slackness, I should stress the *relief* with which I put down her poems and read, oh, parts of Cowper's *The Task* or Byron's *Don Juan,* poems which, compared to hers, look slack. Her preceptor Higginson having visited her, said, "I never was with anyone who drained my nerve power so much. Without touching her, she drew from me. I am glad not to live near her." And Paglia ends her essay by calling Dickinson "frightening." Excessive, but in a milder way I have been illustrating the difficulty of "talking back to Dickinson"—to a poet who (in contradiction to MacLeish's account of her voice) is much of the time *not* speaking to me; who much of the time is doing without the social and dramatic atmospheres and conventions that sustain me in reading Donne or Ben Jonson, Frost or Philip Larkin.

When she sustains me, it is through the sumptuous destitutions of language Richard Wilbur found in her:

> There is a finished feeling
> Experienced at Graves—
> A leisure of the Future—
> A Wilderness of Size.
>
> By Death's bold Exhibition
> Preciser what we are
> And the Eternal function
> Enabled to infer.

> #856

Is this "slight" or not? I at any rate am made "preciser" by such a wholly finished poem with its oblique rhymes (Graves/Size; We are/infer) and its offbeat alliterative swing, from "finished" to "feeling" to "Future" to "function" to "infer." And I don't need further instruction in Dickinson's experience of life, or of death, or of other people, in order to read it with satisfaction.

The "finished feeling" of this poem is an important aspect of many others in her work: but if the emphasis is put instead on her strangeness, or her great cognitive power, or the multiple possibilities or ambiguities held out by the teasing voice, less exciting virtues may be overlooked, and the poems in which they occur will be treated as minor compared to those of "major" difficulty. Sometimes the poem is so finished and inescapable that we suspect it of too-easy resolution:

> The Sky is low—the Clouds are mean.
> A Travelling Flake of Snow

Across a Barn or through a Rut
Debates if it will go—

A Narrow Wind complains all Day
How some one treated him
Nature, like Us is sometimes caught
Without her Diadem.

#1075

Did Frost or Hardy write that? Is it "merely" charming, not up to the tragic Dickinson standard? I'm suggesting that, when with relative ease and comprehension we are taken by one of her lyrics, we feel guilty, as if such ease were a substitute for a worthier difficulty and uncertainty.

On at least one occasion, a sequence of stanzas is so easeful, finished, and elegant, that the poem's conclusion can't live up to it, as in the early one titled by Higginson and Todd "Indian Summer":

These are the days when Birds come back—
A very few—a Bird or two
To take a backward look.

These are the days when skies resume
The old—old sophistries of June—
A blue and gold mistake.

Oh fraud that cannot cheat the Bee—
Almost thy plausibility
Induces my belief.

Till ranks of seeds their witness bear—
And softly thro' the altered air
Hurries a timid leaf.

#130

The line about the old sophistries of June was really written by Lorenz Hart or Cole Porter; the fourth stanza beautifully anticipates A. E. Housman's great tribute to nature's deception, "Tell me not here, it needs not saying." After such brilliances, the concluding fifth and sixth stanzas just sound earnestly exclamatory, for what that matters.

Randall Jarrell, who was meditating an essay on Dickinson at the time he died, made up, as was his wont, a list of her best and next-best poems—his way of talking back to Dickinson. Looking respectfully at the oeuvre of Dickinson criticism that has accumulated over the past decades—responsible, resourceful, ingenious as much of it is—I would welcome more subjectivity, more list makings by individual readers of the fine and not-so-fine poems. This might help in sharpening appreciation and making criticism of her less a sacred act of homage conducted under solemn rubrics like Love, Death, Election, the Woman Question, the Fate of the Soul. As a very small beginning here are two poems that don't make the anthologies or get written about much, but say everything that needs to be said in the smallest space. The first is positive, recuperative, introduced to me by a friend who had come out the other side of desperation and found himself:

> A Death blow is a Life blow to Some
> Who till they died, did not alive become—
> Who had they lived, had died but when
> They died, Vitality begun.

>   #816

The second is mischievous, even wicked, mocking, seeing-through-everything; yet like the one just quoted, exuberant in its formulation, its wild way with words:

> Finding is the first Act
> The second, loss,
> Third, Expedition for
> The "Golden Fleece"
>
> Fourth, no Discovery—
> Fifth, no Crew—
> Finally, no Golden Fleece—
> Jason—sham—too.

>   #870

Sharon Cameron calls it a "poem about disillusionment," which makes the important connection only after it is too late. But not for the reader whose last act, as with "Vitality begun," is a very satisfying finding indeed.

Matthew Arnold's Permanence

❦

"MY POEMS REPRESENT, on the whole, the main movement of mind of the last quarter of a century, and thus they will probably have their day as people become conscious to themselves of what that movement of mind is, and interested in the literary productions which reflect it." Thus Matthew Arnold in 1869, writing to his mother with his usual unapologetic candor. He wasn't just cheering up mother or whistling in the dark, even though his productivity as a poet had been close to zero for some years, and though—in the sentence that follows—he admits to lacking Tennyson's "poetical sentiment" and Browning's "intellectual vigour." Arnold believed he had tapped into something ("the main movement of mind") neither of those more verbally brilliant contemporaries had managed to; and his claim to Mrs. Arnold was, if anything, too modest, since a number of ages later his literary productions—not just his poems—are of the highest interest.

When I was first introduced to Arnold's poetry, in a Harvard graduate school course taught by Douglas Bush ("Tennyson, Browning, and Arnold"), I was unaware of Arnold's claim in that letter. Nevertheless, while I managed to do pretty well reading Tennyson (and not at all well with Browning), it was toward Arnold I gravitated. Lonely, full of unfulfilled yearnings and deep questions, I was a sucker for the poet of "The Buried Life," "Dover Beach," and numerous other sad laments. In the preface to his

A Life of Matthew Arnold, by Nicholas Murray. New York: St. Martin's Press, 1997.

first volume of *Essays in Criticism,* he apostrophized Oxford as the home of "lost causes and forsaken beliefs," and the poems he wrote were full of the sense of loss, of absence—exactly what I wanted to hear to make my own absences feel heroic. I memorized "Memorial Verses," Arnold's 1850 elegy to Wordsworth, and declaimed it aloud while pacing about my small room:

> Ah! since dark days still bring to light
> Man's prudence and man's fiery might,
> Time may restore us in his course,
> Goethe's sage mind and Byron's force;
> But where will Europe's latter hour
> Again find Wordsworth's healing power?

Europe wouldn't; I wasn't expecting to; but meanwhile these were heady sentiments to entertain, courtesy of memorial verses. In reading and rereading Arnold that semester, using an ancient Everyman selection from his works, I began an acquaintance that would be periodically renewed, always with reward.

The new biography of Arnold by Nicholas Murray weighs in at a reasonable four hundred pages and, though it makes use of manuscript material hitherto unavailable, does not cause us to revise our notions of Arnold as either poet or critic (the two halves of the book are divided in this conventional way). This is not a complaint: Mr. Murray's writing is clearheaded and generously appreciative throughout; as a presence he's less intrusive than his predecessor Park Honan, whom he handsomely acknowledges. His account is almost entirely free of the biographical vulgarizing of a subject in which a bit of the poet's life is filled in by reading back into it from a poem. Not quite free: "Dover Beach," written soon after Arnold's marriage to Frances Lucy Wightman, begins as follows:

> The sea is calm to-night,
> The tide is full, the moon lies fair
> Upon the straits;—on the French coast, the light
> Gleams, and is gone; the cliffs of England stand
> Glimmering and vast, out in the tranquil bay.
> Come to the window, sweet is the night air!

In his one venture into how it might have been, Murray writes "One moonlit evening, during that brief stay at Dover, Arnold stood at the hotel window and looked out on the calm sea and the lights of the French coast. Flu [Arnold's wife's nickname] was with him in the room and came to the window to look at the scene and catch the sweet night air." But this is the single exception that proves the rule of biographical probity and good taste.

The modesty with which Murray puts forth certain "tips" for reading Arnold doesn't hector either his subject or his reader. In dealing with what everyone objects to in Arnold's essays—the repetitive intoning of vague and large-sounding phrases like Culture, Sweetness and Light, The Grand Style—he suggests that we get closest to Arnold "when we give these sonorous phrases the slip and catch his mind in its more spontaneous and flexible performances." Just so, and it is equally just to recognize that a number of Arnold's poems forsake the music of verse in their overreaching toward weighty and significant statement. Rather than taking Arnold to task for such overreaching, Murray quietly points out that elegies like "Haworth Churchyard" and "Rugby Chapel" (their respective subjects Charlotte Brontë and Arnold's father) tend to be "a little too prosy and earnestly gravid." We are left to go on and make the necessary discriminations, should we wish to.

If Murray had wished to, he could have followed up on his suggestion that one "slip" Arnold's sonorous words and look for more spontaneous and flexible performance in his writing. One of the most egregious instances of sonorousness, guaranteed to produce curled lips on the part of enlightened modern readers, occurs at the beginning of his greatest essay, "The Function of Criticism at the Present Time." Quoting himself from his lectures "On Translating Homer," he defines the "critical effort" in all branches of knowledge as the attempt "to see the object as in itself it really is." Arnold's own attempt further to unpack and refine on this activity consists, typically, in tying more sonorous phrases to its tail, like "free play of mind," "disinterested," and the endeavor to "know the best that is known and thought in the world." Round and round we go, until Arnold changes the game by naming and ironically saluting some current ways of seeing the object as in itself it really is *not*. He introduces us to Sir Charles Adderley who recently had assured the Warwickshire farmers that the race they represent, "the men and women, the Anglo-Saxon race, are the best breed in the world." He gives us a Mr. Roebuck, telling the Sheffield cutlers that England is a country they can walk from one end of to another in perfect security: "I ask you whether, the world over or in past history, there is anything like it? Nothing. I pray that our unrivalled happiness may last." These proud and uncritical boasts are immediately juxtaposed with a newspaper account of a mother who murdered her illegitimate child, the account concluding with four stark words: "Wragg is in custody." In a brilliant paragraph, Arnold confronts the eulogies of Sir Charles Adderley and Mr. Roebuck with the circumstances of the child murder—"what an element of grimness, bareness, and hideousness . . . the workhouse, the dismal Mapperly hills . . . the gloom, the smoke, the cold, the strangled illegitimate child! And the final touch, —short, bleak, and inhuman: *Wragg is in custody.* The sex lost in the confusion of our unrivalled happiness; or (shall I say?) the superfluous Christian name lopped off by the straightforward vigour of our old Anglo-Saxon breed!"

This way of showing what it's like to see the object as it really is not, or shouldn't be, is an ironic-satiric one. As with his contemporary Carlyle, whom he disliked ("a moral desperado") but to whom his own criticism owes something—it is the blackly comic humor that makes the prose hum. Arnold's irony is more disciplined, less extravagant than Carlyle's, but it animates such classic essays as "The Literary Influence of Academies," "The Study of Poetry," and "On Translating Homer," all of which are concerned to distinguish excellence from the not-so-excellent, authenticity from charlatanism. T. S. Eliot, who wrote disparagingly of Arnold as a critic (Eliot wished, interestingly, that Arnold had "concerned himself with the art of the novel" and given us essays on Thackeray, George Eliot, Dickens) also called comparison and analysis the tools of the critic. Though Arnold's analysis of writers and passages usually stops well short of full-scale demonstration, he had a genius for comparison—for juxtaposing passages and writers in ways that bring with them the exhilaration of humorous surprise. In "The Study of Poetry," for example, by way of leading into the infamous downgrading of Dryden and Pope as, respectively, the founder and high priest of "our age of prose and reason, our excellent and indispensable eighteenth century," Arnold compares three specimens of seventeenth-century English prose—from Chapman, Milton, and Dryden—by way of demonstrating Dryden's achievement as the first writer of "true English prose." What's memorable in the comparison, more than any proven case about how awkward and "obsolete" Chapman and Milton are next to Dryden, is the brio, the sheer pleasure taken in holding up the specimens and inviting us to assent to his argument. The first lecture on translating Homer, comparing Chapman, Pope, and Francis Newman's efforts in that line, contain similarly energetic effects. In *Culture and Anarchy,* his longest though not his most successful excursion into ironic criticism of an English society that consistently sees the object as it is not, there is a moment when, preparing to tackle the difficult question of how the State can embody right reason and authority, Arnold pauses: "And here I think I see my enemies waiting for me with a hungry joy in their eyes. But I shall elude them." A perfect gloss on the "spontaneous and flexible performance" his biographer admires.

By contrast, Arnold's poetry has little humor, its ironies are unsubtle, its prevailing tone elegiac. In this connection we may recall that his admiration for Byron's work was very high; indeed he put him with Wordsworth as "preeminent in actual performance, a glorious pair" among the poets from early in the century. The essay on Byron, an impressive one, goes about placing him by referring, among others, to Milton, Walter Scott, Goethe, Leopardi, Ruskin, and Sainte-Beuve, along with Wordsworth. But his fine lines about Byron in "Stanzas from the Grande Chartreuse"—

> What helps it now, that Byron bore,
> With haughty scorn which mock'd the smart,
> Through Europe to the Aetolian shore
> The pageant of his bleeding heart?

—suggest it was the bleeding heart, the undaunted hero overmastered, that appealed to Arnold. In other words, there's no indication that he was a delighted reader of *Don Juan,* the poem (perhaps the only one) in which Byron is fully alive for us today. Arnold's own poems are most alive when saddest, full of the elegiac "Wandering between two worlds, one dead / The other powerless to be born" he enacts in the Grande Chartreuse stanzas.

He is, it could be argued, the first English poet to make poetry out of the rhetoric of failure, of falling short, a rhetoric rather melodramatically on display in his late poem "The Last Word" ("Creep into thy narrow bed") that ends as follows:

> Charge once more, then, and be dumb!
> Let the victors, when they come,
> When the forts of folly fall,
> Find thy body by the wall!

But from the beginning his imagination warmed to examples of failure: "The Sick King in Bokhara" is about the king's failure to help a dead sinner—"This man my pity could not save"; "The Forsaken Merman" laments the lovely woman who left the merman to his watery round; the "Marguerite" poems are about ways of not getting the girl; and "Dover Beach" memorializes Mr. and Mrs. Arnold's honeymoon by depicting the world as a "darkling plain," devoid of all luminous and benign qualities, in the face of which "Ah Love, let us be true / To one another!" has a really desperate ring, whistling or rather wailing in the dark.

This rhetoric can be traced through the drama of "Empedocles on Etna" whose hero plunges into the volcano while the shepherd Callicles makes sad music. The songs of Callicles show Arnold's lyric art at its highest: Swinburne remembered how, as a schoolboy, they "clove to my ear and memory," and decades later Robert Frost, faced with the death of his beloved daughter Marjorie, had recourse to Callicles' song ("Far, far from here, / The Adriatic breaks in a warm bay / Among the green Illyrian hills") by noting grimly that he and his wife, unlike Cadmus and Harmonia in the song, were "not yet placed safely in changed forms." Even Wyndham Lewis, of all unlikely people, said, in a little-known piece on Arnold, that "no greater poetry was ever written than the concluding song of Callicles." (Two lines from that song—"Not here, O Apollo / Are fit haunts for thee"—were once declaimed by I. A. Richards as he entered a disastrously situated Harvard classroom.) Swinburne was right, and not just about the songs of Callicles: many of Arnold's poems do cleave to the ear and memory, partly because they are so sad. You never know when something wonderful will turn up, even in a rather banal apostrophe ("Poor Matthias") to a dead pet canary. Arnold tells us that birds are, of all "companions," the least available to our understanding, and that in their feathered breasts stirs an unexpressed history of incommunicable wishes and feelings:

> What they want, we cannot guess,
> Fail to track their deep distress—
> Dull look on when death is nigh,
> Note no change and let them die.

One more instance of human failure. Arnold would have approved of, I'm certain, *The Education of Henry Adams.*

And yet in his life the man was fulfilled, with parents he loved and admired, a faithful wife and six children—even though three of his sons died young (Arnold's sad acceptance in letters of their deaths is unbearably poignant). All those years of daily school-inspecting, writing reports, traveling to places he didn't want to go in order to give examinations, dining out too often as he became famous, trying to make time to read a number of lines from Homer before going to bed just to keep his mind in trim—all this endured with so little complaining, even embraced with something like relish. Evident from the letters is the pleasure he took in physical recreation—in skating, fishing, playing billiards: one would like to think that he found a deal of wordless gratification in such nonverbal pursuits. He complained about lecturing in America, but went back to do it a second time, loving the "abundance of fresh fruit and ice" although, Murray tells us, he balked at "an immense beefsteak" presented him at breakfast with the president of Amherst College. Arnold's underappreciated letters reveal that his sanity and clarity and humor—even a dash of sweetness and light—were important parts of making him the most satisfying to contemplate of all the eminent Victorians. A. E. Housman thought so too, but said it rather more passionately in a memorial tribute: "The great critic of our land and time is dead."

American Scholar 67 (1998),
© by the author

What to Do with Carlyle?

❧❧❧

IN ONE OF HIS letters, Robert Frost defined "style" as "the way a man carries himself toward his ideas and deeds," then gave some examples of how different writers such as Stevenson, Swinburne, and Emerson carried themselves stylistically. The only example to receive a bad grade was Thomas Carlyle's, whose way of taking himself, Frost said, "simply infuriates me." Surely Frost's is a reasonable response to the most intractable and cantankerous of Victorian sages. I first encountered Carlyle through snippets from a large double-columned anthology of Victorian prose (Harrold and Templeman) that didn't help to make him appealing. But since I was in search of facts I needed to master for a Ph.D. oral, I read Carlyle's chapters on the Everlasting No and Everlasting Yea, from *Sartor Resartus,* and took careful notes on what he "meant" by those terms. Further pages followed, as I remember, from *The French Revolution, Past and Present,* and—as example of the later Carlyle—"Shooting Niagara." All sputter and invective and self-righteousness, I decided: a most infuriating writer indeed.

In his readable new biography of the sage, Simon Heffer is convinced that Carlyle is a heroic and indispensable figure whose trajectory since his death in 1881 has been "a long and damaging fall from the pedestal he occupied." Carlyle cries out, as Heffer sees it, for "rediscovery and reap-

Moral Desperado: A Life of Thomas Carlyle, by Simon Heffer. London: Weidenfeld and Nicolson, 1995.

praisal," especially with regard to his writings and their contribution to political thought. Heffer's introduction stresses Carlyle's humorousness and his kindness toward his family, and the biographer sums things up as follows: "If he is estranged from polite society today it is because his humour is misunderstood and his candour undervalued in a world based on avoiding truths wherever those truths are uncomfortable." This immediately struck me as unconvincing, since I know of no "polite society" from which Carlyle is estranged: surely academic society, where he is discussed at times, can't be construed as "polite." To blame "the world" for undervaluing Carlyle because that world seeks to avoid unpalatable truths, while not understanding the sage's humor, seems an abstract and unuseful way of blaming anything but Carlyle himself.

Is it true that Carlyle's fall from the pedestal is any more radical than those of his three great Victorian contemporaries—Ruskin, Newman, and Arnold? (Mill has continued to get a good press, especially for *The Subjection of Women*.) Carlyle was the subject, as the others were not, of a great biography by J. A. Froude to which Heffer pays generous tribute. Most recently Fred Kaplan has provided a fully scrupulous, though quite unhumorous, account of the life, which had been earlier told, most succinctly and entertainingly, by Julian Symons, a master of the biographer's trade. Kaplan makes no mention of Symons's book; Heffer mentions neither Kaplan nor Symons; one wonders whether these omissions are made in the fear that one's own biography will seem less groundbreakingly unique. In fact, Heffer's new one has nothing, that I can see, to add to the facts of Carlyle's life; his commentary on the work is however—like Symons's—lively and pertinent (Kaplan does little with Carlyle's writings). But perhaps it is enough justification for a new biography if it can bring us to fresh engagement with its subject. *Moral Desperado* most surely succeeds in doing that.

Of course any biographer of Carlyle must take his bearings in relation to Froude's biography, and not only the biography but the books he brought out after Carlyle's death in 1881: first the *Reminiscences,* containing Carlyle's agonized reflections put down after his wife, Jane Welsh Carlyle, had died and he had discovered, in looking over her letters, how much she suffered during the course of their marriage—how much, in his inattention and silent withdrawal, he was responsible for that suffering. The *Reminiscences* (1881) were quickly followed by the first two volumes of Froude's biography (covering Carlyle's years in Scotland); then, in 1883, *Letters and Memorials of*

Jane Welsh Carlyle, with notes by both Carlyle and Froude; finally, the second half of the biography, detailing the London years and Jane's increasing unhappiness. As the well-known story has it, Carlyle's descendants were outraged by what they felt to be Froude's partiality toward Jane, his suggestion that Carlyle was impotent, and his willingness to write the sort of "warts-and-all" biography Carlyle himself desired. Froude defended himself ably enough, but the counterattack continued.[1] Though Simon Heffer doesn't get caught up in the old quarrel, his sympathies clearly lie with Froude's portrait of the Carlyle marriage; and since Carlyle himself, after Jane's death, contributed so much to filling out the painful picture, it's impossible not to feel strongly toward this forty-year marriage of two extraordinary gifted sufferers. Yet in some heartless way, for all our sympathetic vibrations to each of them, we wouldn't have had it otherwise.

A GOOD place to begin reading Carlyle is a review of two books of philosophy he published in the *Edinburgh Review* in 1831, not long after he came to live in London. Titled "Characteristics," it is less a review than a bold attempt at characterizing the spirit of the age, containing in embryo all Carlyle's later religious and political ideas. In fact, it is a mistake to speak as if "ideas" in Carlyle's writing were something that could be abstracted from the prose and studied at leisure. As John Holloway shrewdly observed, in his still useful book *The Victorian Sage,* rather than being presented with an argument to which one does or doesn't give assent, "the reader is hurried, as if by an all-pervading and irresistible violence, from one problem to another." It's the violence and the hurry that, one suspects, must have infuriated Frost, who was unlikely to have read "Characteristics," where Carlyle proceeds with relative calm and clarity:

> The healthy know not of their health, but only the sick: this is
> the Physician's Aphorism; and applicable in a far wider sense than
> he gives it. We may say, it holds no less in moral, intellectual, politi-

1. In *Keepers of the Flame: Literary Estates and the Rise of Biography from Shakespeare to Plath* (London: Faber and Faber, 1992), Ian Hamilton has an entertaining chapter on the warfare between supporters and detractors of Froude's work on Carlyle. Christopher Ricks, in his essay "Froude's Carlyle," has provided a sensitive defense of Froude's biographical and critical procedures (*Essays in Appreciation* [New York: Oxford University Press, 1996]).

cal, poetical, than in merely corporeal therapeutics; that whatever, or in what shape soever, powers of the sort which can be named *vital* are at work, herein lies the test of their working right or working wrong.

In the Body, for example, as all doctors are agreed, the first condition of complete health is, that each organ perform its function unconsciously, unheeded; let but any organ announce its separate existence, were it even beautifully, and for pleasure, not for pain, then already has one of those unfortunate "false centres of sensibility" established itself, already is derangement there. The perfection of bodily well-being is, that the collective bodily activities seem one, and be manifested, more-over, not in themselves but in the action they accomplish.

He goes on to treat England as a very unhealthy place indeed, cataloguing with some relish the various derangements under which it suffers. In "Characteristics" and in "Signs of the Times" (published a year or so earlier), Carlyle's first significant assault on "machinery," materialism, and the utilitarian calculus, we have, as Heffer notes, "the foundations of his outlook and principles" set forth in accessible, vigorously stated prose.

At a basic enough level, one could even say that these essays said what he had to say about modern civilization. But Carlyle was a *writer,* and writers once they get launched tend not to stop the flow: the early essays and reviews were succeeded by two unique examples of Genius Carlyle: *Sartor Resartus* (1834) and *The French Revolution* (1836). In these two immoderate books he exploited to the full the famous Style toward which readers would have such mixed feelings. In responding to critics of the way he used language in *Sartor,* Carlyle replied that "if one has thoughts not hitherto uttered in English Books, I see nothing for it but that you must use words not found there, must *make* words." From a more disinterested source, Julian Symons, comes the best description of this "making" I know of:

> The style of Carlyle remains unique in English. It is at once breathlessly colloquial and full of elaborate metaphors; connectives are eliminated to gain force; words become displaced in the sentences, as it seems by accident, but always with the effect of increasing power and urgency of expression; the parts of speech abandon their usual functions, and move into new and fantastic patterns. . . .

It brings together in a single paragraph, sometimes in a single sentence, neologisms and compound words, strange nicknames like Teufelsdröckh, and fantastic metaphors: the whole informed with a humour at once extravagant and clownish, obscure yet overflowing with vigour.

Carlyle extinguished, so Symons argues, classical diction in prose.

For at least this reader, the genius of Carlyle's achievement in *The French Revolution* comes through in memorable scenes where the historian's own excess and exhilaration "breathlessly" animate characters and settings. Not the least attractive of Carlyle's appeals is his occasional willingness to confess how much beyond even *his* mortal powers as a writer is the immense subject. Preparing to describe the siege of the Bastille, he pauses, asserting that it "perhaps transcends the talent of mortals. Could one but, after infinite reading, get to understand so much as the plan of the building!" But he plunges on undaunted, after winning us over by his confession of defeat. For all its huffings and puffings, and partly because of them, *The French Revolution* has an attractive, you-are-there feel to it that bears out Carlyle's claim to Mill, who had been critical of Carlyle's stylistic excesses, that "the great business for me, in which alone I feel any comfort, is recording the presence, bodily concrete coloured presence of things."

But the other "genius" book of Carlyle's youth—*Sartor Resartus*—can't similarly be rationalized and justified, at least for one who has butted his head unrewardingly against this monstrous work. In a recent introduction to *Sartor* in the World's Classic series, its editors offer it to us, with some seriousness, as "essentially a work of imaginative fiction that demands a more sensitive and complex response than that in which its formal and stylistic husks are stripped away to reveal the doctrinal kernels." They also recommend it by pointing to Emerson's sponsorship of it, as well as to its influence on Melville's *Moby Dick* and Whitman's *Song of Myself.* Well and good, and surely the days have past when "doctrinal kernels" like the Everlasting Yea (which Christopher Ricks suggests may have been succeeded in our own day, by the Everlasting Yeah), the Centre of Indifference, or The Dandiaical Body are to be lifted out of what the editor in *Sartor* calls "the enormous, amorphous Plumpudding, more like a Scottish Haggis," which Herr Teufelsdröckh "had kneaded for his fellow mortals, to pick out the choicest Plums." There remains the question of just how satisfying, as imaginative fiction, *Sartor* turns out to be in the reading. In response to Mill's worry that its "mode of writing, between sarcasm or irony and earnest" might not have been too unrelievedly employed, Carlyle conceded Mill's point, and said the mode probably had something to do with not knowing "who my audience is, or whether I have any audience"—thus the "Devil-may-care principle" informing the book. And he added, saliently, "Besides I have under all my gloom genuine feeling of the ludicrous; and could have been the merriest of men, *had I not been the sickest & saddest.*" Contemporary readers—assuming they pick up the book at all—must decide for themselves whether and how often Caryle's "ludicrous" mode is all that funny, especially when compared with his acknowledged ancestors, Swift's *Tale of a Tub* and Sterne's *Tristram Shandy.* To my eyes and ears, *Sartor* feels, by comparison with those satirical operations, heavy-footed and haranguing, even as it tries to be madcap and devil-may-care. But then, John Stuart Mill, soberest of critics, eventually came round to reading it with keen delight.

These two works from the 1830s were—with the exception of the later *Reminiscences*—Carlyle's most "literary" performances. More than once—and increasingly—in later years he would contemptuously express his alienation from the world of literature: in a letter from the 1840s to James Spedding, he announces that "I begin very greatly to despise the thing they call 'Literature.'" And even when, in his early reviews, he took on literary figures, he had little to say about their literary qualities. The essay on Croker's edition of Boswell's *Life of Johnson* is very funny about Croker, very appreciative of Boswell's character, but tells us nothing about why Johnson is a great writer. The review of Lockhart's Scott gives us no insight into why Scott as a novelist should be read. And the pages on Shakespeare in *Heroes and Hero-Worship* ("The Poet as Hero"), while full of adulation for the poet's strength, greatness, morality, intellect, what-you-will, have nothing to say about his achievement with words. In a moment like our present one, when the head of Dartmouth College's English department warns us, primly, that we must not "deify" Shakespeare, it is good to read out in response Carlyle's thunderous deification of him: "Such a calmness of depth; placid joyous strength; all things imaged in that great soul of his so true and clear, as in a tranquil unfathomable sea!" But beyond that, there's little to be got from the lecture. Where Carlyle is superb, though in very brief compass, is in his portrait of Coleridge on Highgate Hill (in *The Life of John Sterling*), or of Wordsworth (in *Reminiscences*); what's superb is the evocative portraiture rather than any literary-critical judgment delivered. You can *argue* with Samuel Johnson's extended setting out of Shakespeare's virtues and defects in Johnson's preface to his edition of the poet; with Carlyle one beats the empty air, as one does if one looks to find out, in *Past and Present,* about what "Hero-Worship" should properly consist in, and is given the following: "it is the summary, ultimate essence, and supreme practical perfection of all manner of 'worship,' and true worships and noblenesses whatsoever." No doubt, but where do we go from there?

By the late 1840s Carlyle was turning out the rancorous essays that would be published as *Latter-Day Pamphlets*—to which "The Nigger Question" provided a fittingly unpleasant introduction. He had originally titled it, more politely, "The Negro Question," then when informed that people were outraged by it, proceeded to retitle to make it more offensive. Heffer remarks that Carlyle was "making a career out of being ill-natured in the most entertaining way, albeit often unintentionally." But "The Nigger Question" may not qualify as bona fide entertainment, and even "racism" is an inadequate word for Carlyle's attitude toward black people whom he tolerated as long as they remained slaves, docilely eating pumpkins and drinking rum: "A swift, supple fellow; a merry-hearted, grinning, dancing, singing, affectionate kind of creature, with a great deal of melody and amenability in his composition." (Carlyle may have figured this was a genially entertaining touch of style.) It was about this time that Mill, appalled by some of the things Carlyle was saying, ended their relationship: Carlyle professed not to understand why Mill had so taken offense. The habit of fixing on a colorful phrase, then beating the reader to death with it, more and more substituted for analysis and argument. In "Shooting Niagara" (1867) for example— usually taken as the final exercise in Carlylean negation and despair—he coins the word "swarmeries" to indicate superstitions that hold man in delusive wastefulness. Such is, prominently, literature, "what they call Art, Poetry, and the like. . . that inane region, fallen so inane in our mad era." Art or Poetry is nothing but "a refined Swarmery; the most refined now going; and comes to us in venerable form, from a distance of above a thousand years." Convinced he is seeing through nothing less than everything, Carlyle abandons his mind and his prose to frenzied dithyramb. Here was the moral desperado Matthew Arnold disliked, even as—his biographer points out justly—the "authoritarian" tone in Arnold's own *Culture and Anarchy* owed much to Carlylean doctrines.

Around his house in Chelsea, the moral desperado was also in evidence. Here the witness is Jane Carlyle, who succinctly characterized Carlyle's physical and emotional state: "as usual, never healthy, never absolutely ill—protesting against 'things in general' with the old emphasis—with an increased vehemence just at present." This was in the 1840s, and things would only get worse when Carlyle embarked upon the deadening thirteen-year project of a life of Frederick the Great—Jane would die before he had completed it. "This man of mine will absolutely do nothing but write books and be sick," she had written earlier to John Forster, Dickens's biographer, but the chipper tone is belied by her own prolonged illnesses. The seeds of what Heffer calls "self-flagellatory, self-pitying guilt" that followed her death and informed Carlyle's notes to his portrait of Jane in *Reminiscences* were well-sown early on. His devotion to Lady Harriet Ashburton, his high attentiveness to female aristocratic temperaments even as he managed to devote precious little attention to Jane, made things all the worse: "My husband always *writing*, I always *ailing*" as she neatly put it. Her letters are filled with wonderful sequences in which she manages, through gifts of style and wit, to make the intolerable into something less threatening, indeed amusing, as in an early letter to her aunt written just after the publication of *Sartor*:

> And then there is a young American beauty—such a beauty! "snow and rose-bloom" throughout, not as to clothes merely, but complexion also; large and soft, and without one idea, you would say, to rub upon another! And this charming creature publicly declares herself his "ardent admirer," and I heard her with my own ears call out quite passionately at parting with him, "Oh, Mr. Carlyle, I want to see you to talk a long time about—Sartor!" "Sartor" of all things in this world! What could such a young lady have got to say about "Sartor," can you imagine? And Mrs. Marsh, the moving authoress of "The Old Man's Tales" reads "Sartor" when she is ill in bed; from which one thing at least may be clearly inferred, that her illness is not of the head. In short, my dear friend, the singular author of "Sartor" appears to me at this moment to be in a perilous position,

inasmuch as (with the innocence of a sucking dove to outward appearance) he is leading honourable women, not a few, entirely off their feet. And who can say that he will keep his own? After all, in sober earnest, is it not curious that my husband's writings should be only completely understood and adequately appreciated by women and mad people? I do not know very well what to infer from the fact.

This is marvelous, and one can see how Carlyle, coming across even such a composed piece of discontent, could have used it as more grist for his self-accusatory mill.

Readers unfamiliar with Carlyle's reminiscence of his wife should not, however, think that it is one long gloomy paean emanating from a suffering widower. Parts of it are animated by fierce humor, as in the following sketch of a "Catholic sick-nurse" brought in (but only briefly!) to care for Jane during one of her illnesses. One night Carlyle is awakened (his room was above Jane's) by her violently ringing the bell: the French nun had tried to minister to Jane with "ghostly consolations" such as, perhaps, "Blessed Virgin" or "*Agnus Dei.*" The nun is dismissed next morning "never to reappear, she or any consort of hers," and Carlyle adds:

> I was really sorry for this heavy-laden, pious or quasi-pious and almost broken-hearted Frenchwoman,—though we could perceive she was under the foul tutelage and guidance, probably of some dirty muddy-minded semi-*felonious* Proselytising Irish Priest:— but there was no help for her, in this instance; probably, in all England, she could not have found an agonised human soul more nobly and hopelessly superior to her and her *poisoned-gingerbread* "consolations."

Here it is the poisoned-gingerbread conceit that vitalizes, in a typical manner, Carlyle's writing, as for a moment regret and guilt are put aside in favor of forceful abuse (that "semi-*felonious*" Irish priest is a particularly fine stroke).

Whatever Simon Heffer meant in his introduction by claiming that Carlyle is now in bad repute partly because his "humor" is misunderstood, it's true that, in a broad sense, Carlyle's humorous ways, and not just in writing, are what make him an appealing subject for biography: his long late-night

evening gallops about London on his horse Noggs (named for a character in
Nicholas Nickleby); or his visiting Stonehenge with Emerson on the latter's
second trip to England when, Emerson writes in *English Traits*, after "they
walked round the stones and clambered over them" they "found a nook,
sheltered from the wind among them, where Carlyle lighted his cigar"; or
his penchant for deterring oncoming colds by plunging himself into a freez-
ing bath, evidently to successful effect—the ultimate Boy Scout maneuver.

In his late years he was summoned, along with Browning and a couple of
others, to meet the queen, and wrote afterwards to his sister how she "gently
acknowledged with a nod the silent deep bow of us male monsters." He
described Victoria as a "comely little lady" than whom it was "impossible to
imagine a politer little woman: Nothing the least imperious; all gentle, all
sincere-looking, unembarrassing, rather attractive even; —makes you feel
too (if you have sense in you) that she is Queen." Her response to him, as
recorded in her journal, went as follows: "a strange-looking eccentric old
Scotchman, who holds forth, in a drawling melancholy voice, with a broad
Scotch accent, upon Scotland and upon the utter degeneration of everything." Yes, we feel, they had each other right.

The hero of Wyndham Lewis's novel *Tarr* is characterized as a sort of
anti-Quixote whose "sardonic dream of life" brought him "blows from the
swift arms of windmills and attacks from indignant and perplexed mankind." Tarr possesses, is inflicted with we are told, "the curse of humour . . .
anchoring him at one end of the see-saw whose movement and contradiction was life." Carlyle was, in the same manner, humorously cursed, and
never got off the see-saw until he died at eighty-five, having exhibited, so his
brother-in-law commented, "such tenacity of life and vitality" as he had
never observed in any human being. My single favorite moment from his
writing is one in which he registered comparable tenacity in another human
being, namely Wordsworth in old age, wearing his protective green eye-
shade at a London dinner party amidst an atmosphere of "babble" and
"cackle," "heartily unimportant to gods and men," so Carlyle judges it.
Seated far away at the table from Wordsworth, Carlyle suddenly looks up
and sees the poet:

> there, far off, beautifully screened in the shadow of his vertical
> green circle . . . sat Wordsworth, silent, in rock-like indifference,
> slowly but steadily gnawing some portion of what I judged to be

raisins, with his eye and attention placidly fixed on these and these alone. The sight of whom, and of his rock-like indifference to the babble, quasi-scientific and other, with attention turned on the small practical alone, was comfortable and amusing to me, who felt like him but could not eat raisins.

The curse of dyspeptic humor, turned—especially through the raisins—into a wonderful moment of sympathetic identification, is something even the most unconvinced reader of Carlyle can admire.

Hudson Review 50, no. 2 (Summer 1997)

Henry James on Tour

᪐᪑

ERE ARE SOME OBSERVATIONS by an American traveler arrived in
Rome for the first time:

> If my wits had not been too much congealed, and my fingers too
> numb, I should like to have kept a minute journal of my feelings
> and impressions during the past fortnight. It would have shown
> modern Rome in an aspect in which it has never yet been depicted.
> But I have now grown somewhat acclimated, and the first freshness
> of my discomfort has worn off, so that I shall never be able to
> express how I dislike the place, and how wretched I have been in
> it. . . . Cold, narrow lanes, between tall, ugly, mean-looking, white-
> washed houses, sour bread, pavements most uncomfortable to the
> feet, enormous prices for poor living; beggars, pickpockets, ancient
> temples and broken monuments, and clothes hanging to dry about
> them; French soldiers, monks, and priests of every degree; a shabby
> population, smoking bad cigars, these would have been some of
> the points of my description.

Henry James, *Collected Travel Writings*, ed. Richard Howard. *The Continent* (includes *A Little Tour in France; Italian Hours; Other Travels*). *Great Britain and America* (includes *English Hours; Great Britain; The American Scene; America*). New York: Library of America, 1993.

The passage, from Hawthorne's Italian notebooks, does exactly what it says its writer can no longer do—gives expression, in vivid particulars, to active discomfort. "One cold, bright day after another has pierced me to the heart, and cut me in twain as with a sword, keen and sharp, and poisoned at point and edge": Hawthorne's genius responds most fully to the experience of a new place when it's felt in every way to be inimical, an assault equally on the flesh and spirit. As we read on in the journals and Hawthorne thaws out a bit, appreciating some of the monuments he's been oppressed by, we almost regret losing the acidly depressed tone of those early pages. His original contribution as a travel writer lies in his rendering of how profoundly upsetting it is to find yourself in a new place.

Nothing could be further from the spirit of Henry James's travel writings now imaginatively assembled in two volumes by The Library of America. Unlike the New England–bound Hawthorne who first set foot in Rome in 1858 when he was fifty-three, James was to the Continental manner born. First transported there when he was six months old, he claimed that his earliest memory was of the Place Vendôme; his first adult tour of Europe, mainly France and Italy, was made in 1869 when he was in his twenties. So when, back in America the following year he found himself at Lake George and was informed by a friend that it strongly resembled Lake Como, James could deal urbanely with the matter of such comparative judgments: "Lake George is quite enough like the Lake of Como to impel you, if the image of the latter is fresh in your mind, to pursue the likeness to its inevitable phase of unlikeness." Which he then proceeds to do. Although as a traveler James must have had moments of irritation, fatigue, loneliness, even homesickness (wherever "home" for him could be said to be), as a travel writer he is the very soul of equanimity and composure. One or two exceptions only prove the rule: in the opening pages of *English Hours* he finds himself, preparatory to an extended stay in London, in lodgings that feel "stuffy and unsocial . . . an impersonal black hole in the huge general blackness":

> The uproar of Piccadilly hummed away at the end of the street, and the rattle of a heartless hansom passed close to my ears. A sudden horror of the whole place came over me, like a tiger-pounce of homesickness which had been watching its moment. London was hideous, vicious, cruel, and above all overwhelming. . . . In the

course of an hour I should have to go out for my dinner . . . and that effort assumed the form of a desperate and dangerous quest. It appeared to me that I would rather remain dinnerless, would rather even starve than sally forth into the infernal town, where the natural fate of an obscure stranger would be to be trampled to death in Piccadilly and have his carcass thrown into the Thames.

But, he assures us, he didn't starve, and the mood passed.

Hawthorne of course was writing on the spot, keeping a journal; James's essay "London" appeared many years after the visit in question. But James always moves toward accommodation, toward emotion recollected in the tranquility of composition, and toward a designed scene that may be savored—even the occasional grim bit of it—for its pictorial satisfactions. The relative density of his observations may be suggested by comparing him to Howells, whose *Italian Journeys* (1872) was published just a year before many of the essays in James's *Italian Hours* were written. As always Howells is a wholly agreeable writer who holds nothing back from us in the presence of, say, the Roman Campagna:

> We walked far down the dusty road beyond the city walls, and then struck out from the highway across the wild meadows of the Campagna. They were weedy and desolate, seamed by shaggy grass-grown ditches, and deeply pitted with holes made in search for catacombs. There was here and there a farm-house amid the wide loneliness, but oftener a round, hollow, roofless tomb, from which the dust and memory of the dead had long been blown away, and through the top of which—fringed and overhung with grass, and opening like a great eye—the evening sky looked marvelously sad.

This is perfectly lucid, and the effect of "marvelously sad" that of unabashedly direct confession. By contrast James's pages on the Campagna (in "Roman Rides") bristle with pictorial intent, the insistence that the scene come together into full display, as in his description of wandering near the Claudian Aqueduct:

> It stands knee-deep in the flower-strewn grass, and its rugged piers are hung with ivy as the columns of a church are draped for a festa. Every archway is a picture, massively framed, of the distance beyond—of the snow-tipped Sabines and lonely Soracte. As the

spring advances the whole Campagna smiles and waves with flowers; but I think they are nowhere more rank and lovely than in the
shifting shadow of the aqueducts, where they muffle the feet of the
columns and smother the half-dozen brooks that wander in and
out like silver meshes between the legs of a file of giants. They make
a niche for themselves too in every crevice and tremble on the vault
of the empty conduits.

Howells, whom the Campagna made marvelously sad, is also made to think
of a "wood-pasture in Ohio" as he wearies himself on the "many-memoried
ground." James looks at the fragments of Roman aqueduct and sees something less homey: "They seem the very source of the solitude in which they
stand; they look like architectural spectres and loom through the light mists
of their grassy desert, as you recede along the line, with the same insubstan-
tial vastness as if they rose out of Egyptian sands." Or, instead of an Ohio
wood-scape, he is reminded of Claude Lorrain's paintings, later betaking
himself to the Doria Gallery to inspect a couple of them. This is the cos-
mopolitan speaking.

Most of the material in the travel books published late in James's career—
English Hours (1905) and *Italian Hours* (1909)—appeared as essays, the
early 1870s being an especially fertile period and marking, to my judgment,
James's finest performances in the vein. These books were illustrated by
Joseph Pennell's lovely sketches (preserved in The Library of America volumes) as was, when republished in 1900, *A Little Tour in France.* The usual
word for the book on France is charming, as indeed it is, filled with chatty
talk about HJ's weakness for provincial museums like the one he visits in
Nantes, or how—on romantic, "pictorial" principles—he prefers ruins to
restorations. There are many picturesque portraits of ruins, including human ones like a poor old army veteran who had served in Mexico, encountered near the walls of Carcasonne: "It seemed strange, as he sat there with
those romantic walls behind him and the great picture of the Pyrenees in
front, to think that he had been across the seas to the far-away world, had
made part of a famous expedition, and was now a cripple at the gate of the
medieval city where he had played as a child." This impression was evidently
worth the "small silver coin" James pressed into his palm.

The preparations for writing *A Little Tour* (it was commissioned by an
American publisher) weren't purely pleasurable, and James wrote brother

William that "I pursued my pilgrimage through these rather dull French towns and through a good deal of bad weather. . . . It is rather dreary work." It's the closest thing he ever wrote to a guidebook and could be useful still as a guide to southern France—there are especially attractive sections on the Pont du Gard, Avignon, and Vaucluse. *English Hours,* however, has no particular continuity from chapter to chapter as James goes here and there, at different times, always with a transforming imagination that turns everything from "tramps" to children in a workhouse ("the little multitude of staring and wondering, yet perfectly expressionless, faces") into art. Inevitably the presence of Dickens is pervasive, and after the opening of *Bleak House* it's brave of James to attempt a London fog with attendant snow:

> The thickness that draws down and absorbs the smoke of the housetops, causes it to hang about the streets in impenetrable density, forces it into one's eyes and down one's throat, so that one is half blinded and quite sickened. . . . Just before Christmas, too, there was a heavy snowstorm, and even a tolerably light fall of snow had London quite at its mercy. The emblem of purity is almost immediately converted into a sticky lead-coloured mush, the cabs skulk out of sight or take up their stations before the lurid windows of a public house, which glares through the sleety darkness at the desperate wayfarer with an air of vulgar bravado.

This bit from an 1879 essay is continuous with the London he liked to call "the great, grey Babylon," and it appears in certain of his middle and later tales. Yet the movement of the writing is toward release, toward freedom: "For recovery of one's nervous balance the one course was flight—flight to the country and the confinement of one's vision to the large area of one of those admirable homes which by this season overflow with hospitality and good cheer." A dose of festive comedy is always ready to break into James's ultimately benign account of his traveling self.

Samuel Johnson was clear about the use of travel: "To regulate imagination by reality, and, instead of thinking how things may be, to see them as they are." A contemporary writer about travel books, Paul Fussell, agrees: "Travel books are a sub-species of memoir in which the autobiographical narrative arises from the speaker's encounter with distant or unfamiliar data, and in which the narrative—unlike that in a novel or a romance—claims literal validity by constant reference to actuality." James's relation to

actuality in *English Hours* and *A Little Tour in France* is everywhere respon-
sibly evident; but in his writings about Italy that relation becomes especially
satisfying and his style is felt in its most glowing warmth. Consider this
tribute to Carpaccio's St. Jerome, in San Giorgio degli Schiavoni, Venice:

> It unites the most masterly finish with a kind of universal largeness
> of feeling, and he who has it well in his memory will never hear the
> name of Carpaccio without a throb of almost personal affection.
> Such indeed is the feeling that descends upon you in that wonderful
> little chapel of St. George of the Slaves, where the most personal and
> sociable of artists has expressed all the sweetness of his imagination.
> The place is small and incommodious, and the pictures are out of
> sight and ill-lighted, the custodian is rapacious, the visitors are
> mutually intolerable, but the shabby little chapel is a palace of art.

Here James is a guide of the most personal and sociable sort, unlike John
Ruskin, who is very much looking over the guide's shoulder in Venice and
Florence. With all due respect for his predecessor, James needs to push him
away, even on occasions lecture Ruskin for the incessant way in which he
lectures us. At one point, losing patience with Ruskin's *Mornings in Florence,* James finds himself taking pleasure, in his perambulation of Santa
Maria Novella, of frescoes by Ghirlandio that Ruskin has been severe about.
What Ruskin seems to forget, James says, is the delightful truth "that art
after all is made for us and not we for art":

> And as for Mr. Ruskin's world being a place—his world of art—
> where we may take life easily, woe to the lackless mortal who enters
> it with any such disposition. Instead of a garden of delight, he
> finds a sort of assize court in perpetual session. Instead of a place
> in which human responsibilities are lightened and suspended, he
> finds a region governed by a kind of Draconian legislation.

He concludes, contra Ruskin: "We are not under theological government."
Italian Hours contains some of James's ripest and wisest thought about
the whole matter of "art," these thoughts expressed in an easy, graceful
prose that is a perfect vehicle for them:

> It is the privilege of art to make us friendly to the human mind and
> not to make us suspicious of it. We do in fact as we grow older

unstring the critical bow a little and strike a truce with invidious comparisons. We perceive a certain human solidarity in all cultivated effort, and are conscious of a growing accommodation of judgment. . . . We have in short less of a quarrel with the masters we don't delight in, and less of an impulse to pin all our faith on those in whom, in more zealous days, we fancied that we made out peculiar meanings. The meanings no longer seem quite so peculiar.

This is the tone of a mature sensibility at ease with its own contents and with the actuality of various "cultivated efforts" seen in Italy and elsewhere—like the Torre del Mangia next to the Palazzo Pubblico in Siena:

On the firm edge of the place, from bracketed base to grey-capped summit against the sky, there grows a tall slim tower which soars and soars till it has given notice of the city's greatness over the blue mountains that mark the horizon. It rises as slender and straight as a pennoned lance planted on the steel-shod toe of a mounted knight, and keeps all to itself in the blue air, far above the changing fashions of the market, the proud consciousness or rare arrogance once built into it.

There you have it, and James unerringly shares it with us. What a shock then to encounter, in the "late" part of "Siena Early and Late," the following second look at the city, where he informs us that, after getting to know Siena better over the years, his earlier remarks have fallen short of doing her justice—

True as it may be that I find ever a value, or at least an interest, even in the moods and humours and lapses of any brooding, musing or fantasticating observer to whom the finer sense of things is *on the whole* not closed. If he has on a given occasion nodded or stumbled or strayed, this fact by itself speaks to me of him—speaks to me, that is, of his faculty and his idiosyncrasies, and I care nothing for the application of his faculty unless it be, first of all, in itself interesting.

Whatever is he going on about, piling up those triple adjectives, spluttering, clearing his throat, italicizing *"on the whole"* as if all this were immensely significant? The answer of course is that the second half of "Siena Early and

Late" was written in the first decade of this century and is thus an example of darkest late Jamesian "brooding" (an increasingly favored word by him). No longer, evidently, is he obliged, in Johnson's words, "to regulate imagination by reality" and see things as they are; no longer is "actuality" anything more than what the brooding analyst can construct out of his word-spinnings. The wonderfully relaxed power of the earlier travel writing is gone, its place occupied by a frantic exercise in dithyrambics.

Where, then, does that leave The *American Scene* (1907), the fruit of James's ten-month visit to the United States he hadn't seen for twenty-five years? Established opinion judges it to be a masterpiece: "A triumph of the author's long practice," said Pound in his long essay on James; remarkable for its "exactitude," pronounced T. S. Eliot in his tribute to the Master. Ford Madox Ford called it a "magnificent book of impressions" though he admitted that one "reads for many pages with a sense of deep, of complete, and finally of utter noncomprehension." But, Ford claimed, when one closed the finished book an extraordinary sense of "actuality" overcomes one. Auden in his interesting preface to a 1946 edition of *The American Scene* called it "a prose poem of the first order." "One of his inestimable books and one of the great American documents," said F. W. Dupee. On the other side, standing more or less alone, there is Maxwell Geismar, author of the now pretty much forgotten *Henry James and the Jacobites* (1963), an assault on the James cult that was greeted by most people at the time with disdain. Since I was one of the disdainers, I confess that on a second perusal Geismar doesn't look so foolish. His remarks about *The American Scene* are centered where they should be, on James's "intensely wrought" (Dupee's words) late style about which Geismar says, "Perhaps never have so many words been used for so little content; probably this is really James's worst-written, and mainly most vacant, empty, and chatterbox book; as though the writer's own consciousness as regards his lack of real knowledge about his ostensible subject has impelled him into almost hysterical bursts of verbal virtuosity."

It would be foolish to assume that all this can be sorted out by either analysis or fiat. But reading *The American Scene* in the context of James's earlier travel writing, rather than in the context of *The Golden Bowl* and *A Small Boy and Others,* made me wonder if Geismar hadn't gotten on to something. One fairly long passage will have to do by way of illustrating the problem: it occurs just before James's often quoted outburst, "The *manners,* the manners: where and what are they, and what have they to tell?" and its subject is Cape Cod, "a delightful little triumph of 'impressionism' "

> which, during my short visit at least, never departed, under any provocation, from its type. Its type, so easily formulated, so completely filled, was there the last thing at night and the first thing in the morning; there was rest for the mind—for that, certainly of the restless analyst—in having it so exactly under one's hand. After that one could read into it other meanings without straining or disturbing it. There was a couchant promontory in particular, half bosky with the evergreen boskage of the elegant kakemono, half bare with the bareness of refined, the *most* refined, New England decoration—a low, hospitable headland projected, as by some water-colourist master of the trick, into a mere brave wash of cobalt. It interfered, the sweet promontory, with its generous Boston bungalow, its verandahs still haunted with old summer-times, and so wide that the present could elbow and yet not jostle with the past—it interfered no whit, for all its purity of style, with the human, the social question always dogging the steps of the ancient contemplative person and making him, before each scene, wish really to get *into* the picture, to cross, as it were, the threshold of the frame.

Is it "exactitude" we have here, sentences from "a prose poem of the first order" that give at the end a marvelous sense of a place's "actuality"? Or is it cobweb (the word is Pound's, though not applied to this passage), obliterating in its chatterbox torrent of words any sense of place or actuality, making of the pictorial, the picturesqueness of which the early James is master, a mishmash of fussings on the part of this "restless analyst"—an epithet that James applies to himself with tedious and embarrassing frequency?[1] Auden says in his preface that travel writing is the genre most difficult for the artist because it deprives him of the freedom to invent, since his imagination must be checked by the reality he's attempting to render. If so, James in *The American Scene* demonstrated the freedom to invent at the expense of be-

---

1. Contrast with this the lovely and lucid writing about Cape Cod in chapter 35 of *The Bostonians.*

coming something less—or more, if you feel that way—than a good travel writer.

Auden suggests it would be helpful to think of *The American Scene* as a fairy tale in which things—the landscape, a building, a mountain—speak to the restless analyst, invariably in late-Jamesian accents. (For example, New Hampshire's Mt. Chocorua is heard to utter the following: "Live *with* me, somehow, and let us make out together what we may do for each other— something that is not merely estimable in more or less greasy greenbacks.") My own term for it, borrowed from Kenneth Burke, would be comedy of the grotesque, a comedy that at its best seems aware of the deeply offbeat, deeply mannerist nature of its perceptions. Here is the aging expatriate confronting what he sees as a distinctly American phenomenon, the excellence of our dental care:

> I remember to have heard it remarked by a French friend, of a young woman who had returned to her native land after some years of domestic service in America, that she had acquired there, with other advantages, *le sourire Californien,* and the "Californian" smile, indeed, expressed, more or less copiously, in undissimulated cubes of the precious metal, plays between lips that render scant other tribute to civilization. . . . Every one, in "society" has good, handsome, pretty, has above all cherished and tended, teeth; so that the offered spectacle, frequent in other societies, of strange irregularities, protrusions, deficiencies, fangs and tusks and cavities, is quite refreshingly and consolingly absent.

James finds the consequences "cumulatively charming," an accolade I'm quite willing to bestow on this passage, even if the cumulative effect of *The American Scene* strikes me as something else. No matter: with The Library of America's enterprising gathering together of this material there should be no excuse for anyone missing out on James the travel writer.

Hudson Review 47, no. 2 (Summer 1994)

Yeats's First Fifty Years

❦

O N THE FINAL PAGE of his splendid biography (the first of two volumes), Roy Foster makes a list of what William Butler Yeats would go
on to produce or experience in his later life: "Perhaps his greatest poetry,
political revolution, war, new loves, marriage, fatherhood, still more radical
changes of creative direction, spectacular supernatural revelations, public
controversy and acclaim beyond anything he had yet experienced." Because
in June of 1915, Yeats turned fifty, one might ask just how much his literary
production would weigh had he ceased to write at the point at which this
first volume concludes. There would be the poems, up through *Responsibilities* (1914); a number of plays and essays; the first volume of autobiography, *Reveries over Childhood and Youth* (1914); and some stories and other
fiction, mainly Celtic in nature. On the basis of this work, along with his
political and theatrical endeavors, Yeats's reputation was already immense
("He is the big man here in poetry, of course" wrote Frost in 1913), and yet,
considering what was to come—not just "perhaps," as Foster hazards, but

W. B. Yeats: A Life, by Roy Foster. Volume 1, *The Apprentice Mage, 1865–1914.* New York:
Oxford University Press, 1997. This handsome volume contains not only photographs
but also a number of fine pencil sketches by Yeats's father, John Butler Yeats. The front
and back endpapers feature, in color, details from Yeats's brother, Jack B. Yeats's "Memory Harbour" and Robert Gregory's "Lake at Coole." The book is printed in England by
the Bath Press.

indisputably his greatest poetry; the magnificent *Trembling of the Veil* section of autobiography; *A Vision* and the late plays—one would advise the interested readers of 1914 to hang around, they hadn't seen nothing yet.

Denis Donoghue was originally slated to write the official biography, but soon withdrew over a disagreement with Yeats's heirs. Francis Stewart Leland Lyons worked on a biography of Yeats for ten years until he died in 1983; his archive of transcripts and notes was made available to Foster by Lyons's widow, and Foster dedicates the book to him, terming it "a work of joint collaboration." Describing himself wittily as an "interloping historian" (he is a historian at Oxford), Foster makes clear at the outset that he's not out to write a critical biography, in the sense of giving full discussion to Yeats's publications as they appear. Instead he provides a straightforward, exhaustive, chronological account of Yeats's activities, setting them—and doing so superbly—in the historical, political, and cultural scene. While taking nothing away from his predecessors, especially the notable Richard Ellmann, Foster has wisely decided not to give, as Ellmann mainly did, a thematic account of Yeats's career. Foster praises Ellmann's "psychological penetration" but notes that "we do not, alas, live our lives in themes, but day by day; and WBY [his way of referring to Yeats throughout] is no exception." (Wouldn't most of us prefer to live our lives day by day rather than thematically?)

The influence of Yeats's father, John Butler Yeats, on WBY especially in his early years, was incalculable, not to say tyrannical, and an incident from Yeats's autobiography that Foster doesn't mention may suggest how. The young Yeats came back from his first lesson at a dame school in Sligo and when his father asked him what he learned that day, the son said he had been taught to sing. "Sing then," ordered JBY and Willy proceeded with "Little drops of water, / Little grains of sand, / Make the mighty ocean, / And the pleasant land." Upon hearing which, JBY wrote to the schoolmistress that his son was never to be taught to sing again, and to pass along this directive to the other teachers. Clearly an impossible man, though a brilliant one; in 1903 he remarked in a letter "It is often an astonishment to me that I have not a son or daughter [there were four children] of some extraordinary distinction. Had my poor wife a little more intellect she would have been something very remarkable." (WBY was then a highly successful and admired poet and playwright, age 38.) Perhaps the fact that

JBY does not take up even more space than he does in Foster's account may have to do with the danger that he might run away with the book.[1]

Yeats began to compose poetry when he was fifteen years old, and his family grew used to a "humming" sound as he worked away in his room. My sense of Yeats's ear is that he was pretty much tone-deaf to "serious" music and doesn't seem to have registered the great composers the way he did the great painters and poets. This doesn't mean of course that his early poems don't contain wonderful musical effects, from the simple Tom Moore–ish lilt of "Down by the Salley Gardens," to the ornate splendor of "The Lake Isle of Innisfree," to the perfectly modulated cadences of "The Song of Wandering Aengus" ("The silver apples of the moon, / The golden apples of the sun"). Foster gives an attractive account of the impact of "Innisfree"—an early version of 1888—on the Yeats household as described by his sister Lily:

> In Bedford Park one evening, Helen Acosta & Lolly painting & I there sewing—Willy bursting in having just written, or not even written down but just having brought forth "Innisfree," he re-peated it with all the fire of creation & his youth—he was I suppose about 24. I felt a thrill all through me and saw Sligo beauty, heard lake water lapping, when Helen broke in asking for a paint brush— she had not even pretended to listen. None of us knew what a great moment it was.

The poem's success would eventually irritate Yeats immensely, and Hugh Kingsmill recalls his "reciting [it] with an air of suppressed loathing" to a female audience in Switzerland in 1924 as they "beamed ardently at him, as though ready at a word to fall in behind him and surge towards the bee-loud glade." On another occasion, a note tells us, "Innisfree" was sung in the open air by two thousand Boy Scouts—one would like to have been there for that stirring moment.

"Lanky, untidy, slightly myopic and painfully thin," even possibly tuber-

---

1. William M. Murphy, acknowledged by Foster, wrote an excellent biography of Yeats's father: *Prodigal Father: The Life of John Butler Yeats, 1839–1922* (Ithaca: Cornell University Press, 1978), and has more recently followed it with *Family Secrets: William Butler Yeats and His Relatives* (Syracuse: Syracuse University Press, 1995). One would love to see back in print the edition of JBY's letters to WBY that Joseph Hone edited in 1943, a book filled with marvelous things.

cular as a child, by the time he was twenty Yeats had grown into what his friend Kathleen Tynan, who was herself plain, described as beautiful to look at, "with his dark face, its touch of vivid colouring, the night-black hair, the eager dark eyes." Debarred by his poor academic rank—he seems to have been at the bottom of his class in virtually everything—from matriculation at Trinity College, Dublin, he found his true university in theosophical orders like the Golden Dawn that provided, as a university did, "strictly defined grades, tests, and examinations." While not downplaying the appeal of occult studies to Yeats as avenues into folk myth and ritual, or as metaphors for the poems he was writing, Foster shrewdly suggests that these studies were also a way of gaining influence on and over Maud Gonne, whose immense appeal to Yeats was if anything enhanced by her unattainability as a lover. The discovery and editing of William Blake set Yeats in a tradition of Irish Protestant interest in the occult, a tradition, Foster points out, that included his contemporary George Russell (AE), and went back to include the novelists Joseph Le Fanu and Charles Maturin and forward to Elizabeth Bowen, "all figures from the increasingly marginalized Irish Protestant middle class, from families with strong clerical connections, declining fortunes, and a tenuous hold on landed authority." This sort of placing of Yeats in relation to country, class, and religion, done with a grasp of economic circumstances, is what makes the biographer's treatment throughout so inclusive and solidly convincing—especially to a nonstudent of Irish history.

But it would take a very committed Yeatsian to follow with complete attention the intricate maneuverings WBY performed in the related but also competing worlds of occult research, political debate, and the "theatre business, management of men" he engaged in at the Abbey Theatre in the first decade of this century. Strong women were pulling him in different directions: Maud Gonne wanted him to be more political and to be satisfied with an "astral" rather than a physical connection between them. (They did briefly become lovers, Foster asserts, in 1908.) Lady Gregory wanted him to be more literary, if such a thing could be, and provided him impressively with the facilities of Coole Park—to the extent that Yeats became so accustomed to having the run of the place that friction developed between him and Lady Gregory's son Robert ("An Irish Airman . . ."). Yeats and Lady Gregory were an extremely effective team, especially by way of boosting each other's books, and late in his career, in "The Municipal Gallery Revisited," Yeats would make the two of them, along with the dramatist John Millicent Synge, into a holy trinity:

> John Synge, I and Augusta Gregory, thought
> All that we did, all that we said or sang
> Must come from contact with the soil, from that
> Contact everything Antaeus-like grew strong.
> We three alone in modern times had brought
> Everything down to that sole test again,
> Dream of the noble and the beggarman.

It's sometimes a question of just how much of this heroic idealizing ("contact with the soil"—really?) one can take, and to his credit Foster casts an ironic eye upon many of Yeats's loftier pronouncements. In fact, and without too quickly looking to debunk, it is invigorating to contemplate Yeats's earnestness in a dramatic light that doesn't exclude the humorous touch. Undoubtedly the funniest moment in this biography is Max Beerbohm's account of Yeats and Aubrey Beardsley dealing with each other at a dinner at the New Lyric Club to launch the *Savoy Magazine*. (The menu included bisque d'écrivisses, filet de sole au vin blanc, noisettes de mouton tomates farcies, and a bombe glacé for dessert.) Beerbohm writes that Yeats had been staying in Paris and was full of enthusiasm for Diabolism:

> He had made a profound study of it: and he evidently guessed that Beardsley, whom he met now for the first time, was a confirmed worshipper in that line. So to Beardsley he talked, in deep vibrant tones across the table, of the lore and rites of Diabolism—"Dyahbolism" he called it, thereby making it sound the more fearful. I daresay that Beardsley, who always seemed to know by instinctive erudition all about everything, knew all about Dyahbolism. Anyhow, I could see that stony commonsense which always came uppermost when anyone canvassed the fantastic in him, thought Dyahbolism rather silly. He was too polite not to go on saying at intervals, in his hard, quick voice, "Oh really? How perfectly entrancing!" and "Oh really? How perfectly sweet!" But had I been Yeats, I would have dropped the subject sooner than he did.

Beerbohm is in charge of the humorous superiority here, but on at least one occasion Yeats showed he could regard things occult with something other than reverence. In a letter to Kathleen Tynan of 1888 (not quoted by Foster) he confides to her that "A sad accident happened at Madame Blavatsky's lately, I hear. A big materialist sat on the astral double of a poor young Indian. It was sitting on the sofa and he was too material to be able to see it. Certainly a sad accident!" What larks!

Yeats's *Poems* (1895) containing his verse and plays previous to *The Wind among the Reeds* would prove a key volume in the establishing of his reputation. Over the next three decades he revised the book fourteen times and it continued to provide him with a regular income, "twenty or thirty times as much money as any other book of mine—no twenty or thirty times as much as all my other books together." And much of this success happened while the "Autumn of the Body" phase was still upon him, when he thought poetry should be wavery and elusive and blurred, disdainful of hard outlines and richly soothing to the ear. After *The Wind among the Reeds*, as Yeats plunged himself ever more deeply into drama and away from lyric, more than one of his critics felt he was obeying the wrong voice, and this reader, who has never gotten to first base with the plays can't but agree with them. The change from dreamy verse melody to a strengthened, more wiry line can be observed in the opening lines of "In the Seven Woods" written in 1902:

> I have heard the pigeons of the Seven Woods
> Make their faint thunder, and the garden bees
> Hum in the lime-tree flowers; and put away
> The unavailing outcries and the old bitterness
> That empty the heart.

These lines along with the more famous ones from "Adam's Curse," written about the same time, show that Yeats had mastered a verse movement expressive of what Frost would later call "the sound of sense"—much of that mastery due to his willingness to enjamb lines as he had not previously. But to my ears this development was independent of his playwriting.

Yeats's 1904 American tour, the first of three he made, was a great success: arranged by John Quinn, it took him mainly but not exclusively to colleges and universities. It also put paid to any notions of impracticality on the sensitive poet's part: Yeats was a model of efficiency, "always on time and made the entire Western trip alone and never missed a train," Quinn wrote home to Lady Gregory. During the course of that trip he became an accomplished and confident public speaker, developed a paunch (no doubt from

all the beefsteaks served him), and displayed a long chinchilla fur coat
against the Midwest winter. He was especially successful at women's colleges, to the extent that the wife of his brother, Jack, decided the "girls had
developed crushes on him en masse" and she expected him to come home
married. One guesses that he soft-pedaled the regressive attitudes toward
opinionated women he would proudly display in "Michael Robartes and
the Dancer," and "A Prayer for My Daughter," saying only *in private,* on the
American tour, that he preferred women who were unintellectual.

Foster has a subtle paragraph of analysis of Yeats's character as it developed itself after that first American tour:

> The idea of "masculinity" generated by his American triumph, his
> reading of Nietzsche, and the cataclysmic change in Gonne's cir-
> cumstances [she had married John MacBride, the "drunken, vain-
> glorious lout" of "Easter, 1916"] dictated a new view of himself.
> Throughout the crisis in the theatre he had determinedly stressed
> his own belief in autonomy, his "dangerous" qualities, his "intoler-
> able tongue," his "delight in enemies": he pointedly told Gonne
> that he "revelled in his unpopularity". His sense of self-presenta-
> tion had always been acutely developed, but since America it had
> taken a new and more aggressive form. . . . He remained secretly
> less certain than he claimed, admitting to Gregory that he often did
> not know why he acted decisively, and that he found it hard to
> recapitulate afterwards the circumstances which made him do so.
> But his old, uncertain self would become more and more deeply
> buried beneath the armour of the quarrelsome, self-proclaiming
> public man.

I don't know that it's necessary for a reader of the biography to have feelings
about this new "masculine," "dangerous" Yeats, but he seems to me a not
terribly attractive character, full of self-righteousness and prideful insisting
on the virtues of his pride. Of course among his contemporaries Yeats had
no monopoly on pride: think of Pound's fierce promotion of himself and
others; or Frost's mythical self-creation ("To be perfectly frank with you I
am one of the most notable craftsmen of my times. That will transpire
presently"); or Eliot's conviction, expressed to his mother in 1919, that he is
the most significant critic, if not poet, in England. But they seem to me, in

different ways, to complicate their self-proclamations with astringent kinds of humor and irony—their display of self invites us to see through it, at least to some extent. Yeats's noble lyricism and noble rage, culminating in *Responsibilities*, strikes me as more unyielding, more certain of its essential rightness. As ornate, embroidered, and mellifluous as was his "Autumn of the Body" phase, the reaction when it came seems equally extreme and self-vindicating: "Song, let them take it, / For there's more enterprise / In walking naked."

In fact, at roughly the same time as he was celebrating such heroic intransigence, he managed a few accommodations with the world: accepting a British Civil List pension; aligning himself—as Home Rule seemed incipient—with Protestant ascendancy values rather than the Catholic establishment; even becoming better friends with Bernard Shaw. One tends to remember the remark made after Yeats saw *Arms and the Man* about how in a dream Shaw appeared to him as a sewing machine that "smiled perpetually." In fact Yeats recognized Shaw's genius, and the Abbey Theatre produced *John Bull's Other Island* and *The Shewing-Up of Blanco Posnet*. For all the difference in their respective brands of "word music," the term Shaw liked to use about Shakespeare's art, their creation of dramatic tones of meaning in prose and poetry was, to say the least, noteworthy.

In 1913 he wrote an explanation for his discouragement with what he saw, in Ireland, as "the public mind in decomposition." (Some of this material would appear in the Cuala Press edition of *Responsibilities*.) He singled out three public events that had stirred his imagination profoundly: the death of Parnell; the dispute over Synge's *Playboy of the Western World*; and the refusal of Hugh Lane's bequest for a Dublin picture gallery. Yeats admitted that in each case there were arguments to be made on both sides; that the argument was not "ignoble" but that ignobility lay in the "minds that made use of it" for moralistic and philistine purposes. These events are of course featured in poems from *Responsibilities*—"To a Wealthy Man Who Promised a Second Subscription to the Dublin Municipal Gallery If It Were Proved the People Wanted Pictures," "To a Shade," "On Those That Hated 'The Playboy of the Western World,'" "September 1913," and "To a Friend Whose Work Has Come to Nothing"—that were hailed as a brilliant new departure in Yeats's poetic career. His current biographer finds *Responsibilities* "a strikingly autobiographical collection . . . extraordinarily rich and dense in texture," announcing "a savage energy as well as phenomenal recent creativity." When the book appeared Yeats's early biographer, Joseph Hone, said that the poet's search for a public had produced a new political viewpoint and "an individual protesting voice." So it surely must have seemed in 1914, with "early Yeats" still in readers' ears.

Now, almost a century after *The Wind among the Reeds* and with the twenty-five years of post-*Responsibilities* Yeats in view, that volume may look less like the beginning of something than an interim clearing of the decks, a paying back of insults (as to George Moore in the epilogue), a salute to honored dead poets (the Rhymers, Synge). It may be seen as a holding action, really, on the way to something new, "something" that we will see variously treated in "Ego Dominus Tuus" (the first "mask" poem), "In Memory of Major Robert Gregory," "The Fisherman," "Easter, 1916," "The Second Coming," "A Prayer for My Daughter" and others, right up through the great heroic laments from the 1920s and beyond. We don't need to downgrade middle Yeats, as Harold Bloom has done, by insisting that the early work is superior; we need only suggest that what I've referred to elsewhere as the "style of triumph"—by way of indicating Yeats's vigorous castigation of knaves and fools—is only limited in comparison with what was to come. Consider, say, the difference between "September 1913," a poem Foster makes very high claims for ("Romantic Ireland's dead and gone, / It's with O'Leary in the grave") and a stanza from the fourth section of "Meditations in Time of Civil War," composed ten years later when Yeats had become husband and father:

> Having inherited a vigorous mind
> From my old fathers, I must nourish dreams
> And leave a woman and a man behind
> As vigorous of mind, and yet it seems
> Life scarce can cast a fragrance on the wind,
> Scarce spread a glory to the morning beams,
> But the torn petals strew the garden plot;
> And there's but common greenness after that.

Not even an exceptional group of lines, yet they reveal a syntactical suppleness and human complication of feelings that simply isn't there in *Responsibilities*, geared as those poems were to a more unambiguous form of triumph. I'm saying no more than that in the period we may title Great Yeats—*Michael Robartes and the Dancer, The Tower, The Winding Stair*—he really did become a great poet, one whom we look forward to reading about in Foster's concluding volume when the apprentice mage becomes the masterworker.

Hudson Review 50, no. 3 (Autumn 1997)

T. S. Eliot: A Revaluation

❧

FOR HIS GRADUATION EXERCISES at Smith Academy in St. Louis, Thomas Stearns Eliot composed and recited a poem of fourteen rhymed stanzas in which appropriately lofty and inspiring sentiments were uttered about youth, age, the road of life, sons departing the school to which they would return—changed but still loyal. Most grandly, about the modern world:

> Great duties call—the twentieth century
> More grandly dowered than those which came before,
> Summons—who knows what time may hold in store.

Five years or so later, having graduated from Harvard and having read some French poets, notably Jules Laforgue, Eliot was writing lines like the following:

> Wipe your hand across your mouth, and laugh;
> The worlds revolve like ancient men and women
> Gathering fuel in vacant lots.

From an expansive, large-souled looker into the future and what it held for mankind's great destiny, he had become an imagistic ironist, still making grand and mysterious gestures ("The worlds revolve like ancient women / Gathering fuel") but now in an unillusioned manner. It was the "modern" note, the note that initially strikes a reader picking up Eliot's poetry.

Or so it struck this reader when as an undergraduate I read to myself and read aloud the opening lines of "The Love Song of J. Alfred Prufrock": "Let us go then, you and I, / When the evening is spread out against the sky / Like a patient etherised upon a table." "You and I"—who are we and what sort of relationship is this? "When the evening is spread out against the sky"—when exactly does that occur and how can one tell? "Like a patient etherised upon a table"—how is the evening "like" an etherised patient and what does such a likeness portend? In fact I didn't ask these questions, didn't pause and shake my head in dismay over them, but instead read on, either pretending the difficulties were only temporary and would be resolved, or electing to hear what the poet would say next, what new strange collocation of details would puzzle and excite. Sure enough, within a few lines occurs the infamous couplet—"In the room the women come and go, / Talking of Michelangelo"; utterly memorable, but what did it mean? That whatever sort of women they are in whatever sort of room, coming and going, they are, all of them, talking of Michelangelo. But what are they saying and what does it have to do with the "sawdust restaurants with oyster shells" just preceding, or the patient etherised upon a table with which we began? Is it an unworthy thing to do, to talk of Michelangelo—horribly superficial perhaps? But we are told nothing of how the talk is conducted, in what accents or at what level of perception; no more than with the sawdust restaurants and its oyster shells are we given clear signals on how to regard the talking women. But we remember the couplet in which they appear.

Or so thinks one of the "we" who learned to read poetry during the age of Eliot, an age that began in the early 1920s when "Prufrock," *The Waste Land,* and a number of influential critical essays had given him a reputation as the significant poet-critic of his time. That significance only widened until his death in 1965, even though after *Four Quartets* (1943) he had ceased almost entirely to write poetry. To a college student in the 1950s, Eliot's name was magic, the source of profound wisdom about the chaos of modern civilization and the difficulties—the impossibilities—of successful communication between human beings. Even as we struggled in our lives, sometimes with pretty good results, to know and love some other people, Eliot's work was there as a great looming warning, a grim shaking of the head at the vanity and fragility of human wishes and aspirations. "Between the idea and the reality . . . Falls the shadow," he told us in "The Hollow Men," and the words reverberated. And while his poetry was revered as a source of disenchanted wisdom about life, his critical and historical pronouncements in *The Sacred Wood* and *Selected Essays,* his valuations and comparisons of writers past and present, were deployed in countless undergraduate and graduate English papers. Notions of tradition, or the dissociated sensibility that had overtaken English poetry in the seventeenth century, or the "objective correlative" that Shakespeare in *Hamlet* was unable to discover—these Eliotic formulations were invoked by way of giving authority to whatever argument we were attempting to make. Less important to us were the later attempts at social and religious polemic—the books about culture (*Notes towards the Definition of Culture*) and religion (*The Idea of a Christian Society*) where Eliot spelled out, with maximum qualification and circumspection, his exclusionary notions of life in a world he said was "worm-eaten with liberalism." Nor, despite the popular success of *The Cocktail Party,* did the plays command our lively attention. It was the small body of poems and a selection of essays from a much wider spread of prose writings that constituted his powerful appeal.

The question is whether the appeal is still felt by teachers and students in the last decade of this century. (I am assuming there does not exist a younger nonacademic reading public for Eliot's writings.) His death coincided with a time when American poets were becoming more responsive to William Carlos Williams's experiments in the American grain, than to the "classical" values Eliot espoused and the, by then, too-familiar poems that had made his reputation. And as Wallace Stevens's body of work became increasingly influential, as—under the critical authority of Harold Bloom and Helen Vendler—Stevens's status as our most important poet was asserted, Eliot's reputation enjoyed no comparable enriching. In fact there was a perceptible decline in the capacity of his poetry to make a difference in people's lives. His centennial was celebrated in 1988, and the novelist Cynthia Ozick, writing in *The New Yorker* the following year, put the matter in a way that, though excessive and needlessly melodramatic, is accurate in its estimation of how the winds have been blowing:

> In the early seventies, it was still possible to uncover, here and there, a tenacious English Department offering a vestigial graduate seminar given over to the study of Eliot. But by the close of the eighties only "The Love Song of J. Alfred Prufrock" appears to have survived the indifference of the schools—as two or three pages in

the anthologies, a fleeting assignment for high-school seniors and college freshmen. "Prufrock," and "Prufrock" alone, is what the latest generations know (barely know); not "The Hollow Men," not "La Figlia che Piange," not "Ash-Wednesday"—not even "The Waste Land." Never "Four Quartets." And the mammoth prophetic presence of T. S. Eliot himself—that immortal, sovereign rock—the latest generation do not know at all. (In *Art and Folly*, 1993)

Having herself been one of the generation that eagerly discovered Eliot, Ozick feels saddened by the loss; but she is also unhappy at the reactionary nature of Eliot's political and social attitudes, and she ends her essay by informing us solemnly that it is our "unsparing obligation to dismiss the reactionary Eliot," even as we will probably miss forever "the golden cape of our youth, the power and prestige of high art."

Ozick's conclusion is put forth in a more self-important tone than Eliot used about himself (he once told an audience that since he had a reputation for "affecting pedantic precision" he should not like to lose it). But even more misguided is her attempt to make Eliot less disagreeable to the liberal conscience by telling us we must "dismiss" his reactionary opinions. Surely the business of a good reader consists in something other than condemning qualities in a writer that don't square with certifiably correct morals and politics. If we are uneasy about some or all of Eliot's references to Jews—about, say, his pronouncement in *After Strange Gods* (1934) that since a traditional society needs to be homogeneous, "reasons of race and religion combine to make any large number of free-thinking Jews undesirable"—we should analyze and judge the remark by putting it in relation to comparable assertions and ideas in Eliot's prose and verse. Dismissing it is no more called for than embracing it, and the same may be said of controversial and disturbing moments in the writings of (among others) Milton, Tolstoy, and D. H. Lawrence. It may even be the case that a great writer's power is commensurate with his power to offend.

But I am less interested in quarreling with Ozick than in qualifying her assumption that "the latest generation" doesn't at all know Eliot's poetry. Without asking which poet it is the latest generation knows *well*, it can be said that over the years and right up through a just-completed semester, numbers of students have read Eliot with me in courses called Modern Poetry, Modern British Poetry, and Modern American Poetry, and that these students have found him no less difficult nor less interesting than they find Yeats or Stevens, Robert Lowell or Elizabeth Bishop. Ozick's reading of the world-cultural poetry barometer that registers who's high and who's low must be corrected by the insistence that at least at one college—and I suspect at many more—Eliot is alive and well, his poems, and to some extent his criticism, seriously and satisfyingly engaged with by members of the latest generation.

My attempt in the following pages is to speak not as an impartial, objective observer of the poetry scene, as this century nears its termination, but rather as a critic and teacher who values and is moved by Eliot's work as a whole and who finds parts of it to be of supreme literary quality. While I don't mean to tag certain poems as exclusively the ones in which that quality can be found, I shall mainly focus on three of them from different stages in Eliot's career—"The Love Song of J. Alfred Prufrock," *The Waste Land,* and *Four Quartets*—and on the criticism he wrote in the years roughly from 1917 to 1922.

"PRUFROCK," with the help of Ezra Pound, was first published in *Poetry* in 1915, but it was written in 1910–11, the year Eliot spent abroad, mainly in Paris. It is often pointed out that, as with "Portrait of a Lady" written during the same period, its milieu is Boston. Yet "Prufrock" is the sort of poem that refuses to be located in one topographical cityscape or another, and in fact Eliot's biographer, Peter Ackroyd, terms the "yellow fog" in the poem a St. Louis one. Its landscape is for want of a better word psychological, and in the poem's moment of greatest feeling its protagonist wonders if "it would have been worth it, after all" to have made some large annunciation to the woman, the "she" who lolls and entertains him amidst marmalade and cups of tea. "After" (a key reiterated word in the poem) these and many other pieces of worldly furniture are enumerated, Prufrock suddenly exclaims

> It is impossible to say just what I mean!
> But as if a magic lantern threw the nerves in patterns on a screen.

To say "just" what you mean would be presumably to move beyond the excitements and inadequacies of metaphor into the realm of truth where words mean precisely what they say—a world exactly contrary to the poetic one Eliot creates.

It is as if we were to look at a series of nerve patterns and as if somehow these constituted not a composite visual shape but a musical performance, indeed a love song. "Prufrock" has no plot, no narrative with a beginning, middle, and end; its characters aren't characters but nervous ghosts who mysteriously appear and disappear as elusively as the yellow fog that slides along its street. In the course of various formulations, or half-formulations, the "I" who tells us he has "known" just about everything, decides that he doesn't dare disturb the universe, that he shouldn't "presume" to begin to do anything, that probably he "should have been a pair of ragged claws," that he is not a prophet (even if he's seen his own slightly balding head brought in on a platter), that he really can't manage to pass as either a Lazarus or a Hamlet figure, that he's "almost" (but not quite?) ridiculous, almost (capitalized) "the Fool." Finally, that the mermaids won't sing to him whether he eats a peach and wears white flannel trousers or whether he doesn't. What I'm suggesting by this cavalier assembling of the "facts" about J. Alfred Prufrock is that there aren't any facts, that the "content" of the poem is really a hoax— or rather an occasion for a voice to make haunting music out of them.

To hear that music one must read the poem aloud to a friend, to a class of students, or declaim it silently to the listener within. I can think of no single piece of writing more wholly dependent for its effect on the "performance" that R. P. Blackmur once said was the only way to know literature "afresh"— "in reading and seeing and hearing what is actually in it at this place and this time." For example, one of the important ways Eliot exercises a hold on our ears is to make sequences out of repetitions that don't quite repeat, as in the three quietly lengthening verse paragraphs (from six lines to seven to eight) in the middle of the poem beginning with "For I have known them all already, known them all." Recall the closing questions in each unit: "So how should I presume? . . . "And how should I presume?"; "And how should I begin" (that last one preceded by "And should I then presume?"). Or recall the echoing "And would it have been worth it after all? . . . "Would it have been worth while," and the co-presence, but in varying patterns, of other echoes echoing: "I am Lazarus, come from the dead, / Come back to tell you all, I shall tell you all"; "That is not what I meant at all. / That is not it, at all." What in a reading aloud is heard as ingeniously melodic, subtly compelling, refuses to be carried over into the sentences of a quoting critic at his typewriter.

A contemporary English critic, Barbara Everett, once wrote that the voice in "Prufrock" (it makes more sense to say *in* "Prufrock" the poem rather than *of* Prufrock the character) manages to hold us through its spellbinder's charm. This spell, though, is very much an aural one, depending less upon any sense or point about life that is made—beyond the general declaration of weary futility, of having come too late and missed out on everything—but rather on the seductive drawn-out repetitions, the music of consonantal and vowel echoings. Indeed the theme of weary futility is contradicted by the vitality of the verbal, aural performance. An example from the first of two tercets about the mermaids which end the poem:

> I have seen them riding seaward on the waves
> Combing the white hair of the waves blown back
> When the wind blows the water white and black.

This is really not so much a vision as it is something heard, from "seen" to "seaward," from "waves" to "white" to "waves" to "when" to "wind" to "water" to "white"; from "blown back" to "blows . . . black"—an auditory tour de force surely. For all Eliot's explicitly acknowledged debt in "Prufrock" and the other early poems to Laforgue ("My early vers libre, of course, was started under the endeavor to practice the same form as Laforgue. This meant merely rhyming lines of irregular length, with the rhymes coming in irregular places"), it is the English Tennyson of "The Lotus Eaters" these lines recall:

> . . . but evermore
> Most weary seemed the sea, weary the oar,
> Weary the wandering fields of barren foam.

And rather than asking exactly what the mermaids are doing out there (aside from "combing"), we experience the doing as an effect registered memorably by someone who has "lingered in the chambers of the sea," as Eliot did in the echo chambers of this poem. The astonishing thing about "Prufrock" is of course how it has continued to speak to the most unlikely readers. Or maybe there is no such thing as an unlikely reader: writing about teaching literature in a community college, Clara Clairborne Park remembers one of her students telling her "I must have read that poem fifty times . . . I *am* J. Alfred Prufrock." Such is the power of "a piece of rhythmical grumbling"—Eliot's own phrase about *The Waste Land*, but even more applicable to "Prufrock"—to cast a spell over the responsive ear.

Prufrock and Other Observations was published in 1917. Some of the other observations include, most significantly, "Portrait of a Lady"—probably completed before "Prufrock"—and "La Figlia che Piange." (All three poems involve the central presence of a woman.) "Portrait" is clever and adept at striking off the weary cadences of the lady ("So intimate, this Chopin, that I think his soul / Should be resurrected only among friends") and in opposing them with the furtive, guilty, self-lacerating consciousness of the speaker, an Eliot-like young man who nervously resists being drawn into her orbit. Yet as a poem it now seems less stirring, more dated than "Prufrock." Pound called the latter poem, rather inaccurately, a "portrait satire on futility," but the label might be more justly applied to "Portrait of a Lady" in its probing of the young man's paralyzed responses: "Not knowing what to feel or if I understand / Or whether wise or foolish, tardy or too soon . . ." The line breaks off in an ellipsis, and there is a sense in which the poem does so as well, ending upon two unanswered questions.

A more affecting poem, and rather more mysterious than "Portrait" both in its impulse and its outcome, is the beautiful "La Figlia che Piange." As with "Portrait" and "Prufrock," romantic materials are disguised or displaced by a modernist rearrangement of situation, one not clearly set forth but subjected to fluid definition and redefinition. The opening stanza features an unnamed, unspecified young woman alluded to by the epigraph from the *Aeneid*, "*O quam te memorem virgo.*" In Virgil, Aeneas asks Venus, disguised as an ordinary girl, how he should address her. In Eliot's poem the woman is told to "Stand," to "Lean," to "Weave, weave the sunlight in your hair," to "Clasp your flowers to you with a pained surprise," —as if she were an actress being coached into presenting the most effective romantic posture.

But the second stanza unsettles this scenario by introducing an "I" who tells how he "would have" had the grieving maiden stand, and how he "would have had" her lover take leave of her. Halfway through the stanza he seems to speak as a lover rather than a detached choreographer, when he says that "I should find . . . Some way we both should understand." This doubling of the speaker may be a way of insinuating into "La Figlia" the kinds of hesitations and confusions present, in both "Prufrock" and "Portrait," toward the attractive woman who makes a claim on the protagonist that is both desired and feared. Finally, in stanza three, the "I" tells us that his imagination has been compelled by the woman, "Many days and many hours" and that he wonders "how they should have been together!"—presumably if he had not interfered with *their* scene. Yet by this point in the poem, as the speaker wonders and opines that "I should have lost a gesture and a pose," we must be lost as well, for Eliot has not provided us with any stabilized dramatic situation nor drawn out any clear meaning or implication from the scene. "La Figlia" looks forward to Eliot's major work in that its narrative consciousness is no more or less elusive than it will be in *The Waste Land*. Part of that elusiveness, as well as attractiveness, has to do with the poem's aural richness, its unexpectedly occurring rhymes, its incantatory hieratic repetitions. For all the distance there is between "La Figlia che Piange" and an early poem of Wallace Stevens's like "Peter Quince at the Clavier," or an early poem of Robert Frost's like "October," they can be grouped under the slogan Frost formulated about reading when, in a letter of 1914, he laid it down that "*The ear does it*. The ear is the only true writer and the only true reader." It was a principle that Eliot's poems would consistently embody, right down to the charming one he wrote to Walter de la Mare in 1948—which ended by praising de la Mare for "the delicate, invisible web you wove— / The inexplicable mystery of sound."

In "The Frontiers of Criticism," Eliot's 1956 lecture delivered to fourteen thousand people gathered in the gymnasium at the University of Minnesota, he said, in a typically self-deprecatory disclaimer, "I fail to see any critical movement which can be said to derive from myself." Perhaps the disclaimer is not so much self-deprecatory as a proud fending off of those who come after Eliot the true original: how could you think (we might conceive him saying) that *I* can be held responsible for this or that critical procedure or movement? In fact, for all the academic recycling of Eliotic terms that occurred in the 1940s and 1950s, Eliot's critical convictions and principles do not take kindly to being passed along. We may speak of some critic as a Poundian or Leavisite or a follower of Yvor Winters (Wintersian?) but never as an Eliotian, or even a follower of Eliot. This has to do with the absence in Eliot of a systematic critical method ("the only method is to be very intelligent" he said in his preface to *The Sacred Wood*) or a prescribed routine for conducting literary analysis that we find, to one degree or another, in Pound and Leavis and Winters. As for Eliot's much-used terms which have had such a strong, even notorious, life, they have by now all been thoroughly and adversely criticized; no critic today would use "dissociation of sensibility" or "objective correlative" without the most elaborate qualification.

Still, Eliot remains the major poet-critic of our century, taking a rightful place in the line from Ben Jonson to Dryden, Samuel Johnson, Coleridge, and Matthew Arnold. The last named was felt by Eliot as his immediate predecessor whose work, while it deserved much respect, had also to be firmly placed in perspective. So in introducing his first volume of criticism, *The Sacred Wood,* Eliot saluted Arnold's plea for a criticism that would complement and make more self-aware the work of poets. He agrees with Arnold that this work had not been sufficiently done for the Romantic poets, nor, by implication, for those who were currently writing in English one hundred years later. But he wishes also that Arnold had been more of a practical critic; that he had, in Eliot's examples, taken it upon himself to compare Thackeray with Flaubert, or analyzed Dickens and compared him with George Eliot and Stendhal. Instead Arnold spent too much of his time "attacking the uncritical" and concerned himself more with matters of culture, society, and religion than with literary ones. About which Eliot remarks, adducing his contemporaries H. G. Wells and G. K. Chesterton, "The temptation, to any man who is interested in ideas and primarily in literature, is to put literature into the corner until he has cleaned up the whole country first." So his judgment was that Arnold was more a "propagandist for criticism" than a critic.

Eliot didn't begin by attempting to clean up the whole country; in fact it was not until after his assuming editorship of *The Criterion* in 1922—and especially after his conversion to Anglo-Catholicism in 1927—that his interest shifted from the comparison and analysis of individual writers and literary works, to (in words from his preface to the second, 1928, edition of *The Sacred Wood*) "the relation of poetry to the spiritual and social life of its time and of other times." His most productive, most brilliant years as a "pure" critic of literature were the ones in which his creative work flowered —from the publication of *Prufrock and Other Observations* in 1917 to *The Waste Land* in 1922. After that, although he wrote a number of fine essays about particular writers (perhaps most notably about Dante, Samuel Johnson, Byron, Tennyson, and Yeats), those for which he is most strongly remembered had their birth within a fairly small range of years. (A list of them would include essays on Marlowe, Jonson, *Hamlet,* Philip Massinger, the Metaphysicals, Marvell, Dryden, Blake, and Swinburne.)

Often in the briefest of compasses, Eliot can make a brilliant redirection of our sense of a writer. For example, the Swinburne essay is only six pages long but they are pages in which, as he says approvingly about Aristotle in "The Perfect Critic," Eliot is "swiftly operating the analysis of sensation to the point of principle and definition." In a series of lightning-like comparisons of lines from Swinburne's verse with lines from Thomas Campion, Shakespeare, and Shelley, he establishes his point about how Swinburne's genius was to identify meaning and sound, to present "emotion" that is "never particular, never in direct line of vision, never focussed"—emotion reinforced by "expansion." A moment from these comparisons may suggest Eliot's typical operation in his essays and reviews. He is about to compare Swinburne with Shakespeare, then with Wordsworth:

> It is, in fact, the word that gives him the thrill, not the object. When you take to pieces any verse of Swinburne, you find always that the object was not there—only the word. Compare
>
> > Snowdrops that plead for pardon
> > And pine for fright
>
> with the daffodils that come before the swallow dares. The snowdrop of Swinburne disappears, the daffodil of Shakespeare remains. The swallow of Shakespeare remains in the verse of *Macbeth;* the bird of Wordsworth
>
> > Breaking the silence of the seas
>
> remains; the swallow of "Itylus" disappears.

This is dazzling, virtually sleight-of-hand. Fully to register these comparisons a reader would have to remember Swinburne's "Before the Mirror" (whence the snowdrops), then lines from Act 4 of *The Winter's Tale* about the daffodils, then think of the "temple-haunting martlet" (the "swallow" in *Macbeth* which Duncan invokes as he prepares to enter Macbeth's castle), then Wordsworth's nightingale in "The Solitary Reaper," and finally the evanescence of Swinburne's swallow ("Swallow, my sister, O sister swallow"). Whether readers are able or likely to do all this even as they ponder the convincingness of Eliot's comparisons, is wholly doubtful. More likely we may just nod agreement, impressed by the breezy authority with which the critic proceeds to his conclusion that in Swinburne's verse "the meaning is merely the hallucination of meaning, because language, uprooted, has adapted itself to an independent life of atmospheric nourishment."

Eliot's practical criticism, as instanced in this particularly telescoped example of it, is seldom or never a matter of patient analysis of a poem, but of provocative assertion and invitations to compare one poem or series of lines with another. It is invigorating to read him partly because the twists of his discourse (not typically a soberly conducted "argument") have the surprise and originality of poetry itself. He likes to strew difficulties in the paths of his readers and himself—anything to make things other than cut and dried. In the following sentences from a never-reprinted *Athenaeum* review of 1919, "The Education of Taste," he sets out the difficulties that lie in the way of the practicing critic who must make decisions about how to operate:

> To communicate impressions is difficult; to communicate a coordinated system of impressions is more difficult; to theorize demands vast ingenuity, and to avoid theorizing requires vast honesty. Also there is the generality, which is usually a substitute for both impression and theory.

The neat movement here from theorizing to the avoidance of theorizing, then the capping reference to "generality" in which earlier terms like impression and honesty are brought back, has the force of true wit, Oscar Wilde crossed by Matthew Arnold.

Eliot is especially vigilant toward well-known literary terms a naive, insufficiently disillusioned poet or critic might rely on—terms like "technique." In prefacing the second edition of *The Sacred Wood* he takes us around the mulberry bush by beginning with a definition of poetry that— like Swift's definition of good prose as "proper words in proper places"— says everything and not much of anything in particular. Poetry, he writes, consists of "excellent words in excellent arrangement and excellent metre." But what more can be said?

> That is what is called the technique of verse. But we observe that we cannot define even the technique of verse; we cannot say at what point "technique" begins or where it ends; and if we add to it a "technique of feeling," that glib phrase will carry us only a little farther. We can only say that a poem, in some sense, has its own life.

In other words there is no shortcut, indeed no road through to certainty in literary matters. We can only say that "in some sense" a poem has its own life; or we can say, in Eliot's echo of Bishop Butler, that in considering poetry "we must consider it primarily as poetry and not another thing." Or, in that same playful preface to *The Sacred Wood*, we may agree that poetry is "a superior amusement." Is that a sufficient definition? Not at all:

> I do not mean an amusement for superior people. I call it an amusement, an amusement *pour distraire les honnêtes gens*, not because that is a true definition, but because if you call it anything else you are likely to call it something still more false. If we think of the nature of amusement, then poetry is not amusing; but if we think of anything else that poetry may seem to be, we are led into far greater difficulties.

Such sidestepping and ducking have their perils, and in his later prose Eliot would succumb to them, as in the often lugubrious fussings of *Notes towards the Definition of Culture*. But they also tease and refresh our minds in salutary ways.

Eliot performed similar services with regard to words like tradition, rhetoric, satire—perhaps most importantly to "wit," the promotion of which quality into a major one for great poetry may be his most forceful contribution to literary criticism. In "Andrew Marvell" (1921) he made a memorable attempt to define, even as he deprecated the possibility of clearly defining it, the quality of wit that distinguished Marvell's work and that, over the course of subsequent centuries, had been nearly absent from English poetry. Eliot's account claims that the seventeenth century took the "high" style developed in Marlowe and Jonson and separated it into qualities of wit and magniloquence. While allowing that the terms are fluid, and that the style of Marvell, Cowley, Milton, and others often showed these qualities blended, he attempts to distinguish Caroline wit from what followed it:

> The wit of the Caroline poets is not the wit of Shakespeare, and it is not the wit of Dryden, the great master of contempt, or of Pope, the great master of hatred, or of Swift, the great master of disgust. What is meant is some quality which is common to the songs in *Comus* and Cowley's Anacreontics and Marvell's Horatian Ode. It is more than a technical accomplishment, or the vocabulary and syntax of an epoch; it is, what we have designated tentatively as wit, a tough reasonableness beneath the slight lyric grace. You cannot

find it in Shelley or Keats or Wordsworth; you cannot find more
than an echo of it in Landor, still less in Tennyson or Browning;
and among contemporaries Mr. Yeats is an Irishman and Mr.
Hardy is a modern Englishman—that is to say, Mr. Hardy is without it and Mr. Yeats is outside of the tradition altogether.

It can be found, he goes on to add, in Laforgue and Gautier, two poets Eliot
had managed to make use of in his own work during the decade that had
just concluded itself.

Such an account is itself a specimen of wit, right down to the lyric grace
of naming those three great masters of contempt, hatred, and disgust, and
the tough reasonableness—or so it pretends to be—of excluding both Hardy
and Yeats from any consideration in these terms. Like most exciting passages in Eliot's criticism, we read and silently correct its overstatements: we
can find wit in some of Keats, even in Shelley occasionally; we know that the
dismissal of Yeats and Hardy is too sweeping, unfair. But as Eliot's friend
Wyndham Lewis reminds us, satire is always unfair, and Eliot's early criticism is never far from a satiric—or at least a mischievously subversive—
perspective on things. "Someone said: 'The dead writers are remote from us
because we *know* so much more than they did.' Precisely, and they are that
which we know." These sentences from "Tradition and the Individual Talent" might be turned upon Eliot's own criticism insofar as its formulations
have entered the bloodstream of later generations of readers who were
helped to become critics by having to move beyond the Eliot criticism that
they knew.

I have been suggesting that the challenge and pleasure of reading Eliot's
essays and reviews lie somewhere else than in extracting doctrines or key
terms from them. Nor should we take his comparings of writers and passages as the basis for a systematic account of English literature. At least two
of his successors, F. R. Leavis in *Revaluation* (1936) and Cleanth Brooks in
Modern Poetry and the Tradition (1939), wrote lively books that took Eliot's
inadequate responses to nineteenth-century English poetry as a warrant for
their ignoring, or largely demeaning, the work of Romantic and Victorian
poets, even as Leavis and Brooks exalted the Metaphysicals and admired
Eliot for the way his poems had reestablished connection with seventeenth-
century wit.

In the introduction to a selection from Eliot's prose, Frank Kermode usefully quotes a remark from a 1935 letter to Stephen Spender: "You don't," said Eliot, "really criticize any author to whom you have never surrendered yourself. . . . Even just the bewildering minute counts; you have to give yourself up, and then recover yourself, and the third moment is having something to say, before you have wholly forgotten both surrender and recovery." Kermode points out that this insistence on the primacy of "surrender" to a poet, a poem, a line (the "bewildering minute" referred to here is Eliot's allusion to lines from Tourneur's *The Revenger's Tragedy*), is the opposite of constructing a system, then bringing it to bear on a particular object—"reading to prove one's own point," Kermode calls it. Such an emphasis on surrender perhaps accounts for the scorn Eliot felt for Matthew Arnold's insistence that poetry was a "criticism of life." This was a way of speaking, Eliot said scornfully, "than which no phrase can sound more frigid to anyone who has felt the full surprise and elevation of a new experience of poetry." The surprise and elevation demanded nothing less than surrender, then demanded—in the subsequent "recovery"—a correspondingly fresh and unordinary way of "having something to say." It was here that Eliot's supreme originality as reader and writer made itself felt.

WITH the publication of the first volume of Eliot's letters, reaching to the end of 1922, we have a rich particular sense of what we knew only in outline before: that his marriage to Vivien Haigh-Wood in 1915 became progressively more painful and that both his health and hers worsened. In his case a "breakdown" occurred in 1921 when he took rest cures first in Margate, then in Lausanne, Switzerland, even as he was finishing *The Waste Land*. Epistolary Eliot was able at times to take a sardonically humorous perspective on his problems, saying that he felt himself to be "living in one of Dostoyevsky's novels, you see, not in one of Jane Austen's," or assuring a correspondent that his health wasn't all that bad: "My teeth are falling to pieces, I have to wear spectacles to read, and from time to time I am contorted with rheumatism—otherwise I am pretty well." Meanwhile Vivien was writing his mother about the deplorable condition of "Tom's" wardrobe ("his old underwear is still thick and in *fair* condition, but it needs *incessant darning*. Darning alone takes me hours out of the week"), especially his lack of pyjamas: "He is still worse provided with pyjamas than anything. . . . He is very rough with his pyjamas, and shirts—tears them unmercifully."

It is of interest then to contemplate this hapless creature (as Eliot and his wife present him to others) carrying out brilliantly various public roles in the years 1917–1921: working efficiently in the colonial and foreign department of Lloyd's Bank, teaching night school and extension courses in English literature, turning out enormous amounts of journalism for the *Egoist* and *Athenaeum,* and (in his spare time, one might say) assembling a second volume of verse, *Poems 1920,* consisting of "Gerontion" and a number of poems in quatrains. He praised Wyndham Lewis's *Tarr* when it appeared in 1918 for the "active unpleasantness" of its style, and something of that style permeates the quatrain poems, not only in their references in "Burbank with a Baedeker . . ." to "the Jew" and to Bleistein himself—"Chicago, Semite, Viennese"—but in the milieus of the two Sweeney poems ("The epileptic on the bed / Waiting until the shriek subsides") and the "rank" feline smell distilled by Grishkin in "Whispers of Immortality." The best of these poems may be the most humorous one, "The Hippopotamus," about how the church inevitably capitulates to worldly considerations while the hippo ascends to heaven:

> He shall be washed as white as snow,
> By all the martyr'd virgins kist,
> While the True Church remains below
> Wrapt in the old miasmal mist.

By contrast "A Cooking Egg," one of the most impenetrable of them, has the dubious distinction of having generated a seemingly endless debate in the pages of a learned journal on such matters as the identity of a character named Pipit (it was never satisfactorily explained). The quatrain poems share the quality of being highly memorizable, and they possess arresting individual lines. But they don't add up to a body of work we return to frequently. "In my experience everyone except the fools seem to be warped and stunted," wrote Eliot in 1919; in the quatrain poems he made "fools" like Sweeney or Grishkin or Bleistein the subject of scrupulous caricatural attention. These and their counterparts would perform in *The Waste Land* and in the uncompleted "Sweeney Agonistes" from the late 1920s. But a more important role was reserved for the "warped and stunted," the Gerontion or Tiresias-like protagonist who has foresuffered all, whose existence is characterized by aridity and deliquescence, and whose head is filled with marvelous lines and cadences from earlier poets.

"Gerontion" is Eliot's bleakest, chilliest, most inaccessible poem, virtually "unreadable" by the procedures we use to read more conventional works. It is Eliot at his most complicatedly and concentratedly allusive, as well as his most elusive. What are we to make of a monologue (if it is that) which in seeming to draw itself together near the end proffers the following sentiment—"I would meet you upon this honestly"—in which there is no credible "I," in which the "you" doesn't exist, and in which the adverb "honestly" can't be credited as accurately modifying any credible verb? The referential currency of such a line is about equal to that possessed by the figures—no more than names, really—who momentarily surface in the poem, then just as mysteriously disappear, as Hakagawa bows among the Titians, as Madame de Tornquist shifts the candles, and as Fräulein von Kulp turns in the hall, one hand on the door. Gerontion, whoever "he" may be, puts it thus: "Vacant shuttles weave the wind." The weaving and unweaving of verbal patterns in Eliot's most relentlessly verbal poem has the effect, so it seems to this reader, of rendering the large windy portents about Christianity and history less rather than more intelligible. As always in Eliot, there are wonderfully memorable lines, especially those from the section about history that begins "After such knowledge, what forgiveness?" But they don't contribute to a meditation that sustains itself in moral content as well as in rhetorical flourish. "Whenever a character in Shakespeare makes a direct appeal to us," Eliot wrote in " 'Rhetoric' and Poetic Drama," "we are either the victims of our own sentiment, or we are in the presence of a vicious rhetoric." That he was aware of this assertion in relation to "Gerontion" or that he set out to have the poem's speaker expose himself as fraudulent, is conceivable, yet doubtful. We should remember that he seriously considered using the poem as prologue to *The Waste Land,* desisting only when Pound told him he mustn't.

I should prefer to think that the harassed Eliot—caught in a painful marriage, overworked, plagued by bad teeth and eyesight, contorted by rheumatism, pyjamas falling to pieces, living in, as it were, a novel by Dostoyevsky—cheered himself up by seeing himself in the dramatic light of a poem, as he said Othello was really cheering himself up in his speech before he stabs himself:

> He is endeavouring to escape reality, he has ceased to think about
> Desdemona, and he is thinking about himself. . . . Othello succeeds
> in turning himself into a pathetic figure, by adopting an *aesthetic*

rather than a moral attitude, dramatizing himself against his environment. He takes in the spectator, but the human motive is primarily to take in himself.

The question is perhaps whether either Gerontion or "Gerontion" succeeds in taking *us* in, without the five acts of tortuous dramatic development Shakespeare subjects Othello to and that makes his final end so moving. My answer is that, brilliant as the poem is, it lacks the humor and humanity of "Prufrock." And that for all its evocation of aridity, of "Thoughts of a dry brain in a dry season," it fails to take us in, to take hold of us the way Eliot was about to do in *The Waste Land.*

But how does *The Waste Land* "take hold"? Not so many years ago it seemed important to try to loosen the poem from the interpretive structures critics had attached to it; there was so much "scaffolding"—to use Cleanth Brooks's word about what his own influential essay on the poem provided—that it was all but impossible to see the object the scaffolding surrounded. Now, much of that surrounding material has fallen away, or has become so inert that it's simply no longer of interest. Few critics these days deal with the poem by applying the Fisher King legend, Jessie Weston's *From Ritual to Romance,* or Frazer's *The Golden Bough.* It was of course Eliot himself, in his introductory note, who attached these books and legends to the poem; but the notes to *The Waste Land* are a kind of playful poetry themselves. It is Eliot's superior amusement, for example, to remind us that the hermit-thrush in "What the Thunder Said" is *"Turdus aonalaschkae pallasii,"* that he's heard it in Quebec Province, and that "Its 'water-dripping song' is justly celebrated." Eliot's notes, if not taken too seriously, are harmless and sometimes amusing. But other sorts of notes or glosses adhering to the poem, whether they exist in, say, *The Norton Anthology of Modern Poetry,* or in the mind of an individual reader, can be more insidious, more inhibiting to creative, responsive reading. I am thinking of a gloss such as Norton gives to the Baudelaire allusion at the end of part 1, "The Burial of the Dead": *"You: hypocrite lecteur!—mon semblable,—mon frere!"* After identifying the source, the editor says that "with this line Baudelaire and Eliot assault the reader and draw him accusingly into the same plight as themselves." The problem with this assertion is, of course, that after reading the footnote no sensible reader is going to feel the least bit assaulted. It's just one more allusion to store untroubled in the mind and then read on. Or consider the moment when the narrator, regarding the morning crowd flowing over London Bridge, suddenly recognizes someone named Stetson and addresses him as "You who were with me in the ships at Mylae!" The anthology note identifies Mylae as a battle in the first Punic War between Rome and Carthage, then says: "It merges with the First World War, in which the speaker and Stetson fought; both wars are seen as pointless and futile." This is an example of an editorial anxiety to fill in the blanks that the poem so carefully does *not* fill in: we are told neither that these figures fought in the First World War, nor that the war was pointless. And if— as Eliot's own note claims—all the poem's "characters" merge into Tiresias, it's hard to see how, being blind, he could have fought in any war.

Samuel Johnson's wisdom about notes should be remembered, when in his editorial preface to Shakespeare he wrote "Particular passages are cleared by notes, but the general effect of the work is weakened. The mind is refrigerated by interruption; the thoughts are diverted from the principle subject. . . ." A poem such as *The Waste Land,* just as much as a Shakespeare play, suffers when the reading of it is constantly interrupted by a recurrence to notes or their equivalent. What we need to work at instead is keeping the poem moving, paying attention to the sequence; above all, listening to the voices—for it is voices in motion that make up the poem's substance. Again, Johnson's advice to the reader of Shakespeare is wholly appropriate to reading Eliot: "Let him read on through brightness and obscurity, through integrity and corruption; let him preserve his comprehension of the dialogue and his interest in the fable. And when the pleasures of novelty have ceased, let him attempt exactness, and read the commentators."

Another way of putting it is Wyndham Lewis's way when, decades ago, he said about Joyce's *Ulysses,* recently published, that "No one who looks *at* it will ever want to look *behind* it." Lewis was paying grudging tribute to the incredibly rich surface Joyce's book presents to the reader. And Eliot himself in his essay of 1923, *"Ulysses:* Order and Myth," said that Joyce had given him "all the surprise, delight, and terror that I can require." We may presume that these qualities emanated from looking at and listening to the surface of *Ulysses,* rather than from probing the depths of Joyce's thought or discovering deep meanings supposedly hidden in his book. During the time he wrote *The Waste Land,* Eliot was preoccupied with what he called, in his 1919 essay on Ben Jonson, "poetry of the surface." Many of the things he admired in Jonson's dramatic art he named in terms that could equally well apply to the art of *The Waste Land*: "simplified characters," a "flat distortion" in the drawing, "an art of caricature," "a brutality, a lack of sentiment, a polished surface, a handling of large bold designs in brilliant colours"— one could go on. "We cannot call a man's work superficial when it is the creation of a world; a man cannot be accused of dealing superficially with the world which he himself has created; the superficies *is* the world," wrote Eliot, summing it all up by calling Jonson's drama "a titanic show." The phrase would not be amiss as a collective name for the different "shows" of which *The Waste Land* is composed, whether as conducted at Madame Sosostris's or on London Bridge, or round behind the gashouse, or in the typist's flat.

The challenge lies in saying something relevant and appropriate to these surfaces without saying too much, without foisting a burden of "meaning" on the poem (as do explanatory footnotes, often) that makes it merely portentous. Consider the marvelous and scary utterances of the "neurasthenic" woman, as she is sometimes referred to, in the first section of part 2, "A Game of Chess." "Under the brush, her hair / Spread out in fiery points / Glowed into words, then would be savagely still," as she implores the faceless narrator to "Speak to me," to "Think." Vivien Eliot, who must have been in her husband's mind when he wrote these lines, was reduced to a single marginal response to those words as they appeared in *The Waste Land* manuscript—"Wonderful!" There was no more that needed to be said, and a similar enthusiastic exclamation might be made to the woman in the pub (in the second half of "A Game of Chess") as she runs on about what she told Lil about how to treat her husband Albert who has been in the army and wants a good time: "And if you don't give it him, there's other will, I said. / Oh is there, she said. Something o' that, I said." Neither of these women should be understood as representing or embodying some large important symbolic value—some truth about modern civilization. For if we insist on making the characters representative of something "more," something deeper, we run the risk of missing out on surface intensities, memorable accents and associations—what Lil's friend and critic, referring to the hot gammon Lil and Albert served her, calls "the beauty of it hot." Shakespeare comes to mind again and the critical habit of treating his plays (particularly the last ones) as symbolic utterances, large spiritual meanings about ultimate things. Yet the surface of these plays is so much more active, complex, and just plain interesting than what supposedly lies behind it, that to translate language and events into other terms is simply to dilute and enfeeble them.

Blackmur's name for what Eliot gave us in *The Waste Land* was "sensual metaphysics." In a provocative comment from his Library of Congress lectures (*Anni Mirabiles,* 1921–1925) he confronted the surreal nightmare passage in part 5, "What the Thunder Said," in which "a woman drew her long black hair out tight," in which the towers turn upside down and the bats crawl downward "down a blackened wall" and voices sing "out of empty cisterns and exhausted wells":

> The exegetes tell us, and it is true, that we are in Chapel Perilous and the Perilous Cemetery is no doubt near at hand, and it may be as one of the exegetes says that we hear something like the voice of John the Baptist in the last line. But for myself, I muse and merge and ache and find myself feeling with the very senses of my thought greetings and cries from all the senses that are.

Testimony such as this risks being no more than a fancier version of the professor in the classroom assuring his students how deeply he is moved by a passage; but we can risk it, in the interests of opening up rather than shutting down the poem.

The most challenging of recent reconsiderations of *The Waste Land* is to be found in Christopher Ricks's *T. S. Eliot and Prejudice,* which doesn't address the poem as a whole but selects the openings of part 1 and part 5 with a view to demonstrating how Eliot's poetry is a principled refusal to strike and maintain clear, dramatic postures—the unmistakable postures of sentence sounds that Robert Frost said poetry should provide. As Ricks shows in patient detail, Eliot's openings—"April is the cruelest month" and "After the torchlight red on sweaty faces"—are memorable ones, but the sequences these lines initiate are anything but clearly marked: "The force of this opening [he is speaking of the "April" one] is in its combination of unmistakable directness with all these lurking possibilities of mistaking its direction." For all their differences of vocabulary and emphasis, both Blackmur and Ricks prefer to respond to the volatile surface intensities of language rather than the stable meanings some critics have presumed to lie underneath them. My own experience in teaching the poem is that, if you read it aloud and ask what people hear in it—anywhere in the five parts—the variety of responses, most of them cogent and relevant, will prove *The Waste*

Land to be a work eminently hospitable to divergent reading possibilities, and full of—in Ricks's phrase—"lurking possibilities of mistaking its direction." These qualities make the poem still vibrant after seven decades of interpretation; my procedure here has been, accordingly, not to offer another one but to consider the question of and the necessity for "interpretation."

AN essay on Eliot's work that ignores the part of it produced between *The Waste Land* and "Burnt Norton," first of *Four Quartets,* and indeed that says nothing about the plays or the criticism as they appeared in the 1930s and beyond, can have no pretense at responsible coverage. My excuse, apart from the usual limitations of space, is that some of Eliot's poems from this period, original and distinct as they are, seem to me not particularly to invite further commentary. I am thinking especially of "Ash-Wednesday," in its combination of ritual invocation and private muttering; also of the exquisitely cadenced "Marina." These and the "Ariel" poems are interesting mainly for the way they attempt, with varying degrees of success, to open up channels to a "reality" which, in the language of "Burnt Norton," we are told human kind cannot bear very much of. This opening up of channels is performed so impressively in the *Quartets* that by contrast the earlier "Ash-Wednesday" often seems flashy and desperate in some of its strategies. I am thinking, for example, of the verbal contortions that mar part 5 of that poem, ones in which even though the rhyming extravagances are deliberate—"Where shall the word be found, where will the word / Resound?" or "not on the mainland, in the desert or the rain land," or most egregiously "No place of grace for those who avoid the face," —the effect is too much that of a zany prophet crying out his message, advising us to beware.

Four Quartets has many strategies for opening itself and the reader to "reality," some of them more subtle and engaging than others. Yet if it is true, as Henry James insisted it was in "The Art of Fiction," that "Art lives upon discussion, upon experiment, upon curiosity, upon variety of attempt, upon the exchange of views and the comparison of standpoints," then *Four Quartets* may be the least living poem in Eliot's oeuvre, justifying Cynthia Ozick's statement that the latest generation "never" reads it. Even with the publication in 1978 of Helen Gardner's fine study of the poem's composition, the relative absence of exchange of views, of lively argument about the poem's status, has persisted. Commentators are agreed, for the most part, that it is a mixture of very private and very public poetry, and that as a result its texture is extremely uneven. The question is whether such unevenness is a fault in the poem or the source of its power and beauty.

Donald Davie's way of distinguishing, broadly, the two kinds of characteristic poetry in the *Quartets* is to call one "the sonorous opulence of Mallarmé," the other a "prosaicism so homespun as to be, from time to time, positively 'prosey' or 'prosing.'" And he adds that Eliot's famous remark about how "The poetry does not matter" is directed at the second, prosaic pole. But the statement about poetry not mattering occurs in the second section of "East Coker," part 2, after the Mallarméan opalescence of "What is the late November doing / With the disturbance of the spring." That lyric having concluded itself, there is a blank space after which a voice intones:

> That was a way of putting it—not very satisfactory;
> A periphrastic study in a worn-out poetical fashion.

and we are told that "one" is still left with the "intolerable wrestle / With words and meanings" and that "The poetry does not matter." It is an extravagant thing for a poet who has spent his life wrestling with words and meanings to say, and it surely has just as much reference—perhaps more— to the "poetical" Mallarmé-like passages in the poem as to the prosaic ones it might be seen as rationalizing or justifying. At the same time, the claim about poetry not mattering shouldn't be taken too solemnly, as commentators sometimes do when they compare Eliot's work to the late Beethoven quartets which also, it is said, try to get "beyond" music (as Eliot would get beyond poetry). In fact the differences between listening to Beethoven and reading Eliot are a lot more apparent and significant than the similarities. Let us say rather that they may be compared only to the extent that, despite the innovative, unconventional gestures these artists make in tonality and rhetoric, each remains intractably committed to his medium—Beethoven to music, Eliot to words.

Ten years after he completed "Little Gidding," Eliot published "The Three Voices of Poetry," an essay that contains a number of interesting formulations about the creative act, the most relevant to our purposes being one he uses to distinguish two of these voices—the first and most important of which is that of the poet when he is primarily not attempting "to communicate with anything at all." Eliot draws on Gottfried Benn's lecture "*Probleme der Lyrik*" but prefers to use the term "meditative verse" rather than "lyric" for this first voice. It (the first voice) originates from something germinating in the poet for which he must find words; it is nothing so definite as an idea, not even an emotion—it is what Eliot calls an "obscure impulse," and he says the following about the poet's relation to that impulse:

> He does not know what he has to say until he has said it, and in the effort to say it he is not concerned with making other people understand anything. He is not concerned, at this stage, with other people at all: only with finding the right words or, anyhow the least wrong words . . . he is going to all that trouble, not in order to communicate with anyone, but to gain relief from acute discomfort.

The Waste Land, we remember, was in Eliot's term just a piece of rhythmical grumbling in which various obscure impulses causing active discomfort (a nervous collapse, say) eventually found their way into an order of right—or at least the least wrong—words.

It may be objected that *Four Quartets* is not *The Waste Land,* and that its impulse is less an impulse than an idea, expressed by Eliot in a number of ways over the post-wasteland years: that we lived in a society worm-eaten with liberalism; that the modern world was no longer capable of entertaining the "higher dream," as Dante had; that "The world is trying the experiment of attempting to form a civilized but non-Christian mentality—an experiment which will fail but only after which failure can the world be saved from suicide." That is, *Four Quartets* seems to have issued from an Eliot, or from a part of him, very much concerned with making other people understand that something terribly wrong had happened to the world, and that the poet's task was to warn them of what had happened and to inspire them with the possibilities of another kind of happening.

My contention is that if *Four Quartets* were such a poem, concerned with giving poetic expression to the sentiments Eliot had been expressing—sometimes harshly, even intemperately—in his prose, it would be much less of a poem than it is. His own distinction still holds: that prose may legitimately concern itself with ideals, while poetry can only deal with actuality. Eliot's sense of "actuality" was subtler and more complex than his social polemics could suggest. What is most moving about the *Quartets* is the way the poem tries to talk sense about ideas and ideals, addressing us in the second voice (the poet "talking to other people"), entertaining a formulation, apologizing for it ("That was a way of putting it, not very satisfactory"), faltering and losing confidence in the usefulness of what it is trying to do. Then pausing perhaps and, gathering impetus, beginning again but in a different key; moving out somewhere beyond us, no longer occupied with our needs and interests since it has something more intimate and private in sight. For adequate demonstration of such movement, one needs to read aloud an extended passage; here I simply draw attention to the fifth section of "East Coker" which begins, wearily, with a confession to us that twenty years have been largely wasted ("the years of *L'entre deux guerres*") and that the struggle to use words brings inevitable failure; that each "raid on the inarticulate" is also a deterioration; that the burden of the past is immense and overwhelming; that "conditions" (wartime England in 1940) seem "unpropitious" for any attempt at recovery. But (grimly) "For us, there is only the trying. The rest is not our business."

Then, after a space, the voice resumes, still addressing us evidently but with rather more "poetic" inclinations, speaking intensely about a "lifetime burning in every moment," or of "old stones that cannot be deciphered," and of the respective "times"—under starlight, under lamplight—in which we spend our evenings. After mention of the second evening comes a parenthetical phrase, "The evening with the photograph album," signaling to my ears the moment when the second voice turns into something else (you cannot speak a parenthesis to an audience) and the lines no longer are organized by an order of punctuation:

> Old men ought to be explorers
> Here and there does not matter
> We must be still and still moving
> Into another intensity

Then a glimpsed "union" changing into "communion," as through the cry of wave and wind, through "the vast waters / Of the petrel and the porpoise," the poetry explores, in associative monologue, its subject—the subject of the four poems taken together—continuously winding and unwinding itself. F. R. Leavis once named that subject, with special reference to the beginning of "Burnt Norton," as "a radical inquiry into the nature and methods of his exploration." Let us say rather, "of exploration," by way of noting the poem's reach beyond the merely personal. And what it explores is not merely the conditions of spiritual and religious possibilities, but other matters of intimate and ultimate concern that presented themselves to a man and poet very much in the "middle way" (Eliot was fifty-five when he published "Little Gidding"). It was an attempt to ascertain what things mattered and how much they mattered: questions of present, past, and future time; the writing of poetry; the love of worldly and unworldly things; stillness and speech; one's origins, one's ancestors, one's childhood; the meaning of history, of servitude, of freedom; the circumstances of a nation at war. What it has to "say" about these matters is not to be extracted from its poetry, which turns out to matter very much. When a saying is extracted and contemplated in its "translated" form, the result is unmemorable; but within the poem, from time to time, memorable things happen. In the language of the "dead master" in "Little Gidding" who comes to admonish the "I" about the gifts of old age:

> So I find words I never thought to speak
> In streets I never thought I should revisit
> When I left my body on a distant shore.

In the spring of 1933, during a nine-month stay in the United States (he had determined to separate permanently from his wife), Eliot visited the University of Virginia to deliver some lectures later published as *After Strange Gods*. In their reflections on orthodoxy (the subtitle was "A Primer of Modern Heresy") they figure as Eliot's most controversial prose utterance. But early in the first lecture there is an extraordinary passage in which he describes his impressions of the new world on arriving from England the previous fall:

> My local feelings were stirred very sadly by my first view of New England, on arriving from Montreal, and journeying all one day through the beautiful desolate country of Vermont. Those hills had once, I suppose, been covered with primaeval forest; the forest was razed to make sheep pastures for the English settlers; now the sheep are gone, and most of the descendants of the settlers; and a new forest appeared blazing with the melancholy glory of October maple and beech and birch scattered among the evergreens; and after the processions of scarlet and gold and purple wilderness you descend to the sordor of the half-dead mill towns of southern New Hampshire and Massachusetts.

He goes on to say that the "happiest" lands are those in which the long struggle between man and the environment had brought about a successful accommodation between landscape and "numerous generations of one race," and he concludes that "those New England mountains seemed to me to give evidence of a human success so meagre and transitory as to be more desperate than the desert." He would go on to speak to his Virginia audience about the importance of tradition, and in the preface to the published volume would characterize their university as "one of the older, smaller and most gracious of American educational institutions, one of those in which some vestiges of a traditional education seem to survive."

We need not dwell upon what certainly appears to be a bit of wishful thinking, if not just outright flattery, on Eliot's part; nor will we further consider the context of the previously referred to remark about how free-thinking Jews are undesirable in a traditional society. When called to the bar of judgment Eliot will probably be willing to negotiate with and revise his terms; at any rate he never reprinted the lectures. But non-negotiable, as I hear it, is the description of his stirred local feelings as he ventured through New England, observing and being saddened by the transitoriness of human success. It is the most authentic of Eliotic notes, and—for all the differences between early and late work—is there from the beginning of "Preludes," with its withered leaves and lonely cab-horses, right down to the end of "Little Gidding" with its children in the apple tree, "Quick, now, here, now, always—." Three decades ago, in "Fifty Years of American Poetry," Randall Jarrell surveyed our poets from the first half of this century. When he came to Eliot, Jarrell decided it was appropriate to speak, not from his own voice in the present, but from the point of view he imagined the future would take about this writer:

> Won't the future say to us in helpless astonishment: "But did you actually believe that all these things about objective correlatives, classicism, the tradition, applied to *his* poetry? Surely you must have seen that he was one of the most subjective and daemonic poets who ever lived, the victim and helpless beneficiary of his own inexorable compulsions, obsessions? . . . But for you, of course, after the first few years, his poetry existed undersea, thousands of feet below that deluge of exegesis, explication, source listing, scholarship, and criticism that overwhelmed it. And yet how bravely and

personally it survived, its eyes neither coral nor mother-of-pearl but plainly human, full of human anguish!"

The voice of that future has not yet been heard; we should keep listening for it.

Columbia History of American Poetry, ed. Jay Parini
(New York: Columbia University Press, 1993)

Fabulous Monster: Ford Madox Ford
as Literary Critic

❧❧

T HE FIRST HALF of my title is taken from *Some Do Not . . .* at a
moment when, in exasperated wonder, Sylvia Tietjens so characterizes her husband. But the epithet has general application to Ford Madox
Ford and serves as a suitably outrageous label for his critical audacities and
heresies. Only when we respond to these pronouncements about other
books, writers, and literary forms, with a blend of annoyed disbelief and fascinated attention akin to Sylvia's toward Christopher Tietjens, are we seeing
Ford for the truly interesting critic he seems to me to be. More than forty
years ago, in reviewing his late book of literary portraits, *Mightier Than the
Sword* (published in this country and hereafter referred to as *Portraits from
Life*), V. S. Pritchett caught exactly the right note when he described the
reader of Ford as "stunned by a volubility in which every word strikes and
starts a dozen echoes which distract him to further effects like a boy shouting under an archway." "One sways giddily but enlivened," declared Pritchett, insisting that Ford was "before everything else a personality."

Yet not everyone has been charmed by this personality, at least as it
showed itself in the reminiscences *(Memories and Impressions, Thus to Revisit, Return to Yesterday, It Was the Nightingale),* the appreciations of Henry
James and Joseph Conrad or the ones in *Portraits from Life*—to say nothing
of the more ostensibly critical works *(The Critical Attitude, The English
Novel, The March of Literature).* Early along, the unsigned *Times Literary*

Supplement (22 January 1914) reviewer called Ford's "critical study" of James a "farrago of irrelevancies" and "a piece of trifling" and declared that the author "has a knowing and jaunty style of humour, very freely indulged, which suggests the essay of the schoolboy who discovers, as he approaches his subject, that he has nothing to say." Twenty-five years later, at the time of Ford's death, Edward Sackville-West was appalled by the just-published *The March of Literature* (1938), an "intimidating tome" which would join the books that "lie about the centuries like so many puddings gone cold and uneatable," and which was filled with "the promulgation of enormous and paradoxical views" Sackville-West found absurd. In more friendly and understanding terms, Ford's admirers have apologized for his famous inaccuracies (those tall stories which, repeated, grew ever taller) or warned us not to expect the sort of reasonable behavior one gets from other modern critics of literature. Frank MacShane, to whose labors on Ford's behalf we are all in debt, distinguishes Ford's achievement in criticism from that of John Crowe Ransom or F. R. Leavis by saying about Ford that, "as an enthusiastic pioneer, he was incapable of the balanced and scholarly assessment that characterizes their criticism."[1] The "old man mad about writing" label that Ford hung around his own neck in prefacing *The March of Literature* could in these terms be a gloss on his whole career as a critic: young or old, he was in more than one sense mad about writing, an enthusiast whose opinions evidently need to be taken with a grain of salt, a bit of discounting.

This way lies patronizing, and although MacShane does not indulge in it, his distinguishing of Ford from presumably more responsible critics like Ransom and Leavis seems to me a step in the wrong direction. We need not argue the ways in which "balanced and scholarly assessment" will not quite do as a description of either the moral fierceness or the homely elegance with which Leavis and Ransom, respectively, conducted their critical operations. But it may be suggested that as the major nonacademic modern critics of literature recede into historical distance, their interest for us (in a phrase Leavis hated) becomes increasingly a purely literary one. We no longer read them for news about their responses to a particular writer, or for their theoretical or ideational content (which we are already familiar with, having read them more than once). Instead they appear and appeal to

---

1. Frank MacShane, introduction to *Critical Writings of Ford Madox Ford* (Lincoln: University of Nebraska Press, 1963).

us in ways that more closely resemble those of a good poem or piece of fiction: it is their powers of imaginative creation, rather than the demonstrated truth of their judgments, which engage us.

Already it may sound suspiciously as if I am setting up a special plea for Ford by converting his critical irresponsibilities and excesses into exactly the things to be delighted in. This may be true, but if so, I am convinced that other significant modern artist-critics must be similarly apologized for: I am thinking, for example, of such names as Ezra Pound, T. S. Eliot, D. H. Lawrence, Wyndham Lewis; or on a lesser scale, of William Carlos Williams, Robert Graves, or Ransom. (Even though he wrote no literature himself, Leavis belongs with this group.) Not all artist-critics fall inevitably into this category of "strong" practitioners: one might adduce E. M. Forster, or Virginia Woolf, or W. H. Auden, or (perhaps) George Orwell, or Edwin Muir, as appreciators with more catholic tastes, reviewers who give at least the illusion of seeing the object as in itself it really is, rather than pressing the claims of some special vision. Strictly on the basis of Ford's last book, the immensely long *The March of Literature* with its patient surveying of the whole of literature "from Confucius' day to our own," Ford himself bids to be included in the second, "catholic" category. But for more compelling reasons I propose to assign him a place in the first one, in the ranks of Pound, Eliot, Lawrence, and Lewis.

Of this intimidating foursome, the only one really to speak well of Ford was Pound, who prefaced his 1914 review of Ford's *Collected Poems* by calling him the lonely possessor of a "vision of perfection."[2] "Mr. Hueffer" had committed the crime of insisting on the importance of "good writing as opposed to the opalescent word, the rhetorical tradition." He, like Pound, admired Stendhal, Flaubert, Maupassant, and Turgenev; therefore it was inevitable that he be disliked or ignored in London—"a capital where everybody's Aunt Lucy or Uncle George has written something or other, and where the victory of any standard save that of mediocrity would at once banish so many nice people from the temple of immortality." Pound has

---

2. "Mr. Hueffer and the Prose Tradition in Verse," *Poetry* (June 1914). Both Lawrence and Lewis were interested in Ford while he was publishing them in the *English Review*, but became markedly less so after he ceased to edit the magazine. Eliot never appears to have taken an interest in Ford.

only to say these words to establish, as it were, Hueffer as the best critic in England, "one might say the only critic of any importance."

It may be observed that one sure way to make yourself more disliked was to be extravagantly praised by Pound: at the same moment Pound was booming Ford, Robert Frost was successfully detaching himself from the ministrations of his "discoverer"; Lewis was to do the same during the 1920s. Ford never did so; indeed the connection with Pound was used explicitly, in Sackville-West's attack on *The March of Literature,* as indicative of Ford's unsoundness as a critic. But it is important to insist that—while we recognize the strong affiliations between Pound and Ford, particularly in their dislike for the "rhetorical tradition" as it showed itself most egregiously in the Victorian novel, and in their compensatory adulation of Continental practitioners of "the prose tradition"—we cannot rest content with Pound's way of praising Ford. There is no more inert idea to be discovered at present than that Stendhal's sentences or *Trois Contes* are healthy prose, whereas the periods of Thackeray, Dickens, or George Eliot are diseased, at least "opalescent." If we are to appreciate Ford rightly, in other words, it will not do to abstract the doctrine and pin it on the wall for daily contemplation and agreement.

Another way of putting this caveat is to say that however much we respect Pound for his perspicuity about Ford's intelligence as a critic, there was some sentimentality about the portrait, since Pound presumed to make the fabulous monster nothing more or less than a lonely, sane, accurate perceiver of "good writing." Pound says winningly that if a man insists on talking about perfection he is going to get himself "disliked." What in retrospect we see about Ford is the extent of his alienation from what, in words from *Hugh Selwyn Mauberley,* "the age demanded." In the tenth section of *Mauberley* we are introduced to what is usually understood as a Ford-like artist who has, as Pound is about to do, forsaken the "march of events" and what passes for culture in postwar London:

> Beneath the sagging roof
> The stylist has taken shelter
> Unpaid, uncelebrated,
> At last from the world's welter
>
> Nature receives him. . . .

And we are told that "the soil meets his distress." Of course one should not hold Ford responsible for Pound's heroic or mock-heroic portrait of him. But in setting himself off from what the age demanded, Ford accentuated and cultivated certain human tendencies that had been there all along, were there in his *English Review* essays and in his book on James. The remainder of this essay will direct attention to some ways and instances in which those human tendencies expressed themselves in his literary criticism.

It may help to compare Ford's critical personality with those of two other English writers whose procedures seem to me interestingly related to his. The first is Coleridge, a writer whom he barely mentions ever and then only to be named (in *The March of Literature*) as one more English Romantic. Yet is it not possible to think of Ford's critical writings as constituting one book, a biographia literaria that must be perused with excitement, exasperation, and disbelief: a book in which marvelous bits of humor and irony alternate with self-defensive exculpations, boastings, "digressions" that set out to undermine the notion of a digression; in which lists of bad names and good ones are called up for catcalls or admiration; and in which the general sense is that there are no limits to what may be expressed? As Randall Jarrell once said of William Carlos Williams, "Why he'd say anything, so long as he believed it was true." With both Coleridge and Ford, the reader often gasps at something he cannot quite believe they believe to be true; yet they have said it. And in both men there is a feckless quality, something in the voice, in their stance toward "the world's welter," that makes us want to sympathize with their "distress," be indignant that their visions of perfection are so little appreciated and valued by all those other successful authors and worldlings.

One thinks of chapter 10, the long, thirty-six page ramble from the *Biographia* in which Coleridge sets forth "a chapter of digression and anecdotes" as an "interlude" preceding his tackling the question of the imagination. Yet even as he postpones explicit dealings with his subject, his style demonstrates the very "poetic power" in question. Ford's indirections similarly work to coax a reader into acceptance of his truth about the only way to write a novel; as when, in *It Was the Nightingale* (part 2, chapter 2), we hear successively about (among other things) classical scholarship, Harold Monro's villa in the south of France in 1922, memories of World War I and Ford's loss of memory, the death of Proust, the death of Marie Lloyd, Joyce and the Parisian literary scene, a Pen Club lunch in Paris, the possibility that Ford might have become a French writer, Pound, memories of Arthur Marwood (the prototype of Christopher Tietjens), how Ford found the "Sylvia" of *Some Do Not . . .*—and then at last the following "truth":

> The first thing that you have to consider when writing a novel is your story, and then your story—and then your story! If you wish to feel more dignified you may call it your "subject." Once started it must go on and on to its appointed end. . . .
>
> Of course you must appear to digress. That is the art which conceals your Art. The reader, you should premise, will always dislike you and your book. He thinks it an insult that you should dare to claim his attention, and if lunch is announced or there is a ring at the bell he will welcome the digression. So you will provide him with what he thinks are digressions with occasions on which he thinks he may let his attention relax. . . . But really not one single thread must ever escape your purpose.

What is promised or recommended here has already been performed in the previous pages of the chapter.

Ford may also be usefully compared with his contemporary Wyndham Lewis, whose earliest story he published in the *English Review* but from whom he seems thereafter to have kept his distance. And no wonder, if Lewis acted at all as Ford says he did. In "There Were Strong Men," the final chapter in *Portraits from Life,* Lewis catches Ford "mysteriously by the elbow" (a nice way to catch anybody) and delivers, inaudibly, the message that the elder novelist is a has-been: "You and Mr. Conrad and Mr. James and all those old fellows are done. . . . Exploded! . . . *"Fichus! . . . Vieux jeu! . . .* No good! . . . Finished!" These old fellows take infinite pains to convince their readers that they are undergoing a character's experience; they are after something called "verisimilitude," but, Lewis continues, that is not what people want any more:

> They want to be amused. . . . By brilliant fellows like me. Letting off brilliant fireworks. Performing like dogs on tight ropes. Something to give them the idea they're at a performance. You fellows try to efface yourselves; to make people think that there isn't any author and that they're living in the affairs you . . . adumbrate, isn't

that your word? . . . What balls! What rot! . . . What's the good of being an author if you don't get any fun out of it?

There may be some truth in the distinction this amusingly rendered scene makes between Ford's careful novelistic composition and Lewis's breezier efforts, although *Tarr* and Lewis's other early fictions look to have been carefully enough composed. But Ford's critical procedures do not provide analogous examples of self-effacement and can be assimilated more naturally to the performance-showman aspect Lewis speaks up for here. The brilliance, the fireworks, the amusement—indeed the self-justifications, the boastings, the "digressions"—are at least as much to be found in Ford's pages as in those of his ill-mannered younger contemporary. Neither of them puts much stock in disinterested, rational, "objective" critical demonstration.

It should also be noted that, in a most important sense, neither Ford nor Lewis was English. Lewis, born on his mysterious American father's yacht anchored off the coast of Nova Scotia, then brought up by his mother and sent to Rugby as if he belonged there, left England at the beginning of this century and, in Paris and in Germany, formed a self that was to dedicate much of its future energies to castigating English humor and the English inability ever to know what Art was really about. Ford, born in Surrey and brought up in Hammersmith, liked to think of himself as not to the English manner born. Decades later in *It Was the Nightingale,* he delightedly spun out a moment when, lying on a grassy knoll in Kent and talking to E. V. Lucas, the editor of Charles Lamb, he abuses Lucas for admiring that "buttered-toast-clean-fire-clear-hearth-spirit-of-the-game-beery-gin-sodden sentimentalism." The invective continues for the next two pages, while Lucas takes long puffs at his pipe and eventually, when challenged to say why Ford *cannot* appreciate Charles Lamb, gently tells Ford that he is "not really English." Ford protests, producing his credentials as a cricketer and golfer, a public schoolboy who takes cold baths in the morning, knows about sheep and flower-gardening, has a tailor in Sackville Street and a barber in Bond Street. Why then is he not English?

> Mr. Lucas said with dejection:
> "Because you do not appreciate. . . ." He paused; I supplied: "Charles Lamb?"
> He said:
> "No, I am thinking." He added: *"Punch."*

That did it, and Ford admits defeat; indeed, the reader feels, Ford is quite pleased by the whole exchange and wouldn't have missed giving us the full benefit of it.

Thus it was that in *The Critical Attitude* (1911), made up of pieces published in the *English Review,* he insisted that the title of the magazine was a contradiction in terms. Nothing on earth will make an Englishman adopt the critical attitude, since nothing can make him review his thoughts: "The ass draws his cart; the respectable journal preaches respectability; the hyena disinters and crunches his bones; but the Englishman—he is just God's Englishman." This complaint picks up where Matthew Arnold had left off, but in an airier, more disillusioned way. Englishmen go around grunting that they "like" something or do not like something; whereas the critic, Ford says, exists to point out defects, the defects of a writer's qualities, or to point out the difference between "commercial books" and works of art. To behave in this way is supposedly to make unpopular, un-English discriminations against, in Pound's colorful words, "everybody's Aunt Lucy and Uncle George."

Ten years later in *Thus to Revisit* (1921), when Ford considered the contemporary prose writers ("Prosateurs" is his chapter title) who wrote not commercial books but authentic works of art, he confronted the English reader, not surprisingly, with somebody more pure, more purely The Writer, than they had imagined could exist. Conrad and James were supreme novelists, but their effects can be studied, their books admiringly understood for the craftsmanship with which "life" is rendered. But "the unapproached master of the English tongue," the writer whose gift is "immense, tranquil or consummate," is . . . W. H. Hudson! Not only, like Conrad and James, has Hudson escaped the perils of being English, and thus of having been influenced by such monuments as the Authorized Version, Shakespeare, and Sir Thomas Browne, but—unlike Conrad and James—his effects are unaccountable. " 'You can't tell how this fellow gets his effects!' " Ford quotes Conrad, who said as he looked up one day from reading *Green Mansions:* " 'he writes as the grass grows. The Good God makes it be there. And that is all there is to it!' " This state of affairs Ford finds irresistible. In Hudson he can admire a writer who, like Ford's beloved Turgenev (the "beautiful genius" as he too often refers to him), is quite beyond critical categories of description. After devoting a full-length chapter in *Portraits from Life* to Turgenev, he finally admits that he has said nothing about the "technique" employed by this writer, because it cannot be done: "No one can say anything valid about the technique of Turgenev. It consisted probably in nothing but politeness . . . in consideration for his readers." Remarks like these would of course put out of business all those aspiring to write books on Turgenev's art, since its technique is really all politeness and thus all really inexpressible. And it is exactly the sort of remark for which one reads Ford and that when encountered makes the reading worth the effort.

Hudson's effects are not in fact inexpressible; at least Ford is able to write vividly about them in *Thus to Revisit* by comparing him to Turgenev, who watched humanity as raptly, with as much engrossment as Hudson gave to nature. It is "that note—of the enamoured, of the rapt, watcher" which Ford rightly finds consummately there in Turgenev's " Byelshin Prairie" ("Bezhin Lea" or "Bezhin Meadow" as it is also called), and to express his impression of this note in Hudson's writing, Ford has to write hard himself. He comments that in Hudson "the watcher disappears, becoming merely part of the surrounding atmosphere amidst which, with no self-consciousness, the men, the forests or the birds act and interact"; and he continues to render this "selflessness" in the following paragraph:

> It is no doubt this faculty that gives to Mr. Hudson's work the power to suggest vast, very tranquil space and a man absolutely at home in it, or motionless vegetation, a huge forest and a traveller who wishes to go nowhere, nor ever to reach the forest bounds. For you can suggest immensity in your rendering of the smallest of British birds if you know an immense deal about the bird itself; if you have watched innumerable similar birds, travelling over shires, countries, duchies, kingdoms, hemispheres and always selflessly. So the rendering of one individual bird will connote to the mind of your reader—if you happen to be Mr. Hudson!—the great distances of country in which you have travelled in order that, having seen so many such birds, you may so perfectly describe this one. Great plains will rise up before your reader's mind: immensely high skies; distant blue ranges, woodlands a long way off. . . .

The style here sounds as if Christopher Tietjens had added another feather to his cap, revealing himself to be a fine naturalist and splendid writer, along with his abilities as analyst of government financial figures and computer of the trajectory of golf balls. The paragraph breaks off perfectly with the expressive ellipsis (though often in Ford's writing the ellipsis feels merely habitual), inviting us now to contemplate for ourselves, and raptly, the "distant blue ranges, woodlands a long way off. . . ." What Ford does here, and at other good moments in his writing about another writer, is to imagine a richly responsive reader—more responsive perhaps than we are able to be when we put down Ford and pick up Hudson—as large and capacious in his sympathies as is presumably the writer who evokes them. This reader would be able fully to appreciate the immense consideration, the politeness being shown him by Turgenev; would be fully in tune with Hudson's expressive effects, though like Conrad he cannot describe how they come about. Ford is most irresistible as a critic when, rather than pointing out a writer's defects (as *The Critical Attitude* said the critic must do) he devotes his own verbal resources to imagining the virtues of those whom most he admires.

ONE of the best recent critics of Ford's art, Samuel Hynes, has usefully noted the centrality of Romance to his subject's behavior in both his novels and his other prose works. Hynes suggests that we should read books like *Thus to Revisit* or the memoir of Conrad—and we can add *Portraits from Life,* even by extension *The English Novel* and *The March of Literature*—as "experience transformed by memory, idealized versions of people, books, places, conversations which never occurred but somehow should have." This is the method of Impressionism: in Hynes's formulation, "the method by which experience, transformed by romancing memory, may be rendered."[3] It was in part his possession of such a memory that must have caused Sylvia Tietjens to throw up her hands in dismay at the fabulous character she had married.

But Romance was also a habit of imagination Ford looked for, and often found, in the contemporaries he cared most about. In *Henry James* he calls *The Spoils of Poynton,* surprisingly, James's best novel, "a romance of English grab." *What Maisie Knew* and *The Turn of the Screw* are also romances: the former, "a romance of the English habit of trying to shift responsibility"; the latter, "a romance of the English habit of leaving young children to

---

3. "Ford and the Spirit of Romance," in *Edwardian Occasions* (New York: Oxford University Press, 1972), p. 78.

the care of improper maids and salacious ostlers" (a quite good description, that). In *Portraits from Life*, Hudson's *The Purple Land* is the "supreme—is the only—rendering of Romance in the English language." As for Conrad: "*The Secret Agent* is the romance of international communism . . . *The Arrow of Gold* is the romance of royalist machinations . . . *Under Western Eyes* is the romance of Russian-Swiss nihilism." Even when he does not use the term, one sees the concept behind his preference for certain books over other ones. He is much taken with Galsworthy's character and with that writer's admiration for Turgenev, but the only book of Galsworthy that Ford seems to admire is the early *Villa Rubein*, "a work of sunlit genius." After it, however, Galsworthy's humanitarianism got the better of him, and he wrote satirically pointed novels with Ideas in them. From Romance to Reform, one might put it. H. G. Wells is called a "lost leader" because he deserted the "glories" of works like *The Invisible Man* (and how right Ford is to admire that piece of fiction), "The Country of the Blind," and "The Time Machine," for novels with political and social purpose. He is eloquent in lamenting such desertion when he says at the end of the Wells portrait that "every real artist in words who deserts the occupation of pure imaginative writing to immerse himself in the Public Affairs that have ruined our world, takes away a little of our chance of coming alive through these lugubrious times." We remember that these words are uttered by the writer who spent much time in collaborating with Conrad on a novel eventually called *Romance*, a piece of "pure imaginative writing" if ever there was one. That book, at least to my eyes, is virtually unreadable; yet I never tire of listening to Ford talk about its composition. It is the romance of *Romance* that has remained.

Until the end of his life, Ford liked to pretend to himself and his readers that criticism was a calmly judicious activity—"not the warm expression of sentiment but the cool exposition of a man standing back and viewing with relatively cold eyes the object on which he is to descant." There was a part of him that remained Arnoldian and "objective" in its aims. Yet, as has been evident from my emphasis thus far, I do not think Ford succeeded very often in being this sort of critic; his descanting, whether in praise or in blame of the writer, is usually a good deal warmer in expression than his above definition of it leads one to expect. Take for example the following comparison of Donne with Herbert, from *The March of Literature*. The page is titled "Unhappy Donne," and Ford describes him as "a man who has seen into Hell and conceived of Heaven otherwise than on the smooth paths about the country vicarage's hedge"—which brings him to Herbert:

> Heaven forbid that one should seem to despise Bemerton and its parsonage. Herbert's vision of a perfected High Church Earth, near Salisbury Plain with its high elms and smooth pastures, and Love's table set is of a beauty and confidence that we could ill, indeed, do without.
>
> "You must sit down," says Love, "and taste my meat."
> So I did sit and eat.
>
> may well mark the final height to which devotional poetry may attain. But one has, if one lets oneself be fanciful, the image that round the vicarage hedge, mumbling a mildewed crust, stands hunched a great, hobo figure, the fruit of whose despairing meditations strike in English poetry a note that, lacking which, English poetry would have been something narrower, something merely regional with a tang at once of lavender and of the unimportant provincial.

If one is Ford, one does indeed let oneself be fanciful, and the result is a memorable, fabulous construction: Donne the "great, hobo figure" standing outside the table where Herbert so shyly and successfully dines. As is often true in Ford's portraits, it verges on the sentimental but is saved from that by the vigorous originality of its language. It is typical of much that one encounters in *The March of Literature*.

When we come to a writer or book Ford really dislikes, he can be equally invigorating. "God forbid that I should say anything really condemnatory of any book by any brother-novelist alive or dead," he solemnly swears in *The English Novel* before launching into a full-scale disparagement of Fielding, especially of *Tom Jones*, than which there are few books he more cordially dislikes:

> But as regards *Tom Jones* my personal dislike goes along with a certain cold-blooded critical condemnation. I dislike Tom Jones, the character, because he is a lewd, stupid, and treacherous phenomenon; I dislike Fielding, his chronicler, because he is a bad sort of hypocrite. Had Fielding been in the least genuine in his moral

aspirations it is Blifil that he would have painted attractively and Jones who would have come to the electric chair as would have been the case had Jones lived today.

Ford dislikes this "papier-mâché figure" on which a morality "of the most leering and disastrous kind" is exercised; and "fellows like Fielding who pretend that if you are a gay drunkard, lecher, squanderer of your goods and fumbler in placket-holes you will eventually find a benevolent uncle . . . who will shower on you bags of tens of thousands of guineas . . . these fellows are danger to the body-politic and horribly bad constructors of plots."

I think it undeniable that Fielding is made here to bear the brunt of Ford's personal experience that squandering and sexual imprudence lead to worldly success only in bad novels, bad because they are idealized versions of the word. When it came time, in *The March of Literature,* to take up Fielding again Ford accuses him of "smart-Aleckery," of engaging in verbal juggling or any trick that will delight a reader. At which point he introduces, this time anonymously, the Wyndham Lewis figure who presumably lectured Ford on how modern readers do not care about verisimilitude but want to be amused by showman-performers. This, Ford insists, is what Fielding himself might have said to Defoe, or Richardson, or even to Smollett. An interesting connection is thus made, not for the first time in his writing, between the desire to perform in a "brilliant" manner and a disregard for Jamesian-Conradian form. Fielding was, at least partly because of his self-indulgent penchant for display, a " horribly bad constructor of plots." (One would like, incidentally, to have had Ford's opinion of R. S. Crane's lengthy and admiring essay, "The Plot of *Tom Jones.*")

Ford's long-standing quarrel with English literature was that its most famous writers had too much personality and expressed that personality by imposing richly idealized versions of existence on the overwhelmed reader (he himself practiced, in his criticism, what he preached against). So "the novels of Dickens, Fielding, and Shakespeare are in form (leaving aside the question of texture) fairy tales for adults," and—snorts Ford, pulling himself up—"there are other occupations for grown men." Of significance here is the parenthetical "leaving aside" of something called "texture"; one may suppose that Ford was responsive enough to the poetry in Shakespeare, or the great feats of verbal play in Dickens's novels (if not in Fielding's) but that, or perhaps for that very reason, he insisted upon leaving them aside, speaking as if "form"—the telling of a story, the rendering of an affair—were what counted and what had been horribly mishandled in English novels written between Richardson and Conrad. One may also suppose that the reason (for all Pound's tributes to Ford as the man who *knew* about poetry, the "best critic in England," and so forth) his criticisms of poets are less trenchant than those he made of novelists is that modern poems do not render affairs, but get their effects through "texture." When in *Thus to Revisit* he turns his attention to recent poets he has admired, we hear praise of Robert Bridges, Walter de la Mare, Christina Rossetti, and Robert Browning for "the simplicity of the wording; the beauty of the image evoked by the contact of simple words one beside the other." As criticism this appears to be itself rather simple, not to say simplistic; one has the sense that Ford is being protective of the species, and certainly he was shockingly easy on some of his own poetic compositions he allowed into print.

Ford's attitude toward novels was fully formed by the time he came to edit the *English Review,* and its most essential opposition was between the writer who merely renders, or presents, or records, and the one who shows off or writes fairy tales for adults. In *The Critical Attitude* he uses Trollope and George Eliot to show why "we can take up with interest 'Barchester Towers' in a hand from which nervelessly 'Adam Bede' drops." It is not that Trollope cares about "form," but that

> never taking himself with any attempt at solemnity [he] was con-
> tent to observe and to record, whereas George Eliot, as if she had
> converted herself into another Frankenstein, went on evolving
> obedient monsters who had no particular relation to the life of her
> time—monsters who seduced or admitted themselves to be se-
> duced, who murdered their infants or quoted the Scriptures just as
> it suited the creator of their ordered world.

Did Ford ever read *Middlemarch?* He certainly never modified his opinion of George Eliot, and she appears in *The March of Literature* only as one of the writers he is forced to skip over. But Trollope returns, indeed plays a rather large role in Ford's discussion of nineteenth-century English fiction, since he belongs to a select group, which includes Jane Austen and Stendhal, of "realist" or "psychological" writers from whom almost all the rest of the century's novels fall away.

The marvelous thing about Jane Austen, Ford says, is that she is "free from the moral preoccupation that troubles the waters of that greatest of her predecessors, Richardson himself." She does not "denounce or scarify the vices of her age" (nor did the author of *The Good Soldier*) but freely indulges her "continually lambent humor that plays around the weaknesses" of her characters. You have to go back to Chaucer, Ford declares, to find her spiritual counterpart; and even Henry James is heavy-handed in comparison. Jane Austen then is admired for what she managed to avoid; for the way, in T. S. Eliot's phrase about James, her mind was fine enough to be unviolated by the "ideas," the idealizations which, say, George Eliot was prey to. Here one wants to interrupt again and ask whether Ford had read *Mansfield Park*. The answer is yes, since he cites as evidence of Jane Austen's "vividness" her rendering of the theatrical rehearsal at the moment when, unannounced, Sir Thomas Bertram returns. But Ford was a good deal less interested in the moral judgments about people and society that *Mansfield Park* and Jane Austen endorse than in the purer activity of listening to the "gossip," or watching Mrs. Norris prepare conserves, or hearing about the troubles of a neighbor.

It takes a pure imagination to be interested in gossip. Trollope then is admired as "The Master Snooper," the writer who heard more gossip than anybody else, and—having the advantage over Jane Austen of being male—more varied gossip. "Trollope, in short, was an English gentleman" (unlike Thackeray, who sympathized with rogues, and Balzac, who was French) who was somehow, always, just *there*—not "sympathizing," not idealizing, not denouncing:

> When he entered a club smoking-room no one interrupted his conversation; when he shot no one noticed his bag. Synge said that, occasionally, when Trollope was the last member in the lounge of the old club, St. George's Hanover Square, the waiters would put out the lights, not noticing Trollope, although he was under their eyes.

Here, spectacularly compressed, are the essential elements of Ford's criticism: the honoring of the recorder, the man who was there just to render an affair; the romancing memory that delights in impossible moments when life is no different from art; and the appeal to the charm of that rendered moment as substantiating the judgment, rather than making an argued case from a careful inspection of the novels themselves. (Ford admits that *Framley Parsonage* is his special favorite among English novels—and that is about the limit of his reference to Trollope's books.)

But the fine thing about *The March of Literature,* and the reason it seems to me far and away the best book of criticism Ford ever wrote (although *Portraits from Life,* the series of memoir-essays, is also fine), is that it shows him not wholly at the mercy of the system of judgments and preferences on which his own creative and critical work was based. In other words, there are surprises, moments when, as in Matthew Arnold's phrase about Edmund Burke, "the return of Burke upon himself" is suddenly and gratifyingly evident. For example, when Dickens is brought on stage in the long last chapter of *March,* it will only be, we expect, to be pilloried once more as an exaggerator, a writer of fairy tales for adults. Ford begins that way, complaining that, like Thackeray and Fielding, he "overdraws" characters, especially his hypocrites, who may be roared over but not believed in. Whereas Jane Austen, Stendhal, and Trollope were masters of getting into their books "that element of queer surprise" which only the impressionist rendering of life can achieve, in Dickens there is no surprise—"you always know beforehand what Dickens will do with the fraudulent lawyer on whose machinations hang the fate of a score of his characters."

So it is surprising that a couple of pages on we learn that, at least on the basis of one book, Dickens can be called "the founder of the realistic school." That book is *Great Expectations,* which Ford dares to compare with the *Divine Comedy. Great Expectations,* and Thackeray's *Vanity Fair* as well, "are infused with the views of life of two writers who have lived intensely, who have known real griefs, and who have attained to wealth and celebrity at the expense of disillusionment." Dickens's novel qualifies for those reasons as an authentic realist product, unconcerned with propounding a moral solution to some evil; it (and *Vanity Fair,* though less convincingly it seems to me) "are simply records, that from time to time attain to the height of renderings, of life transfused by the light of their writers' temperaments as modified by their vicissitudes." Ford continues to reflect upon *Great Expectations* as "a product of world-weariness . . . of a passionate world-weariness with humanity and humanity's contrivance." He imagines Dickens as an early Christian eremite "who should have grown weary with denunciation and was set merely on depicting the failure of his efforts." It is a "muted book," inspired by "deep pessimism"—

And the hero is no hero and the heroine, no heroine; and their hands are not in the end united; and there is no immense fortune to be chanted over by a triumphant Wilkins Micawber; no conspiracy to be unveiled; no great wrong righted. The book is, in fact, one of those works, rare in the English language, that can be read by a grown man without the feeling that he is condoning childishness and would be better employed over John Stuart Mill.

It is as if, during this discussion, Ford has truly discovered Dickens, and not just the untypical *Great Expectations,* since there is also expressed a more general admiration, forced out of him as it were against his Pre-Raphaelite upbringing. Although on the one hand, Dickens overwrites and exaggerates and is full of "literary faults": "on the other hand, like Homer, he gave us a world and his writings were epic because his illustrations of life came from the commonest popular object. And it is impossible not to see that Anglo-Saxondom was a better double world because he had passed through it." A better world, even if the writer was no master of *progression d'effets.* At such a moment it becomes possible, without sentimentality, to speak of the humanity of Ford's imagination. Then he leaves Dickens simply by quoting without further comment what he calls the "masterly opening" of *Great Expectations,* its early paragraphs, the marsh country, the churchyard, the convict. After such writing the only place to go, so it seems, is to Flaubert, James, Conrad; though it is fascinating that *The March of Literature* ends with, of all people, Dostoyevsky —"the greatest single influence on the world of today"—who is too large for any terms the critic can bring to him (Ford must have been a bit tired at this point, having achieved page 850). The concluding bow to Dostoyevsky is another instance of Ford's willingness to honor giants who break the rules of critical systems and snatch whatever is there beyond the reach of art.

WITH these impressions of Ford's practice as a literary critic I have tried to suggest the kind of reader he was as well as the kind of reader we must be to appreciate him. I am convinced at any rate that his criticism is filled with lovely moments, *mots justes* (but not too *juste,* as R. L. Stevenson was guilty of) and equally just paragraphs of creative characterization that bring their subject—Donne, Hudson, Charles Lamb, Dickens—to new life. I am convinced also that the familiarity of reencountering these characterizations breeds the opposite of contempt; that Ford's effects gain in subtlety and in the pleasure they provide upon rereading—though in as unsystematic a way as were his own operations conducted. "One of the scamps of literature" as Graham Greene called him in his obituary review, he was also surely a scamp of a literary critic. But perhaps also, as Greene insisted, a great writer; and if not quite that, one whose like we shall not come across again in this century, let alone beyond.

The Presence of Ford Madox Ford: A Memorial Volume
of Essays, Poems, and Memoirs, ed. Sondra J. Stang
(Philadelphia: University of Pennsylvania Press, 1981)

R. P. Blackmur's Last Song

❧❦

A week ago as I was walking through a street, little frequented, in the suburbs of this city, I was suddenly conscious of a rushing noise behind me, and before I knew what was the matter, I was struck violently by a soft substance on the back of the head, and flung to the ground so quickly that I did not even make an effort to save myself. I was somewhat stunned and a good deal hurt, but I jumped up mechanically, with the desire one always has to escape ridicule and appear as though one's internal anguish were a pleasure and quite the sort of thing one likes. Bewildered by the blow from behind and the equally severe fall; covered with sand from beard to boots; my gloves torn; one finger flayed; two others nearly dislocated, and a painful swelling raised over my knee, I staggered to my hat, and picked it up. Perhaps in my foggy condition I should have hurried on without stopping to search the cause of my disaster, had the cause not been too evident. There, on the ground half a rod in front, flapping painfully, and gazing at me with eyes to the full as amazed and bewildered as my own, was a huge, white, tame goose.

ALTHOUGH LITERARY PEOPLE can quote "Leda and the Swan" at the drop of a shuddering blow (the great wings beating still), few of them are familiar with Henry Adams and the Goose. Which is a pity since, as

R. P. Blackmur, *Henry Adams,* ed. and with an introduction by Veronica A. Makowsky. Foreword by Denis Donoghue. New York: Harcourt Brace Jovanovich, 1980.

Adams went on to note in this letter of 1869 to Charles Milnes Gaskell, the event will have, he is convinced, "some mysterious and portentous connection with my future fate." He invites Gaskell to compose some Latin verses describing how he, Adams, met his end

> not like the poetic bird, by one of my own feathers, but by the entire carcass of the beast whose feathers had made my wings. Daedalus was nothing in comparison. He melted at the rays of the sun. But I was floored by the stupidest, dirtiest and coarsest of domestic dung-hill fowl.

Since as far as one knows, Gaskell didn't come through with the requested verses, we might at least supply a title to the episode: Historian Forcibly Goosed, or The Sum and Term of Education. And I would guess that despite the sore knee and flayed finger, that goose's visitation made the historian's day. Aside from the obvious pleasure and pains Adams has taken in writing it up for his friend Gaskell, there must have been a sense of confirmation: here, once more, an unimaginable, unforeseen force by which defenseless man was floored. The event could be sad, tragic even; but when one considers that the huge goose was at least as bewildered as Adams, then one smiles, or grimaces, and proceeds to rise again, to go about one's business with, it may be, renewed energies.

I discovered the goose only while reading Adams's letters this past summer, under the stimulus of R. P. Blackmur's posthumously published book about him. But the combination of playfulness and portentousness, of mock heroic stylishness, was memorably impressed on me thirty years ago when as a college sophomore I was introduced to *The Education of Henry Adams*. Much of it, not surprisingly, went over my head; but I knew that I'd never encountered anything like it before. In its magnificent first chapter ("Quincy") we are told that "The New England light is glare, and the atmosphere harshens color. The boy was a full man before he ever knew what was meant by atmosphere"; and that "After a January blizzard, the boy who could look with pleasure into the violent snow-glare of the cold white sunshine, with its intense light and shade, scarcely knew what was meant by tone. He could reach it only by education." That atmosphere, that tone, is what the *Education* creates superbly and continuingly; the elegiac and the humorous wonderfully mixed; portent nudged into something other than the merely portentous.

Now if there is any critic of literature in this century whose writing is full of atmosphere and tone, it was Richard Blackmur. When, especially in his essays on modern poets—Eliot, Crane, Lawrence, Pound, Stevens, Cummings—that atmosphere provided a medium in which the words on the page were studied and their music evoked, the result was breathtaking and Blackmur's achievement beyond praise. When, more frequently in his later work from the postwar 1940s and '50s, he became speculative and his essays began to bear titles like "Between the Numen and the Moha," atmosphere became all-pervasive and stifling, the tone sometimes too hushed and elevated for its prose's own good. Without trying to sound superior to a superior intelligence, I think it right to have mixed feelings about (in a favorite word of his) Blackmur's "ad-libbing," his vamping till the ready which never comes. At any rate, all Blackmur's readers knew that for years he had been at work on Henry Adams, and that the long book he was writing would provide the sacred word by interpreting Adams with a sympathy and inwardness beyond the reach of ordinary critics. The book never appeared; but now, fifteen years after Blackmur's death, an edited version of it has given us as much as we had any right to expect. Gratitude to the editor and the publisher must be one's first word.

In his foreword to the book, Denis Donoghue suggests that perhaps Blackmur's failure to complete it might have had something to do with the fact that his mind worked best in the twenty-five-page essay format (those essays from the 1930s on poets), and that since the only way to go at Adams was through one foray (Adams would say "failure") after another, there was no true sense in which the book could be completed. This seems to me likely, but I am less convinced by another remark Donoghue makes in the course of describing Blackmur's characteristic critical operation as "a supplication of texts": "In supplication you create the thing you see . . . you respond to one form of energy, enhancing it with your own," says Donoghue. But supplication means presenting a humble petition, with religious overtones to the fore, and in this sense Blackmur didn't "supplicate" the poetry of Lawrence or Hart Crane or Stevens; he analyzed its use of language, compared it to other uses, and made a judgment (sometimes an adverse one) about the result. In other words, he did criticism. With Henry Adams, to whom he devoted so much of his energies and with whom, I think it is fair to say, he felt the deepest kinship and identification, no such critical detachment was possible. And the resulting "supplication" needs to be criticized more strongly than Donoghue is willing to do in his celebratory foreword.

Related to the matter of supplication, there is Veronica Makowsky's claim in her editorial introduction that Blackmur's "most luminous and sustained work on Adams came, as one would expect, during the late 1940's and early 1950's, when Blackmur—at the height of his powers—turned his attention to the final and most fruitful decades of Adams's life." The result of that attention makes up by far the bulk of this book: "The Virgin and the Dynamo" is a 250-page explication of the *Education* and of *Mont-St-Michel and Chartres,* while "King Richard's Prison Song" is a 60-page portrait of Adams's last years. Yet I would argue that Blackmur reached the height of his powers in his earlier essays, published in *The Double Agent* (1935) and *The Expense of Greatness* (1940), that he never wrote anything as fine thereafter, and that his writing on Adams did not gain in strength and comprehensibility the more he did of it. In support of this claim that his best pieces of writing about Adams were done early on: "The Expense of Greatness: Three Emphases on Henry Adams" was published in 1936 and has been chosen by the editor to lead off this volume; while "King Richard's Prison Song," with which the volume concludes and which the editor speaks of as a product of late 1940s–1950s "mature" Blackmur, first appeared, in a shortened but essentially the same version, as "Henry Adams: Three Late Moments" in the *Kenyon Review* in 1940. In other words, I don't think it unfair to say that Blackmur's best writing about Adams was done in the 1930s, at the time when he was turning out his other classic essays. What happened later on, and not perhaps for the best, was elaboration and extension, the further supplication which makes the long central essay "The Virgin and the Dynamo" an unsatisfactory, even at times a tedious, reading experience.

As Blackmur saw it in the first chapter of this long essay, with reference to the *Education* his job was

> deliberately to detach and rehearse the symbolic elements in the effort to catch the echo. At the right point an analogous exploration of the *Chartres* must be made; and finally, if possible, the symbolic values of the two books must be compared and joined and encouraged to work upon each other, so that we may feel them, however complex and disparate in structure, as a single echo, fading and fulling in our own minds.

Already here there seems to be a bit of incantation, the Pateresque single echo, alliteratively "fading and fulling" [*sic?*] in the mind, as if something more and something more delicate were to be attempted here than in mere ordinary criticism made up of comparison and analysis. In fact when Blackmur attempts to "catch the echo" by rehearsing certain symbolic elements in the *Education,* the rehearsal often turns out to be more elusive, harder to hear correctly, than was the tune itself. For example, perhaps the most vivid and amusing chapters in the book are the ones describing Adams's diplomatic and social life as assistant secretary to Charles Francis Adams's ministry to England during the Civil War. One of these chapters, "The Battle of the Rams," consists of the most complicated diplomatic maneuvers involving Palmerston, Lord Russell, Gladstone, and the American statesmen who were trying to keep England neutral during the conflict. Each time I read "The Battle of the Rams" I resolve to follow the maneuverings, tease out the connective thread which renders them intelligible in Adams's narrative. Each time I fail, to the point where I've persuaded myself that this is what Adams wants me to do, and that in diplomacy your opponents may have even less policy, be more confused and unintelligible in their actions, than you yourself are. But consider the following sentences by Blackmur, reflecting on what "he" (Adams) learned from this experience:

> The more he reflected on what they taught, the clearer it seemed that they taught the limitations and relative intensities of their different types of character as they pressed, or were pressed by, the mass of government in motion. Though government is set up of laws not men, men still sit at the center and filter laws through their personality. So it is also true that men must filter their words through the acts to which they are impelled by laws and interests. The filters alter the force and value of the laws without altering either the intent of the laws or the interests. Thus there is conflict and contradiction which require treatment, either by self-deception or readjustment, by the men who experience them, in order to make action possible. Action emphasizes the values actually at work, with expense to the consistency of the principles which are supposed to guide the action. Action is a constant revelation of the inadequacy of principle to a given situation without necessarily

affecting the adequacy of principle to all situations. The lesson is
simple in the abstract but aggravating in the concrete instance.

Something is wrong with this writing. It is surely less vivid, more toneless,
than anything in the chapter from Adams. It formulates, painstakingly and
without Adams's playful, dramatic sense of things, a moral insight one can't
deny the truth of (if one understands it) but that seems remote from, even
irrelevant to, the experience of reading Henry Adams. Do I need to be told
this? one asks, unconvinced that it's a true "echo" of the *Education*.

Often Blackmur begins his sentences the way Adams begins them, with a
"To Adams," say, and the result is eerily like and unlike the original: "To
Adams the English mind of the 'sixties, and all its motives, seemed an
eccentric version of the American mind. It either worked off center or its
center was not located where the American center was and had other attractive forces unknown to Americans—especially to Americans from Quincy."
Now Chapter 12 of the *Education,* "Eccentricity," says in its first paragraph,
"The English mind was one-sided, eccentric, systematically unsystematic,
and logically illogical. The less one knew of it, the better." It would be a poor
thing to charge Blackmur with the Heresy of Paraphrase, and admittedly he
is not attempting to render one particular sentence. But I think that his
sentence is less "eccentric" than Adams's, less playful—even with the flourish at the end about Americans from Quincy—and that it loses rather than
catches the echo. To sound *almost* like Adams may be more dangerous than
not sounding like him at all.

Blackmur says that the full meaning of Adams's symbols is elusive, and
(with regard to the recurrent *Pteraspis*—the sturgeonlike first vertebrate
who appears in the Darwinism chapter of the *Education* and keeps cropping
up later on) even admits that "there is a little plain nonsense in them too, a
little of *hoc est corpus* turned hocus pocus." Recognizing that Adams culti-
vates such effects is a step in the right direction, certainly as far as reading
the *Education is* concerned. But when Blackmur comes to consider the
recurrence of *Pteraspis* late in the book (after Adams has been to the Chicago Exhibition and the South Seas) to illustrate "what survives every moral
improvement . . . in society," he expatiates in this manner:

> There had been an interlude of shark education in the South Seas,
> for there the shark was divine, and Adams had become a member

of the royal, or Salmon, family, whose source of power was in that divinity. And there, too, the women had measured like Venus, and Adams had made himself an image that brought the Greeks on an argosy there. *Pteraspis* indeed! Venus too! His exile had been in a strange land, in which numerical sequences, the shark, and Venus came to have a relation. Failing Nirvana in Japan (though not giving up) he had found the shark-Venus in Tahiti, and had there changed his name in deepening his service. Thus his nieces became *Salmonidae*, and Rodin's *Psyche*, when transplanted to the Beverly Woods, became Fishy. On the edges of life Pteraspis was divine energy: in its center, brute.

Even if one has just reread the *Education* this piece of hocus pocus leaves one baffled and irritated. At such a point it is good to pick up Yvor Winters's chapter on Adams in *The Anatomy of Nonsense* where Winters says, with regard to Adams on geology, "His procedure is to be witty rather than intelligent, and, having established a state of confusion for the sake of the wit, to deduce his spiritual suffering from it. . . . The result is a certain iridescence of emotional surface but nothing precisely of sanity." If Winters could say this about Adams, what would he have said about the above paragraph in which Blackmur attempts to do his subject one better? Again, with reference to Adams's effort to distinguish kinds of eccentricity in Whistler and John LaFarge, Blackmur makes distinctions in an elliptical way that makes Adams seem clear by comparison:

> LaFarge's eccentricity was of perception, Whistler's of temper, and Adams's, perhaps, of reason that expressed some admixture of temper and perception. LaFarge in glass ran to insubordination, Whistler in life ran to the commonplace, Adams in thought to principle, to summarized intelligence. LaFarge left out wholeness, Whistler actual perception, Adams—did not know what he left out. . . .

Hocus pocus: now you see it, now you don't.

A final example of Blackmur's making things even harder than they are in the original comes in his discussion of the "movement" of five late chapters in the *Education* beginning with "The Dynamo and the Virgin." Surely these chapters are difficult of access and, for me at least, represent the least satisfying part of the book. But Blackmur tells me this about them:

The movement of the five chapters is thus continuous—as if circular—along the three sides of a triangle, with each angle representing the juncture of two contrasted conceptions of force, the Dynamo and the Virgin, the human machine and its energies, and lastly the human animal and his own force, where at the limit of the third leg of the triangle the end is identified with the beginning of the motion. The force of thought, the trope of Psyche, is itself the outside force, like the Dynamo or the Virgin, and as occult as either. But it is an identity only by dialectic, by reversal, by experience; and the question is how to translate an ambiguity into an ambivalence.

In my judgment he is pretending to hear things that just aren't there in the music; at least any reader who might be said to experience "movement" in such terms would be a very ideal type indeed, not necessarily to be encouraged.

But my chief sticking-point with Blackmur's Adams is not his analysis of the *Education*—overwrought as I think it often is—but with his conviction that *Mont-St-Michel and Chartres* is Adams's "chief imaginative pilgrimage" (the editor, Veronica Makowsky, also regards it as a "masterpiece") and that "those who complain that he romanticizes a fantastic or an eccentric impulse have not thought from what depths that impulse came, nor how ancient and universal its human history is." Blackmur must be speaking about the likes of myself who find *Chartres* precious and long-winded and full of, yes, mariolatry, of a piece with Adams's generally embarrassing reverence for Woman. For Blackmur, it represents "The Full Return" (as the chapter is titled) and the culmination of a life's work. But would it be perverse to suggest instead that the great work of Adams's life had already been done; that, though the *Education* is a magnificent book and the one of Adams's that will continue to be read, his unread masterpiece is the nine volume *History of the United States during the Administrations of Jefferson and Madison,* a book I urge you, reader, to devote next summer to. In this great history, Adams's expressive powers are fully displayed, his language is wholly adequate to what he wants to say, his irony and humor are strong and unsoured. It is without archness or whimsicality—nothing in it ever feels forced. And perhaps the reason why Blackmur neglects it in favor of the later Adams is that it is all *there* on the surface; no need then for the critic to "supplicate," or to "rehearse the symbolic element in an effort to catch the echo," since it is the historian's voice, not the echo, to which we attend.[1]

What will turn out, I suspect, to be the section of Blackmur's book that will be returned to (aside from the reprinted "Expense of Greatness" essay) is "King Richard's Prison Song," his loving and luminous (a favorite Blackmurian word, justly applied to his writing here) portrait of Henry Adams's old age.[2] Here we are served with, among much else, wonderful comparisons between Adams and Henry James, or a brilliant juxtaposition of Henry Adams with his brother Charles Francis about whom Henry would think (when he saw Charles, nearing eighty, still riding his horse daily) "There goes my 'idjut' brother Charles!" Or we hear of Adams, after his stroke, drinking only champagne and taking it by the pint in a single gulp since "the full mouth was the only way to get the taste of all of it all at once." Finally there are a couple of extraordinary pages in which Blackmur improvises on a paragraph from Mrs. Winthrop Chanler's *Roman Spring,* which describes "Uncle Henry" alone in his library with Gabrielle Chanler, one of his "junior nieces": "The small old man nearing eighty, in dark clothes, with white beard and shirt, and the young girl of sixteen, sitting opposite each other in the low, deep maroon leather chairs. . . ." Blackmur continues to hover, Jamesianly, over the scene and eventually concludes with the following sentences:

1. The best study of the *History,* recently published, is William Dusinberre's *Henry Adams: The Myth of Failure* (Charlottesville: University Press of Virginia, 1980). An English historian, Dusinberre devotes a long chapter ("History as Art") to Adams's style, identifying and admiring its salient features; "His precision of vocabulary, vividness of imagery, extravagance of syntax, fertility in inventing synonyms and in exploiting the resources of iteration; capacity to generalize, courage to trust the reader's power of comprehension; passionate engagement in past politics, yet discretion in expressing his own judgments; sophistication in proposing contrary points of view for the reader's consideration—these and other qualities conjoin to make Adams's prose something exceptional." Dusinberre goes on to compare the *History* with the great works of Gibbon and Macaulay.

2. John Quincy Adams had been much taken with a song from André Grétey's opera, *Richard Coeur-de-lion,* which begins "O Richard! O, mon Roi! / L'univers t'abandonne." Henry Adams quotes it in *Chartres* and devoted much energy in his later years to studying and paraphrasing it. Is it fanciful to guess that Richard Blackmur was also extremely moved by the earlier Richard's prison song?

No wonder the old man Adams, coming back, as we put it, to himself—to the loneliness which we feel as echo—should have found safety in the conviction that what was shared was not understood—it was beyond that—and have found comfort in the assurance that his words could no more be quoted than the look on his face. Who would wish, really, experience to be otherwise than fleeting? It is enough ever afterward to be haunted.

It is for such fleeting moments that we will keep reading Richard Blackmur, and if this monument, this last song to Henry Adams, is not his "masterpiece," we can respect the depths from which the impulse behind such writing must have come, and even feel the loneliness and the hauntedness as echo.

Hudson Review 33, no. 4 (Winter 1981)

Anthony Powell's Serious Comedy

❧

T HE MOST HEARTENING, if uncelebrated, literary event of recent months is the publication by the University of Chicago Press of Anthony Powell's masterwork, *A Dance to the Music of Time,* in anticipation of Powell's ninetieth birthday. Each volume of three novels makes up one "movement" in the twelve-novel sequence. Each features on its cover a detail from Poussin's painting in the Wallace Collection, "A Dance to the Music of Time," with black-and-white reproduction of the painting inside the cover. The books are well bound; their type is large and reader-friendly; they look as if they will be around for some time.

A Dance to the Music of Time began to unfold in 1951, when Powell published *A Question of Upbringing,* largely concerned with the life of the narrator, Nicholas Jenkins, at "school"—Eton and Oxford, though neither of them is named. The novel introduces us to a number of characters who will play significant or minor roles in the sequence to come, among them Nick's roommates, Peter Templer and Charles Stringham. Even as a young man Templer is good with the ladies, not much with the books; Stringham, ironic and literary, is already detaching himself from conventional social expectations. We also meet figures who will surface later on, "characters" such as Nick's housemaster, the hellenizing LeBas and his stock of bad

A Dance to the Music of Time, by Anthony Powell. 4 vols. Chicago: University of Chicago Press, 1995.

Victorian verse, and Nick's relative, Uncle Giles, "a bit of a radical" (as he likes to think of himself) who always turns up at the wrong time. But the figure with whom—after a short prologue—the novel begins is that of Kenneth Widmerpool, another school acquaintance. Except for Nick himself, Widmerpool will play the most significant role in *Dance,* turning up in each successive volume, never less than substantially.

We are introduced to him as he is taking "a run"—something he does voluntarily every afternoon—"in a sweater once white and cap at least a size too small, hobbling unevenly, though with determination, on the flat heels of spiked running-shoes." Nick continues:

> It was on the bleak December tarmac of that Saturday afternoon . . . that Widmerpool, fairly heavily built, thick lips and metal-rimmed spectacles giving his face as usual an aggrieved expression, first took coherent form in my mind. As the damp, insistent cold struck up from the road, two thin jets of steam drifted out of his nostrils, by nature much distended, and all at once he seemed to possess a painful solidarity that talk about him had never conveyed.

Thus "stiffly, almost majestically, Widmerpool moved on his heels, out of the mists."

Dance concluded in 1974 with *Hearing Secret Harmonies,* Jenkins now living, as Powell has for decades, in the country, observing and commenting with his usual wit and dispassion, on the social, political, and sexual turbulences in the early 1970s. Previous novels in the sequence have taken Nick through the years between the wars as he works in publishing, then screenwriting, publishes a couple of novels, gets married, lives in London. He serves as an officer in the army during World War II and afterwards participates in the London literary scene. Meanwhile all about him characters appear, disappear, then—like Widmerpool—once more rise up out of the mists, usually causing a surprise when they do.

The presiding metaphor of a dance is set forth in two opening paragraphs to the whole sequence, as an anonymous narrator encounters some road repair work in which a number of workmen, taking a break, are gathered round a bucket of coke burning in front of their shelter. Snow begins to fall; the workmen go back to work; the day draws in. Gradually the narrator begins to emerge, being reminded first of the ancient world ("legionaries in sheepskin warming themselves at a brazier") then of Poussin's painting, "in which the Seasons, hand in hand and facing outward, tread in rhythm to the notes of the lyre that the winged and naked greybeard plays." There follows an often-quoted piece of writing in Powell's high style that gives eloquent expression to the project on which he and we are about to embark:

> The image of Time brought thoughts of mortality: of human be-
> ings, facing outward like the Seasons, moving hand and hand in
> intricate measure: stepping slowly, methodically, sometimes a trifle
> awkwardly, in evolutions that take recognizable shape: or breaking
> into seeming meaningless gyrations, while partners disappear only
> to reappear again, once more giving pattern to the spectacle: un-
> able to control the melody, unable, perhaps, to control the steps of
> the dance.

At which point "classical associations" remind him of his days at school and the narrative proper launches itself.

TWENTY years after the dance so launched was brought to its close, it should be possible to arrive at an estimate of Powell's literary contribution. To an extent he is a cult figure, admired by an informed and devoted group of Anglo-American readers able at a moment's challenge to distinguish a character named Bithel from one named Borrit (I once failed to do this), or not to confuse Lady Anne Stepney with her sister Lady Peggy. But that cult status makes it harder to decide how much Powell counts. To be the sort of writer whose work invites guidebooks in which characters, plots, births, deaths, and marriages may be charted at length, is to risk accusations of triviality—just the thing that Anglophiles get carried away by. The reader who doesn't get on with *Dance* is put off by the worry or the certainty that it's all just gossip, and gossip about a particular social stratum at the end of its tether: the English upper-class, public school, privileged network of old boys and the girls they do or don't marry, 1920–1970. (It's interesting that, though a similar devaluation could be made of Proust on the grounds that he inspects a privileged class in *A la recherche*, it is not made—Marcel's intensities and the magic of Proust's name evidently making any such de-murring impossible.) For those who don't get on with Powell, Marvin Mudrick will have said the last word when he mocked the sequence as "the most interminable soap-opera since Australopithecus": "Powell's method of getting on with the story must be the most ponderously inefficient of all time," Mudrick began, noting that when a character is introduced, the narrator, Jenkins, spends a few pages speculating on the probable nature of this figure who, it may be, "is blond, has small ears, and wears a black raincoat." Later on, as the character turns up more than once, Jenkins will proceed, says Mudrick, to add further uninteresting though precise details to the portrait. Mudrick called this procedure less a narrative method than "a spreading tumor of speculation," and said that Powell suffered from "an elephantiasis of the will, making harrumphing preparations for something that never happens."

There is no point surely in "arguing" with such a colorful onslaught; there is point in noting that, by never descending to quoting anything from the novel, Mudrick assumes (or assures us) that no one could be interested in *listening* to the narrator's speculating voice as it slyly presents and protracts character in action. But if slyness is attributable to Powell the novelist, it does not at all describe the blend of modestly thoughtful and intimate speculation that characterizes Nick Jenkins's voice. Nick is perhaps the least aggressive, least willful, most reasonable narrator ever to show up in a novel; by contrast, even the self-effacing apologies of Fitzgerald's Nick Carraway are memorably eloquent. Jenkins's virtue, or limitation, is to avoid self-dramatizing theatrics, indeed to make reticence about private matters a mark of character. When, in an especially charged moment, he lays eyes for the first time upon Isobel Tolland, one of a large number of brothers and sisters in an aristocratic family, he addresses us with a question: "Would it be too explicit, too exaggerated, to say that when I set eyes on Isobel Tolland, I knew at once that I should marry her?" Never did a question more invite the negative answer, and we hear virtually no more about Isobel at this or subsequent moments. She marries Nick, has children by him, shares a joke or a quiet exchange with him now and then, but that's all. Although it would be misleading to call Nick reticent in his dealings with and speculations about other characters, those speculations always feel tentative, capable of revision, not to be laid in stone. The more offensive and egregious are the words or behavior of someone, like Widmerpool, with whom Nick has to deal, the more he will bend over backward to insist that there's perhaps something to what Widmerpool is saying. Nick is very good at seeing what there is to be said in defense of even the most indefensible person or attitude; he provides us with the kind of detached consideration of the foibles of others which, in life, we're scarcely able to manage. Much of the time, since this is a work of comedy, his perspective on things, the tone in which he registers them, is open, watchful; if not amused, at least interested in what's going on.

Consider a moment from *A Question of Upbringing* in which a practical joke misfires. Nick is visiting his roommate Peter Templer, at whose father's house the guests include a somewhat disagreeable man named Jimmy Stripling, married to Templer's older sister Babs, and a rather more attractive one named A. Sunderland ("Sunny") Farebrother. One evening Farebrother attempts to demonstrate a handy gadget for turning white shirt collars, thus saving money. Stripling offers one of his collars for demonstration, and eventually the contraption manages to tear, dirty, or ruin several of them. In revenge, Stripling plans a trick on the night before Farebrother's departure, after the party has returned from a dance. A load of baggage outside the latter's door—suitcases, fishing rod and landing net, a gun case—includes a leather hatbox containing the bowler required for Sunny's business in the City. As Nick and Templer's sister watch, Stripling appears, approaching Farebrother's closed door, carrying a small green chamber-pot in his hand, the plan being to substitute it for the hat:

> My immediate thought was that relative size might prevent this plan from being put successfully into execution; though I had not examined the inside of the hat-box, obviously itself larger than normal (no doubt built to house more commodious hats of an earlier generation), the cardboard interior of which might have been removed to make room for odds and ends. Such economy of space would not have been out of keeping with the character of its owner. In any case it was a point upon which Stripling had evidently satisfied himself, because the slight smile on his face indicated that he was absolutely certain of his ground. No doubt to make an even more entertaining spectacle of what he was about to do, he shifted the china receptacle from the handle by which he was carrying it, placing it between his two hands, holding it in front of him, as if it were a sacrificial urn. Seeing it in this position, I changed my mind about its volume, deciding that it could indeed be contained in the hatbox. However, before this question of size and shape could be settled one way or the other, something happened that materially altered the course that events seemed to

be taking; because Farebrother's door suddenly swung open, and Farebrother himself appeared, still wearing his stiff shirt and evening trousers, but without a collar. It occurred to me that perhaps he knew of some mysterious process by which butterfly collars, too, could be revived, as well as those of an up-and-down sort, and that he was already engaged in metamorphosing the evening collar he had worn at the Horabins'.

There the long paragraph ends, a new one beginning with this short sentence: "Stripling was taken completely by surprise." Farebrother remains silent, only raising his eyebrows a little; whereas Stripling's features, as he strides on down the hall, "looked not so much angry, or thwarted, as in actual physical pain." "With an air of being hurt, or worried," Farebrother quietly shuts his door; the narrator, feeling uncommonly tired, also retires. And that is that. Mudrick might call it a perfect example of harrumphing aimlessly, as Nick's cautious, even pedantic deliberations unfold: he hadn't examined the inside of the hat-box, isn't sure the chamber-pot will fit—though perhaps this box, built for former "more commodious" hats, and with its cardboard removed, may do the trick. Yes, he decides as Stripling holds it up urnlike in front of him, the chamber-pot *will* fit.

In one sense all this fussing has nothing to do with the fact that Farebrother opens the door and catches Stripling in the act of behaving, as he thinks, very oddly. In a more important sense, however, the fussing, the qualification and requalification, the leisurely focus, are the whole point of such comic writing. After all, Powell has read his Proust and knows that his readers most likely will have done so as well. Are there not satisfactions in writing post-Proust about chamber-pots and hat-boxes as if they constituted the stuff of imaginative recapture, the remembrance of things past? Although Powell's humorous writing is often compared with Evelyn Waugh's, it has more affinities with early Samuel Beckett, especially the Beckett of *Murphy* who, at the beginning of his literary career, wrote a monograph on Proust. Beckett's comedy is louder, more slapstick, but it unfolds like Powell's, through the narrator's mock-pedantic treatment of his subject. If one doesn't take the trouble to listen to Beckett's or Powell's sentences as the voice unrolls them, the writing will provoke not pleasure but active annoyance.

Assuming, though, that you are pleased rather than provoked by the hatbox incident, you may become curious to hear more about the potential victim turned conqueror, Sunny Farebrother. We come immediately to the second great pleasure of *Dance*—second only to its narrative voice: the disappearance and reappearance of characters who, facing outward like Poussin's Seasons, are "moving hand in hand in intricate measure." The following morning Nick finds himself on the same train to London with Farebrother who, in puzzlement, tells Nick about Stripling's strange behavior—"Marching down the passage holding a *jerry* in front of him as if he were taking part in some ceremony." What could he have been doing, and was it a joke? Nick plays the innocent. Sunny finally decides that it wasn't a joke, since "we are always hearing that his health is not good." In other words, Stripling's involvement with the "jerry" might be accounted for by serious intestinal problems. At any rate, Farebrother concludes with a vague and pleasantly irrelevant reflection about Stripling: "Coupled with the rest of his way of going on . . . it made a bad impression." Farebrother's futile attempt to make sense of Stripling's behavior stands on its own with minimum narrative comment, Powell taking care not to spoil the comedy by explicit underlining. Abruptly the section ends:

> We passed on towards London. When we parted company Sunny Farebrother gave me one of his very open smiles, and said: "You must come and lunch with me one of these days. No good my offering you a lift as I'm heading Citywards." He piled his luggage, bit by bit, on to a taxi; and passed out of my life for some twenty years.

From time to time, in the novels that follow, Farebrother is briefly thought of, in connection with Stripling's attempted joke. In *The Soldier's Art* (book eight) he reappears in person, skirmishing with Widmerpool, both of them now officers in the army. Finally, in *Hearing Secret Harmonies,* Nick recalls meeting Farebrother, now nearly eighty, in the tube, coming back from Kensal Green cemetery where Farebrother has attended the funeral of none other than Jimmy Stripling. He makes a point of going to funerals, Farebrother confides, "because you always meet a lot of people at them you haven't seen for years, and that often comes in useful later." Stripling's, however, was the exception to this rule, the turnout embarrassingly small, the assembly a poor lot ("I shall never expect to set eyes on mourners like his again, Kensal Green, or anywhere else"). Preparing to depart the train, Nick asks after Sunny's health and Sunny replies, "Top-hole form, top-hole. Saw my vet last week. Said he's never inspected a fitter man of my age." A widower now, he invites Nick and his wife to come and see his roses ("I can always manage a cup of tea. Bless you, Nicholas, bless you"):

> As I walked along the platform towards the Exit staircase the train moved on past me. I saw Farebrother once more through the window as the pace increased. He was still sitting bolt upright, and had begun to smile again. At the visit to which he had himself referred, the time when Stripling's practical joke had fallen so flat, Peter Templer had pronounced a judgment on Farebrother. It remained a valid one.
>
> "He's a downy old bird."

Whatever, exactly, a downy old bird might look like, we have undeniably met him in the person of Sunny Farebrother.

Farebrother's quirky memorableness, like so many other figures that populate the pages of *Dance,* is grounds for reflection on the novelist's technique of characterization, especially since, as the individual books appeared, reviewers fell into the habit—encouraged by Nick's own commentary—of classifying characters either as representing the Will or the Imagination. Men of the Will are power hungry, like Widmerpool, or the critic J. G. Quiggin, or the industrialist, Sir Magnus Donners; men of Imagination like Stringham, or Nick's composer friend Hugh Moreland, or Nick himself, care about poetry, art and music, are sometimes careless of their own best interests—at least in the eyes of others. This distinction between will and imagination is harmless and true enough, but it doesn't go far toward reminding us that, as his treatment of Farebrother may suggest, Powell's art is importantly an art of the surface, insofar as it asks us to be interested in what the character *is* rather than what he or she represents. After all, Poussin's Seasons are facing outward, not inward. Powell, who admired the Wyndham Lewis of *Tarr* and *The Wild Body* stories, has his own predilection for "external" art, a predilection to be noted especially in his brilliant prewar novels *Afternoon Men* (1931) and *From a View to a Death* (1933). But the external treatment is to be found in *Dance* as well. The essential things about Farebrother are his smile, his roses, his expressions ("jerry," "Tophole," the doctor as a "vet"), and of course his name itself. In response to those who call Powell's characters and their world superficial, there is Eliot to quote on Ben Jonson: "We cannot call a man's work superficial when it is the creation of a world; a man cannot be accused of dealing superficially

with the world which he himself has created; the superficies *is* the world."
This is not the whole story of Powell's art, but it's an important part of it.

In calling *Dance* the most interminable soap opera since Australopithecus, Mudrick must have thought he'd scored a good hit, since what is more
damning to art than a comparison to trash? But Powell's art is not necessarily undone by the comparison. As with daily episodes in a soap opera,
you could skip parts of any particular novel from *Dance* and still be able to
locate yourself well enough in its successor. For although both *Dance* and
the soap have plenty of plots, they lack an overall Plot. A master plot would
imply a conclusion, when in fact the show aspires to run on forever. Powell
has said that he conceived of *Dance* because he didn't think he was especially good at making up plots that would begin, develop, and conclude
themselves in 225 pages. To write a twelve-novel sequence is, time and again,
to defer conclusion. *Dance* eventually concludes, but we don't read it with
the excited sense that we're following an action that's working itself out.

It is also possible to develop kinds of affection for and interest in a
character, whether in novel or in soap opera, that depend upon acquaintance developed over the long haul. Experiencing the self-contained characters of *Dance,* with their amusing, often striking surfaces, their distinctive
idioms and vocabularies, their styles of address, is a more complex version
of the way we get to know long-enduring characters in a soap. Of course the
psychology of a soap character's "inner life" is laughable, sketched only in
the crudest of fashions; but over the course of time spent watching, we build
up a pleased recognition as characters reappear, sometimes even come back
from the dead, once more to do their thing. Increased acquaintance with
rather than deeper knowledge about these characters is the name of the
game. So it is with most, if not all, of the personages in *Dance.* But, unlike
the effect of a soap, the illusion of Powell's art is to make us feel that, oddly
enough, the more we're acquainted with a character, the more his ultimate
inaccessibility to us and to the narrative understanding that presents him
becomes apparent. For the reader who takes Powell seriously, there are of
course innumerable other aspects and qualities of the work with which to
be concerned: the rendering of period details from the twenties to the
seventies; the pervasive mythological, historical and occult lore that deeply
fascinates some of the characters and in a playful way Powell himself; the
unusual pungent sexual language ("I only stuffed her once," says Bob Duport of the notorious Pamela Flitton, "Against a shed in the back parts of

Cairo airport, but even then I could see she might drive you round the bend"). Questions of literary value might be raised as well: does the sequence reach its high point in the three war volumes, then fall away somewhat in the last three, or are those final volumes an intensification of earlier ones? Is the abject death of Widmerpool in *Hearing Secret Harmonies,* a believable metamorphosis or an example of what, with reference to Milton's treatment of Satan in *Paradise Lost,* A. J. Waldock called the "technique of degradation"?

Rather than exploring such matters, I want—by considering some examples of it—to touch on an enduring pleasure of *Dance* not enough remarked on by critics of Powell's work. This pleasure comes from the densely allusive way in which poems, hymns, and popular songs pervade the sequence. (The going word for it these days is "intertextuality," a term that would doubtless afford Powell some amusement.) An appealing instance is found in the character of Ted Jeavons, second husband of the Lady Molly whose name gives the fourth novel its title. Jeavons was wounded in the stomach in the First World War and has suffered ever since ("I feel bilious most of the time"). Given to long silences, he has no visible employment, but is interested in various gadgets and attempts without success to interest others in them. Every so often Jeavons needs to kick up the traces and go out on his own for a night of serious drinking (incapacitating himself for days thereafter), perhaps flirt with a "tart" or two. His finest moment comes at the end of *The Kindly Ones,* just half-way through *Dance,* at the point where England has gone to war with Germany and Nick is trying to get commissioned in the army. At the end of a small party, Nick is sitting with Ted and his brother Stanley in the Jeavonses' South Kensington flat, the room blacked out in response to German air raids. Ted Jeavons is wandering about in his mackintosh and pajamas and Stanley, who "evidently found his brother's life inexplicable," has given Nick a useful lead on getting into an infantry regiment. Whereupon Ted Jeavons

> moved towards the table where the beer bottles stood. Suddenly he began to sing in that full, deep, unexpectedly attractive voice, so different from the croaking tones in which he ordinarily conversed:

> There's a long, long trail a-winding
> Into the land of   . . . my dreams,
> Where the night . . .   ingale is singing

> And the white moon beams.
> There's a long, long night of waiting,
> Until my dreams all . . .   come true . . .

He broke off as suddenly as he had begun. Stanley Jeavons began tapping out his pipe again, perhaps to put a stop to that refrain.

"Used to sing that while we were blanco-ing," said Jeavons. "God, how fed up I got cleaning that bloody equipment."

At which point Nick says good night and makes his way home. Abrupt, inexplicable, unexpectedly attractive, mysterious in its point of ending as well as its motive for beginning, the moment makes Ted Jeavons stranger as well as more familiar to us.

What difference does it make if one knows the tune to "There's a long, long trail . . ."? All the difference, insofar as we can perform in our head the heightened, sentimental execution of a song that calls out to be suitably lingered over, drawn out mightily in an exaggerated style. (My father used to embarrass me by singing "The Sweetheart of Sigma Chi" in such a style.) By the same token, it helps to know the song "South of the Border" if we are to experience properly the moment in *The Valley of Bones* (book seven) when Nick, joining his regiment in Wales, with his mind full of Celtic lore and thoughts of the Seven Churches of Asia (one of which, Sardis, is the name for the cavelike "tabernacle" where his company is billeted), views the "asymmetrical rows of double-decker bunks upon which piles of grey-brown blankets were folded in regulated manner." As he looks, he hears from the far end of the "cave"

> like the anthem of the soloist bursting gloriously from a hidden choir, a man's voice, deep-throated and penetrating [that] sounded, rose, swelled, in a lament of heartbreaking melancholy:

> That's where I fell in love
> While stars above
> Came out to play;
> For it was *mañana,*
> And we were so gay,
> South of the border,
> Down Mexico way . . .

My 1939 sheet music of "South of the Border" reveals a couple of words out of place ("For it was fiesta," is correct), so either the soldier or Powell erred slightly. No matter, for nothing could be more incongruous than this song that surfaced briefly on "Your Hit Parade" and, I had thought, disappeared forever. How odd to have it called up decades later by an English novelist! But then, incongruity is the reigning principle in *Dance*, to be accepted as perfectly appropriate the way life is:

> The mournful, long-drawn out notes died for a moment. Glancing round, I thought the singer, too, was praying then saw his crouched position had been adopted the better to sweep under one of the bunks. . . . Rising, he burst out again with renewed, agonized persistence:
>
> > . . . The Mission bell told me
> > That I mustn't stay
> > South of the border,
> > Down Mexico way . . .
>
> The message of the bell, the singer's tragic tone announcing it, underlined life's inflexible call to order, reaffirming the illusory nature of love and pleasure.

And Nick girds his own loins for the new professional life of the soldier he has embraced. As always at memorable moments in *Dance*, the pleasure lies in the complex mixture of feeling, the narrative "tone" that constitutes Powell's unique blend of things. The soldier who was singing may have adopted a tragic tone, but the vehicle doesn't quite measure up to tragedy—however attractive, in its faded recall, "South of the Border" is to us. To speak grandly, as Nick does here, of "the illusory nature of love and plea-sure" may suggest that Powell is inviting us to reach into the depths with such a grand formulation. But in fact the formulation won't bear much thinking about—you can't do anything interesting with it. What we do instead is take pleasure in the vivid juxtaposition of the banal tune and lyric with whatever feelings—deep or shallow—the singing soldier is giving ex-pression to.

Finally I want to suggest, by way of a more lengthy example, the kinds of allusive satisfactions *Dance* provides and the way the book, at one such moment, touches upon greatness. These satisfactions are splendidly present in the six-and-a-half pages of *The Military Philosophers* (book nine) when Nick attends the service of General Thanksgiving in St. Paul's to commemorate the end of World War II. In these pages we give ourselves over to the meanderings of an intricate if reticent sensibility as it responds to various lines and passages from the Bible and from English poetry, while becoming itself densely poetic in its associations. After the Royal Party is seated there are prayers, then a hymn:

> Angels in the height, adore him;
> Ye behold him face to face;
> Saints triumphant, bow before him
> Gather'd in from every race.

Nick thinks that, whether saints or no, under the great dome are gathered together, in the various Allied representatives, every race. He remembers how Stringham, dead in a Japanese POW camp in Singapore, used to quote hymns because they "described people and places so well." Thoughts of Stringham bring to mind others dead in the war, like his old roommate Peter Templer and his cousin George Tolland.

The minister begins to read from the book of Isaiah about how, in the new dispensation "The wilderness and the solitary place shall be glad for them; and the desert shall rejoice, and blossom as the rose." Mention of "the wayfaring men" who "though fools, shall not err within," makes Nick wonder who these "fools" are: one would surely be the drunken, endearing Bithel (whom Widmerpool had sacked from the Mobile Laundry). But what about the perennially unsatisfied Borrit, another of Nick's wartime companions? Borrit once told of marveling at how, traveling in Spain on business, he noticed honeymoon couples being shown to their bedrooms, then not being visible for a fortnight ("They've got their own ways, the Spaniards"). We remember that Borrit was sexually disappointed; that, as he put it once, he "never had a free poke in his life. Subject doesn't seem to arise when you're talking to a respectable woman." Now Borrit, too, is dead, and Nick wonders whether he ever got that "free poke" before the grave claimed him.

More prayers, a psalm, a dull bit of preaching by the Archbishop, then all rise to sing Blake's *Jerusalem*:

> Bring me my bow of burning gold;
> Bring me my arrows of desire;
> Bring me my spear; O Clouds unfold!
> Bring me my chariot of fire!

Was that also about sex, Nick wonders, and if so why are they singing it at the victory service? He thinks about Blake, "a genius, but not one for the classical taste. He was too cranky." Further reflections on changes in poetic fashions and on Blake's phrase "arrows of desire" makes Nick think of Cowley, a once famous poet who didn't survive his own age but (unlike Blake) is buried in Westminster Abbey. Nick recalls Pope's question about the man ("Who now reads Cowley?") and his "Pindarique art." Yet, remembering some witty lines from Cowley about lust ("Thou with strange adultery / Doest in each breast a vigil keep; / Awake, all men do lust for thee, / And some enjoy thee when they sleep"), Nick decides that the poet who wrote them shouldn't be forgotten. He compares them favorably with lines from "poor old Edgar Allan Poe" on a similar theme, Poe having recourse to "ethereal dances" and "ethereal streams." Yet it was the lines from Poe, Nick reflects, that used to run in his head when many years previously he was in love with Jean Duport.

The audience stands to sing "Now thank we all our God"—was this hymn of German origin chosen by design or inadvertence? Finally comes the national anthem and Nick decides that its second verse ("O Lord our God arise / Scatter his enemies, / And make them fall. / Confound their politics / Frustrate their knavish tricks"), is the best part, since "the verbiage of high thinking had not yet cloaked such petitions." But then and finally, in one of those gestures that permeate *Dance*, where a formulation is slightly taken back, criticized, and qualified, Nick questions his own verbiage:

> Such a mental picture of the past was no doubt largely unhistorical, indeed totally illusory, freedom from one sort of humbug merely implying, with human beings of any epoch, thraldom to another. The past, just as the present, had to be accepted for what it thought and what it was.

So ends the service and Nick's accompanying monologue, whose concluding sentence is a fine and moving example of the cast of Powell's mind. Nick and his creator resist the temptation to take a nostalgic view of history, to believe that back there somewhere people and song lyrics said what they meant, without "the verbiage of high thinking." Such a view of the past is rejected by what appears to be a theoretical idea that goes deeper into things, that explains and accounts for them; but the idea is a formula that doesn't quite formulate, since it leaves us with both past and present "to be accepted for what it thought and what it was." The surface of things, of history and character, is too much itself to be gone behind, to be violated by something less real than the way words and things look and feel and say. Like Henry James's mind according to Eliot, the narrative poise of *Dance* is so fine that no idea can violate it. So the only thing to do is reread, something any lover of Powell will do abundantly.

At the service in St. Paul's, Nick calls Blake "a genius, though not one for the classical taste. He was too cranky." Compared to Powell, the other two central writers of English comedy in recent decades, Evelyn Waugh and Kingsley Amis, seem for all their brilliance, cranky rejecters and mockers of modern civilization. In his registration of different people, different historical periods—including the present one—Powell by contrast offers something that might be called classical. Or call it neo-classical, as summed up in Pope's fine couplet: "Let the strict life of graver mortals be/A long, exact, and serious comedy."

New Republic, August 19 and 26, 1996

Appreciating Kingsley Amis

❦

E VEN AS, A FEW years ago, he became Sir Kingsley and settled into the
process of surviving his seventies (he is now seventy-three), Kingsley
Amis was largely regarded in this country as a relic, an antic reactionary
whose work could be taken seriously only by illiberal males predisposed to
chauvinism. His detractors might grant that, yes, his first novel, *Lucky Jim*,
was highly entertaining and that there were things to praise in some of the
work to follow in the 1950s and 1960s. But his alleged misogyny, increasingly
retrograde views on education, race, and the Russian Threat—even on alcohol, whose praise he continued to sing as enlightened times frowned—all
together conspired to leave him out there alone on his limb. In *Jake's Thing*
and *Stanley and the Women* especially he was accused of purveying jaun-
diced attitudes toward human brings that excoriated many of the men but
almost all of the women: the all-purpose comedian had become a sharp-
fanged, cruelly unfair satirist. Anyway, why should Americans take him to
their hearts when, in *Difficulties with Girls*, the only thing adulterous Patrick Standish can say to his latest conquest after she has postcoitally observed "The sky is blue, and I feel gay," is "Are you an American?" Currently

Kingsley Amis: Modern Novelist, by Dale Salwak. Lanham, Md.: Barnes & Noble Imports,
1992. *Understanding Kingsley Amis*, by Merritt Moseley. Columbia: University of South
Carolina Press, 1993. *The Anti-Egoist: Kingsley Amis, Man of Letters*, by Paul Fussell. New
York: Oxford University Press, 1994.

the other Amis has more of his fiction in print here than does Dad, and perhaps this is a payback for Dad's inability, so he claims, to read son Martin's works with pleasure. The point is that most American novel readers gave up on Kingsley Amis awhile back.

Thus has injustice been done to this increasingly impressive writer whose forty years' worth of fiction shows no signs of drying up. For Amis is no less than what one of his critics called "a serious comic novelist": and if the comedy has recently been underappreciated, the seriousness has never been properly recognized and valued for what it is—a highly intelligent, absolutely distinctive take on life that instructs through hugely pleasing art. It's therefore a good sign that, though they've attracted little notice from reviewers or academics, some recent books about Amis have been appearing. In 1989 Richard Bradford and John McDermott both produced short, critically perceptive studies of the novels, and in 1990 Dale Salwak edited a lively collection of essays by English and American writers about the man and his work. More recently Salwak has followed up with a biographical and critical account; Merritt Moseley has surveyed the novels briefly; and, most agreeably, Paul Fussell has written a passionate apologia for Amis as a man of letters. There remain plenty of distinctions to be made about the novels in relation to one another and their collective force as an achievement.

In titling his book *The Anti-Egoist*, Fussell must have expected that more than one reader, seeing the epithet applied to Kingsley Amis, would respond, "Are you kidding?" For no one ever accused the novelist of undervaluing his own ego. I remember a symposium about something or other, in London twenty years ago, in which Amis, when he was introduced as a participant, stood up and swung his clasped hands above him like a heavyweight acknowledging the crowd. Instead of egotism, Fussell stresses Amis's disinterested devotion to writing, to literary tradition, to language, also his generosity toward his readers. The focus is on Amis's nonfiction and literary learning, "his performance as a critic, a learned anthologist, a memoirist, a teacher, and a poet—in short, a man of letters in the old sense, a writer conspicuous for complex literary knowledge and subtle taste as well as for vigorous views on politics and society." In these terms Amis would take his place as a late example of a tradition in British letters sketched by John Gross in *The Rise and Fall of the Man of Letters*. Predecessors in that tradition include George Saintsbury, who resembles Amis in his devotion to drink as well as to books—the Saintsbury whom Amis once characterized as "debarred by nature from writing anything not worth reading." The comment suits Amis as well, whose literary knowledge is surely not as wide as Saintsbury's (whose is?) but who, unlike Saintsbury, produces novels and poems of his own.

Early in the book it looks as if Fussell's friendship with Amis, which he makes no attempt to conceal, may get in the way of objectivity in this portrait of the artist as anti-egotist. I at least was pulled up short when, by way of arguing for Amis's "generosity" as not just "a literary or abstract value" but a very tangible one, Fussell confides to us that one Christmas, Amis "loaded my young son with wonderful costly gifts, including his first typewriter, because he wanted to augment his self-respect and make him happy." Doubtless the case, but it puts us in a slightly awkward position of having looked in on a private act we really have no business knowing about—this is the risk of Fussell's avowedly personal treatment. As another example of generosity he notes that once Amis, at a lunch party in Wales, gave the waitress an extravagant tip (the equivalent of fifty dollars or so) because he was so struck by her "intelligence, charm, generosity, and humor." I've no doubt she was a splendid person but would be interested to know more about what she looked like, especially whether she was, as the expression goes, full-figured. There are moments, in other words, when Fussell sounds a little too eager to attest to his friend's sterling moral qualities; whereas readers of the novels get used to thinking of him always as a bit of an old devil.

But if in a couple of places claims for Amis's stalwart nature sound a little like a friend's warm recollection of good acts performed, the claims Fussell makes about Amis's contribution as a man of letters are eminently valid and presented with a documentation—admittedly in the brief span of this short book—that strikes me as undeniable. In particular he draws attention to Amis's performance in areas insufficiently remarked, such as his work as an anthologist, his writing about food and drink, his "amateur" comments on classical music, and his poetry. Amis has done a number of anthologies, all of them distinctive and rewarding (though I have not seen his most recent, *The Pleasures of Poetry*, a collection of poems, each accompanied by brief commentary, which appeared over the course of a year in *The Daily Mail*). Of these anthologies, the most autobiographical is *The Amis Anthology* (1988), a gathering of his favorite poems, not the "best" poems in English. He says that a "favorite" poem is attractive to an individual in part for reasons that are unfathomable. A favorite poem must produce "the illusion that it was written specially for me, however well I may know that it was in fact written for the whole nation . . . or for nobody in particular." Of course no one else would title a collection *The Amis Anthology,* and no one but the compiler would include Matthew Arnold's "Rugby Chapel," a surely over-long and rhythmically undistinguished elegy for Arnold's father ("Fifteen years have gone round / Since thou arosest to tread, / In the summer morn-ing, the road / Of death, at a call unforeseen, / Sudden . . ."). But include it Amis does, and in the notes that follow the anthology (thirty-seven pages of explanation and comment) Amis says about "Rugby Chapel" that

> It is hard for us today not to feel from time to time, when words, like *arosest* or *beckonedst* come along, that the forms of the second person plural would have been more natural. But to Arnold's read-ers in the 1850s, in that context, they might very well have seemed intolerably familiar and indecorous. If faced with the counter-argument that a poet should make a point of not catering to his readers' expectations, one could answer in turn that he should not bother with such trivial concerns when writing about something as important as his father's life and death.

This direct appeal to what "we" might feel and to what readers in 1850 might be imagined to have felt, is extremely thoughtful in the unobvious point it worries, and could only have come from an editor who can't or won't tell us why "Rugby Chapel" is a favorite, but who protects its manner of address by invoking subject matter rather than technique. This is a small example of how personal choice gets embodied in the selection.

As for food and drink, which Amis has taken pains not to deny himself over the years, his performance as a restaurant critic is memorable for its vigorous response to pretentious language and to restaurants that fail to deliver the goods. Thus the venerable Rules, of London, gets its dues for serving "two of the most disgusting full-dress meals I have ever tried to eat in my life" (details follow). Of a fellow food reviewer who announces that "A Hong Kong meal . . . is a statement to which customers are secondary," Amis replies, "I know that sort of meal and the statement is Fuck You, and you don't have to go to Hong Kong for it. Soho is far enough." As for the drink part, over twenty years ago Amis wrote a masterwork on the subject, *On Drink,* a guide to the pleasures and perils of alcohol that is surprisingly little known. (I've loaned it to a number of friends and miraculously still retain my copy.) The best parts of *On Drink* aren't the recipes for drinks you've never heard of before and probably won't get around to trying,[1] but rather the section titled "Mean Sod's Guide," a handbook to stinting your male guests "while seeming, at any rate to their wives, to have done them rather well." (The idea is to provoke a quarrel on the way home between the couple in which "she" defends you as sweet and thoughtful, while "he" labels you a drunk.) Out of many tips I select one, the procedure for dealing with the person who refuses to be content with your predinner serving of a punch made with cheap red wine, soda water, and some cooking sherry, to be served in small glasses. A recalcitrant guest who insists, say, on Scotch should receive the following treatment: "Go to your pantry and read the paper for a few minutes before filling the order. Hand the glass over with plenty of emphasis, perhaps bawling as you do so, 'One large Scotch whisky delivered as ordered, *sah!*' "

But the most original part of this wholly original book is its section on dealing with the Hangover. No reader of *Lucky Jim* will be surprised in the least at Amis's mastery of the subject; even so it is with painful pleasure that we follow him through the steps in dealing, first, with the Physical Hangover ("I must assume that you can devote at least a good part of the day to yourself and your condition"), then, more significantly, the Metaphysical Hangover. For the latter Amis prescribes short courses in literature and music, on the principle that you must feel worse emotionally before you can start to feel better, so that a good cry is essential. For the reading course he prescribes the final scene of *Paradise Lost*, or—if you want something less "horribly great"—A. E. Housman's poems. For music, don't set your sights too high by going for Mozart. Pick someone instead who is "merely a towering genius," like Tchaikovsky, preferably the *Pathétique* symphony. Or perhaps Brahms's *Alto Rhapsody* which, especially in the Kathleen Ferrier version, would "fetch tears from a stone."

Mention of these musical treatments for the Metaphysical Hangover is

---

1. Such as Queen Victoria's Tipple (1/2 tumbler red wine, Scotch) or The Lucky Jim (12 to 15 parts vodka, 1 part dry vermouth, 2 parts cucumber juice, cucumber slices, ice cubes). Obviously the cucumber juice makes all the difference to the latter. Or there is the Tigne Rose (1 tot gin, 1 tot whisky, 1 tot rum, 1 tot vodka, 1 tot brandy). That one, says Amis, is "a drink to dream of, not to drink."

occasion for a word on Amis's interest as, every now and then, a writer
about classical music. From Philip Larkin's account of Oxford days we
know how much time he and Amis spent listening to American jazz; less
well known, especially after letting Jim Dixon refer to "filthy Mozart"—is
how much Amis cares about "serious" music and how that caring gets into
his writing. At a farcical level it was first evident to me when I realized that
in *Lucky Jim*, the "Welch tune" "featured in the 'rondo' of some boring
piano concerto" and which Dixon sings to himself ("You *i*gnorant clod, you
*stu*pid old sod, you *ha*vering, *sla*vering get . . . You *wor*dy old *tur*dy old
scum, you *gri*ping old, *pi*ping old bum") is in fact the main theme from the
last movement of Beethoven's First. For some years I thought this my private discovery, but Amis has since made it public knowledge in a 1982 piece
on the summer Proms concerts at the Albert Hall. Then there is his poem,
"A Chromatic Passing-Note," that begins

> "That slimy tune" I said, and got a laugh,
> In the middle of old Franck's D minor thing:
> The dotted-rhythm clarinet motif.

It's a good poem partly because at a certain state of musical "sophistication" one might well be on guard against possibly sentimental tunes like
that dotted clarinet motif in Franck's symphony. That Amis (in the same
"Proms" piece) refers to the symphony as "miraculous" suggests that his
later self has more than come to terms with it. No such accommodation,
apparently, has been made with Mahler; at least to the opening of the first
movement of his First Symphony. The narrator of *Girl, 20*, hearing the piece
rehearsed, reflects that its length was

> a considerable mercy, seeing that it might so easily have been some-
> thing broad, full, ample, spacious, massive, leisurely and going on
> for over half an hour from the Second or the Third. Thanks to
> some paroxysm of curtailment on the composer's part, I was in for
> little more than fifteen minutes' worth.

You don't have to agree with Douglas Yandell (and I'm pretty sure Amis as
well) about Mahler's "enormous talentlessness" to note that the passage—
which contains further particulars—could have been written only by someone who's spent time registering the works of "Gus"; while the phrase
"paroxysm of curtailment" marks one more in a long list of Amis's fine-

tuned surprises. At the end of a piece entitled "Rondo for My Funeral" (1973) he wrote that as a source of pleasure music took precedence for him over literature, but that as an amateur he could never do more than "catch glimpses of the world of mysterious, ideal beauty that music offers." It takes courage to say this, as well as courage to admit that your favorite composer (not the Greatest composer) is Tchaikovsky. I have heard no one but Amis admit this, and it recommends him to me since my favorite composer is Tchaikovsky.

Elsewhere I've expressed my admiration for Amis's poetry, now a thing of his past evidently. That leaves us with the novels, which like Tchaikovsky's music are pervaded by a melancholy that's grown as Amis has aged. Yet at the root of them is something other than melancholy though not incompatible with it, a comic-satiric energy that carries the novelist again and again into the things of this world that call out to be rendered, sometimes rended. There is a fine moment at the close of Robert Frost's 1960 *Paris Review* interview when he ponders the nature of what young people call poetic "inspiration":

> But I tell them it's just the same as when you feel a joke coming. You see somebody coming down the street that you're accustomed to abuse, and you feel it rising in you, something to say as you pass each other. . . . Something does it to you. It's him coming toward you that gives you the animus, you know. When they want to know about inspiration, I tell them it's mostly animus.

Amis's inspiration is mostly animus and I suppose only readers who delight in this "abuse" will find tonic and indispensable such astringencies. Yet the animus may sound merely windy unless it finds the right words for itself, and no English novelist of the last few decades has paid closer attention to his words—indeed to language itself—than has Amis. Almost thirty years ago, in what was perhaps the first incisive piece of criticism provoked by his early novels, David Lodge declared unequivocally that Amis's use of language was "as inextricably part of his importance as Henry James's was of his or Joyce's was of his." Lodge was countering the tendency to consider those novels as social documents showing off the angry young man at odds with English conventions and society. By way of redirecting readers, Lodge noted Amis's habit of picking up words and subjecting them to skeptical, playful attention, as in Jim Dixon's mockery of the mindless article he's written, "The Economic Influence of the Developments in Shipbuilding Techniques, 1450–1485": " 'In considering this strangely neglected topic,' it began. This what neglected topic? This strangely what topic? This strangely neglected what?" In "superficially clumsy prose," said Lodge, Amis explored and exploited his fastidious contempt for and large pleasure in "strange locutions, odd pronunciations, verbal errors and unconscious puns."

The Russian Girl, his most recent novel published in this country, won't cause anyone to claim that it's his best since *Lucky Jim,* but it's a wholly professional tale about a Russian scholar at a London institute who falls in love with a visiting Russian poet named Anna Danilova. The trouble is that Anna's poetry is dreadful and the scholar, Richard Vaisey, knows it, even as she enlists him in a political cause—the freeing of her brother who's been arrested, with or without justice, back in the motherland. There is much interesting talk about poetry, politics, love, and sex, which bears out Fussell's observation of how Amis's novels sometimes resemble "anthologies of opinions" more than they do fictions. But the places where the book comes to its sharpest and funniest pitch are those in which Richard's wife, Cordelia, is on stage, either in her own person or as the subject of others' disbelieving conversation:

> "Cordelia's the sort of woman—"
> "If you mention her again I'm leaving," said Richard quite violently. "Not another word on that subject while I'm here. And by the way she isn't a *sort* of woman."
> "And it's even doubtful if she's a sort of *woman,*" said Godfrey.

Her very name inspires another character's awe: "What a *name* for Christ's sake—Cordelia or Nggornndeenlia as I suppose she calls it. What's wrong with Cordy? Or Deely? See you down the boozer, Cordy. She'd vanish in a puff of smoke." ("Old Cordybags" is yet another riff on the name.) When the woman in question is herself on the phone, she provokes a "plebeian-voiced" caller into the following:

> "Paki, are you, love?"
> "I beg your pardon."
> "Well, I beg yours and all, madam. I just thought, the way you talk, ennit. Was it Europe, then? I said was it Europe?"
> "Vug of, uzzhaul," she said in an eerily unchanged voice, cut him off and punched another number.

When Richard leaves his wife for the Russian Girl, Cordelia launches a series of fiendishly successful attacks on his library, unfinished manuscript, car, and credit card account in a dazzling burst of creative malice. The wife who turns out a shrew has been a recurrent feature in Amis's more recent fiction, especially Susan Duke in *Stanley and the Women.* But never before has there been one as magnificently awful as the perfectly misnamed Cordelia. One can argue about whether Amis is misogynist; or one can wonder at the astonishing energy he accords his female targets, thus magnifying rather than diminishing them.

Henry James once provided "a delightful young man from Texas" named Stark Young with two lists of his novels as guidance for reading the Master's work, on both of which lists were *The Wings of the Dove* and *The Golden Bowl.* On the pretense that some similarly delightful person should ask me for similar help with respect to Amis's work, my two lists would both contain *Lucky Jim* and *The Old Devils.* The former, endlessly rereadable, always fresh and newly funny, is the comic masterwork of our century's second half; while the latter, in some ways Amis's most difficult book stylistically, is dense not only with satiric energies but with two scenes between characters that touch the heart. At least they elicited tears from this hardboiled reader who never expected to shed them over Amis. On at least one of my lists I'd want *Ending Up,* his shortest novel and most ingeniously verbal working out of the end of five octogenarians living together in a small cottage. And I'd hate for any reader to miss *Girl, 20,* in its ironic celebration of Swinging London and the attempts of a classical music conductor, Sir Roy Vandervane, to swing with it.[2] After that the lists would include *Stanley and the Women,* Amis's strongest onslaught on the psychiatric profession; or *I Want It Now,* in which the rich get their comeuppance; or *The Alteration,* a dystopian-futuristic vision of a Roman Catholic world; or *The Riverside Villas Murder,* a delightful visit to the mind of an adolescent youth growing up in the late 1930s and awakening to sex (the murder part is less interesting). And what about *The Anti-Death League* or *The Green Man* or *Jake's Thing* or *The Folks That Live on the Hill?* Two lists of five aren't big enough, no more than they are with James.[3]

---

2. *Girl, 20* contains one of Amis's finest inventions, the "Fuckettes" wielded by Sir Roy Vandervane as "obscenity-savers." They include School of Thought, Christian Gentleman, Puck-Like Theme, and other phrases to be used in moments of stress.

3. There should now be added to one of the lists, *You Can't Do Both* (Hutchinson:

A recent, strikingly candid and unillusioned interview in a *London Times* Saturday Supplement reveals the following about Amis: no, he tells the interviewer, he doesn't suffer from self-disgust exactly (Auberon Waugh had guessed that he did). But maybe a little bit "when you wish you weren't so fat and so old." Self-hatred? "Yes, from time to time." The interviewer is emboldened to ask Amis whether he likes himself: "No, I don't think I do like myself all that much . . . but I don't want to have to think about that." Dale Salwak quotes him as saying that writing is the only meaningful activity he enjoys, the only possible antidote to the "terrible feeling of gloom and panic and Christ knows what that a combination of drink and the aging process seemed to usher in." That out of such feelings the novels still keep coming regularly, each one giving us something a little different from anything given before, each a fresh entry into the English language and English humor, seems grounds for making the strongest insistence on his absolutely unique and irreplaceable contribution to the art of fiction in our time.

Hudson Review 48, no. 1 (Spring 1995)

London, 1994), still—for reasons unknown but deplorable—not published in this country. One of Amis's strongest pieces of comic realism, it treats the hero's parents, wife, and homosexual friend in an expansive, even exploratory way quite different from the jokey, hardboiled presentation of character Amis is associated with. Put it with *Lucky Jim* and *The Old Devils* at the top of the pile.

Naipaul's Written World

❧ ❦ ❧

V. S. NAIPAUL'S TWENTY-SECOND book is an occasion for looking over his extraordinary career and considering how much it weighs and what parts of it weigh most. That he hasn't yet won the Nobel Prize is continuing matter for speculation and doubtless has to do with his out-spoken airings of prejudices that are insufficiently liberal. Reviewing the new book's predecessor, *The Enigma of Arrival* (1987), Derek Walcott—a Nobel winner—both praised it as writing and deplored Naipaul's disdainful attitudes toward black people and the West Indian world. Even so, said Walcott, Trinidadians had large enough hearts to forgive him for choosing England as the place of authority and tradition from which other places were judged and found wanting. One has the sense, then, of Naipaul as a politically incorrect figure whose views on things political count more than does his art as a writer (though everybody says he "writes well"), to the extent that the art has not been properly examined and evaluated.[1]

In particular one wants to ask about the sort of novelist we have on our hands. *A Way in the World*, like *The Enigma of Arrival*, insists on its title page

---

A Way in the World, by V. S. Naipaul. New York: Alfred A. Knopf, 1994.

1. On Naipaul as politically incorrect I can say that some years ago there was talk of inviting him to lecture at the college where I teach. Three members of the English department objected on the grounds that he was racist, sexist, and homophobic, all rolled into one. The invitation never materialized.

217

that it is a novel. Yet by no stretch of my imagination can either book be called a novel in any but the loosest and most unhelpful sense. Randall Jarrell's witty definition of the genre as a prose work of some length that has something wrong with it, will hardly do to characterize *A Way in the World*. Unlike *Enigma*, which concentrated obsessively and minutely on the narrator's life in a Wiltshire cottage over a period of years, the new book has no unifying thread of time or place; nor is its nine-part scheme of biographical reminiscence, historical fable, and portraiture of imaginary-real figures consistently "voiced" in such a way as to assure us we can trust the narrator. Sink or swim, is more like it, and a number of times I sank.

You could say that Naipaul began as a writer of novels and late in his career has become a writer of "novels." (The English edition of *A Way in the World* calls it a "sequence," which is safe enough.) In what to my taste was the most engaging section of this sequence, "Passenger: A Figure from the Thirties," Naipaul recounts his relationship with an English writer he calls Foster Morris, who encouraged Naipaul at the beginning of his career as a novelist. In 1937 Morris had written a book about Trinidad centering on a strike in the oilfields and on the leader of the strike, a preacher named Tubal Uriah Buzz Butler. In "Passenger," Naipaul (we scarcely need to call him "the narrator") praises Morris's book for the way it depicted Trinidad people "with the utmost seriousness," treating them without irony, as if they were English. But, adds Naipaul, well intentioned as *The Shadowed Livery* was, it was also wrong, since it suppressed "the sense of the absurd, the idea of comedy"—the "preserver," Naipaul calls it. His own earliest efforts at fiction, in which he attempted to use English settings and people encountered after he settled in London in 1956, were, he soon decided, misconceived, since they suppressed his comic inheritance. The comedy inherited was a double one, from his story-telling Hindu family and from the street life in Port of Spain. More than once he has described how his true direction became apparent to him one afternoon when, sitting in the offices of the BBC for whom he was an occasional worker, he wrote the opening paragraphs of the opening story in what would be *Miguel Street* (his third published book, though the first to be written):

> Every morning when he got up Hat would sit on the banister of his back verandah and shout across, "What happening there, Bogart?"
>   Bogart would turn in his bed and mumble softly, so that no one heard, "What happening there, Hat?"

In Naipaul's "Prologue to an Autobiography" (in *Finding the Center*, 1984) he writes about this opening:

> The first sentence was true, the second was invention. But to-gether—to me, the writer—they had done something extraordi-nary. Though they had left out everything—the setting, the histor-ical time, the racial and social complexities of the people of the street—they had suggested it all; they had created the world of the street. And together, as sentences, words, they had set up a rhythm, a speed, which dictated all that was to follow.

Of note in this portrait of the artist by himself, is Naipaul's confident assumption that the difference between truth and invention is perfectly clear, and that the account given here of his beginnings as a writer is ob-viously true, not invented.

Naipaul's emphasis on the pace and idiom of comedy, with its roots in local observation and its dependence on artfully combined sentences and words, surely characterizes with accuracy the feel of the stories in *Miguel Street* and—even more satisfying—his first two novels, *The Mystic Masseur* (1957) and *The Suffrage of Elvira* (1958). In *The Mystic Masseur*, Ganesh—the struggling masseur who turns himself into a famous writer and healer—observes a shop notice written by Leela, his bride-to-be, who is being recommended to Ganesh by her father, Ramlogan:

> "Is Leela self who write that," Ramlogan said. "I didn't ask she to write it, mind you. She just sit down quiet quiet one morning after tea and write it off."
>
> It read:
>
> NOTICE:
> Notice, is. Hereby; provided: That, Seats!
> Are, Provided. For; Female: Shop, Assistants!
>
> Ganesh said, "Leela know a lot of punctuation marks."
> "That is it, sahib. All day the girl just sitting down and talking about these punctuation marks. She is like that, sahib."

Later, to the surprise of those around him, Ganesh writes his first book, titled *A Hundred and One Questions and Answers on the Hindu Religion*, which contains sticklers such as number 46, "Who is the greatest modern Hindu?" (Ans. Mahatma Gandhi), and 47, "Who is the second greatest modern Hindu?" (Ans. Pandit Jawaharlal Nehru), and 48, "Who is the third greatest modern Hindu?" (Ans. not revealed to us). Ramlogan is delighted: "Is the sort of book, sahib, they should give to children in school and make them learn it by heart."

The idiom is as memorable as the inventive comedy it conveys: Ganesh's aunt is known by him as "The Great Belcher" for reasons of her expressive dyspepsia; Ramlogan says that having to look after himself since he was five years old has given him "cha'acter and sensa values, sahib. That's what it gives me. Cha'acter and sensa values." In The _Suffrage of Elvira_, about a political campaign in one of Trinidad's first free elections, the tone is even broader and more farcical, with many fine scenes, one of which involves a dead chicken that someone lays squarely in the middle of Ramlogan's door-way, just after he has luxuriously rubbed himself with Canadian Healing Oil (the "Canadian" touch is especially good in this Caribbean venue). When one of the characters is told by his son that the son will no longer support his father's candidate in the election, the older man doesn't attempt to argue with him since "You is a big man. Your pee making _froth_." Many further ex-amples of a living idiom could be adduced as proof of the way, in Naipaul's retrospective phrase about it, "the world of the street" has been created.

The "Passenger" section from Naipaul's new work throws interesting light on how he sees the relation between his first three "street" books and what is generally acknowledged to be his masterwork, _A House for Mr. Biswas_ (1961), by any standards among the major novels of our century. Naipaul tells us that though his early way of writing had given him confidence and gotten him started, by 1960 or thereabouts he had begun to be bothered by its "jokeyness," a humor that seemed to lie "on the other side of hysteria," just as did the colonial society he had written about. He says—it must be in reference to _Mr. Biswas_, though he doesn't name it directly—that he was "absolutely secure in this new book" which was taking him much longer to finish than the previous ones. And although the six hundred pages of _Biswas_ contain much comedy—especially in the verbal inventiveness of the protagonist's name-calling of his Tulsi in-laws—and much fiercely sar-donic humor in Mr. Biswas' struggle with the world's stupidities and follies, the novel frequently takes on a deeper note. Mr. Biswas could be said to exist, like the comedy Naipaul had become adept at creating, on the other side of hysteria or anxiety, that "deeper root of comedy" that had become this novelist's subject. Biswas suffers a major nervous collapse during the book as well as countless smaller defeats and depressions; so when Naipaul provides him with a momentary vision of self-possession, of peace, the effect on a reader is strong and satisfying, as in this memory of morning in Port of Spain:

> The newspaper, delivered free, still warm, the ink still wet, sprawled on the concrete steps down which the sun was moving. Dew lay on trees and roofs; the empty street, freshly swept and washed, was in cool shadow, and water ran clear in the gutters whose green bases had been scratched and striped by the sweepers' harsh brooms.

Or this moment, in his final dwelling place two weeks before he dies:

> He thought of the house as his own, though for years it had been irretrievably mortgaged. And during these months of illness and despair, he was struck again and again by the wonder of being in his own house, the audacity of it; to walk in through his own front gate, to bar entry to whoever he wished, to close his doors and windows every night, to hear no noises except those of his family, to wander freely from room to room, and about his yard . . .

A House for Mr. Biswas is invariably called "Dickensian" by critics, as I suppose any big book teeming with characters (many of them caricatures), disdaining economy of effort and moving always toward expansion, determined to leave nothing out, could be so called. But except for the reflective gravity of some of the narrative in *Great Expectations*, Dickens, whose "jokeyness" is always cropping up, contains little of the sustained depths and glooms that lie not very far beneath Mohun Biswas's story.

Having published, at age twenty-nine, a novel containing as much life as did *Mr. Biswas*, what was Naipaul to do next? A possibility, frequently made use of by English novelists of this century, was to travel, then write up your travels: accordingly Naipaul went back to the Caribbean, then to India, and produced absorbing accounts of these places in *The Middle Passage* (1962) and *An Area of Darkness* (1964). But while in India he also wrote, one presumes fairly rapidly, the oddest and in some ways most delightful book of his career, *Mr. Stone and the Knights' Companion*, the one novel of his set wholly in England and with English characters. To those familiar with Naipaul's other fiction, both early and late, *Mr. Stone* reads like a ventriloquist's performance, as if Muriel Spark or Elizabeth Taylor were at the controls. The tone and irony of the novel is delicate and mischievous, with yearning and melancholy in it as well. It was as if Naipaul were saying, if you think I'm merely a regionalist entertainer, let me show you what I can do as well or better than any contemporary English novelist. By the same token, it was something only to be done once.

Naipaul's decline as a novelist—or at least his metamorphosis into a very different, and to my eyes less appealing, one—began with the award-winning *The Mimic Men* (1967). His first novel in the first person, it is an example of what Henry James, speaking of that mode, called "the terrible fluidity of self-revelation." Whether we are meant to identify the narrator, one Ralph Singh, with Naipaul, or whether Singh is the object of authorial irony, is impossible to determine. What is damagingly evident is that comedy has been thoroughly laid aside in favor of Singh's largely toneless recitation of his career in London, his childhood in the Caribbean, his marriage and its dissolution, his decision to write a memoir. Instead of comedy, we have endless assertion and declaration (the book is only 250 pages long but feels much longer). Nothing is dramatized; the mode of presentation is as flat and uninflected as Singh's life seems to have been. Here for the first time we see Naipaul—as he characterized himself in a recent *New Yorker* profile— as a hater of "style" in prose: "I want the writer not to be there. . . . In my writing there's no self-consciousness, there's no beauty." He says in the profile he is against "smoothness," against rhythm, against Santayana and Gibbon and the King James Bible ("Unbearable—*unbearable*"); he is against plot (Trollope would be all right if he weren't always plotting); he is in favor of Richard Jeffries and William Cobbett as admirable nineteenth-century writers, rather than Jane Austen and Henry James. Although these prejudices don't express themselves fully in his writing until the last two "novels," they begin to be felt in *The Mimic Men* and in the three political novels of the 1970s which followed.

In 1974, the year before the second of these books, *Guerillas,* was published (*In a Free State* appeared in 1971, *A Bend in the River* in 1979), Naipaul wrote an essay about Joseph Conrad in which, rather tortuously, he delineated his relation to that writer. As criticism, it is a curious performance: "An Outpost of Progress," an early Conrad story, is designated "the finest thing Conrad wrote," while "The Lagoon" (also an early story) provided Naipaul with something "strong and direct" that he was never again to find in Conrad. By contrast, *Lord Jim, The Secret Agent, Under Western Eyes,* and

Victory are in their different ways unsatisfactory, and he couldn't finish *Nostromo*. Yet, and this is the burden of the essay, Naipaul eventually discovers that Conrad has been there before him: that Naipaul's desire to make a romantic career for himself as a writer was doomed to fail, since the world had changed:

> The new politics, the curious reliance of men on institutions they were yet working to undermine, the simplicity of belief and the hideous simplicity of actions, the corruption of causes, half-made societies that seemed doomed to remain half-made: these were the things that began to preoccupy me.

This had been Conrad's experience, and Naipaul attempted to match it, he says, by losing "one's preconceptions of what the novel should do and, above all, to rid oneself of the subtle corruptions of the novel or comedy of manners." These words are extremely revealing: the corruption of causes, of half-made societies, of "politics" necessitates something different from the subtle corruptions of fiction. If "novel" equals "comedy of manners," then it can't relevantly deal with politics. Perhaps Naipaul believes that Conrad's austerity and lack of comedy were also to be emulated; yet *The Secret Agent* and *Under Western Eyes* are full of a sardonic humor directed at institutions and at "the hideous simplicity of actions." Indeed you might even say that in them Conrad came closest to writing the comedy of manners and they are perhaps the novels of his that wear best. What I find disturbing in Naipaul's political novels from the 1970s is a tonelessness at their center; an absence of narrative performance—of "style" if you will—that novels have not often tried to do without. Bent on displaying the corruption of causes in African and Caribbean "half-made societies," these books do so at the price of readerly pleasure. Even admirers of them might admit that they're not much fun to read; for Naipaul has deliberately moved beyond the "fun" that was so importantly a part of his pre–*Mimic Men* fiction. Taking the long view, we see that this was the way he had to go—to "develop": yet such development exacts its price. *Mr. Biswas* will be read when *Guerillas* is barely remembered, because the earlier book is art, the later one closer to a cautionary tale told in icy, noncommittal prose that doesn't admit any mixed feelings.

With *The Enigma of Arrival* and *A Way in the World,* Naipaul has ceased to write novels in favor of densely meditative prose excursions, linked together through something other than story ("Yes—oh dear yes—the novel tells a story," squeaked E. M. Forster). Or put it that the story has been internalized and historicized into something presumably deeper and more profound than a mere piece of fiction. In the *New Yorker* interview, Naipaul spoke of himself as a man who weighs his words, doesn't just say what comes into his head, and that therefore his books demand special treatment: "My paragraphs are very rich—they have to be read. Many things are happening in the paragraph. If you miss a paragraph—if you miss a page—it's hard to get back into it." He thinks that "twenty good pages" at a stretch is about as much as a careful reader of him can manage. *The Enigma of Arrival* contains a hundred or so rich pages ("The Journey") describing Naipaul's leaving Trinidad and early sojourn in England. But the rest of the book, centered on the manor-cottage life he lived in Wiltshire, is not so rich as it is labored. The assumption behind his remark about weighing words carefully is that a writer who does so will be neither vain nor prolix. Yet the minutiae of observation and speculation, the teasing out of the people and places that surround him—done without humor, largely without irony in *Enigma*—constitute an obstacle course that can be traversed only with much effort and frequent stops along the way. Naipaul's power and authority as a writer is such that to admit to failure on a reader's part, to lapse into inattention or boredom, makes for a guilty sense of inadequacy. Isn't there something really *deep* here that, if I were a better reader, I could discover?

On the basis of *A Way in the World*, I'd have to say—not necessarily. As with *Enigma*, the best parts of it are distinctly autobiographical: early memories ("A Smell of Fish-glue") of administrative work in the Red House in Port of Spain; the aforementioned sequence with Foster Morris; and at least part of the section about the revolutionary Lebrun (a C. L. R. James–like figure). But much of the book is devoted to what Naipaul calls three "unwritten stories," one of which is about Sir Walter Raleigh in his old age coming back to Trinidad, still occupied with the fading possibility of an El Dorado to be discovered up the Orinoco; another, even longer, story is about the career of the Venezuelan revolutionary, Francisco Miranda, a late-eighteenth-century precursor of Simón Bolívar. By calling them unwritten stories, Naipaul, it seems to me, bids to disarm us by deconstructing the business of writing fiction (these are not "stories," you understand, not "written" in the usual sense), then taking the liberty to spin out at some length combinations of imaginative-historical embroidery. But their power to make us ask the crucial narrative question—what happened next?—is too often absent, with the effect that they feel, in the main, contrived and willed: interesting ideas that end up being overwritten rather than unwritten.

A Way in the World is a strange book, and though it has been called (along with *Enigma*) Proustian, there seems to me a huge difference between the densely psychological, often playful-painful exploration Proust gives his narrator, and what Naipaul does to the "I" in the presumably more autobiographical sections of the new work. A single instance will have to do to show what I mean and why it's a problem. In the section dealing with the revolutionary Lebrun ("On the Road"), Naipaul is invited to a dinner in London for the man, at which West Indian food is served—a dish called "coo-coo" or "foo-foo" consisting of "a heavy glistening mound" of yams and green bananas and peppers. Repelled by it, Naipaul leaves it on his plate (no one noticed, he tells us). Eight pages later he is in New York City, again at dinner with friends of Lebrun with whom he has been put in touch. The host has promised him that gefilte fish will be served, a "special dish" which Naipaul says he's never had. When it appears this is what happens:

> I didn't like the way it looked, and have no memory of it. The idea of something pounded to paste, then spiced or oiled, worked on by fingers, brought to mind something of hand lotions and other things. I became fearful of smelling it. I couldn't eat it. With the coo-coo or foo-foo in the Maida Vale flat I had been able to hide what I did to the things on my plate. That couldn't be done here; everyone knew that the gefilte fish had been specially prepared for Lebrun's friend from London.
>
> Manners never frayed. Conversation revived. But the embarrassment that began in the dining room lasted until I was taken back to the Manhattan hotel.

This is as much as we are told. What is the meaning of it and why should it be presented as imaginatively significant? We know that Naipaul is an extremely fastidious man, a strict vegetarian, prey to disgust at certain kinds of culinary treats. And that he is as fastidious about what he writes (he weighs the words) as about what he eats. But for the life of me I can't see anything more to this passage than that gefilte fish didn't pass his scrutiny and embarrassment ensued. What does this have to do with Lebrun, or with the world about which Naipaul moves with such deliberate complication?

By banishing irony and humor, the staple of comedy of manners and of a certain kind of novel, Naipaul has put himself out there on a limb with little besides his righteous, proud sense of himself as a man of integrity. Too often, in *A Way in the World,* that's all we're left with, and it feels flat, merely asserted. This is by way of saying that the new book (a strong bid for the Nobel?) is not the crown, but a curious outgrowth rather, of his distinguished writing life.

Hudson Review 47, no. 4 (Winter 1995)

Looking Back at Lessing

❧

A LITTLE OVER TWO DECADES ago when Doris Lessing published her ninth novel, *The Summer before the Dark* (1973), she could lay claim to consideration as the foremost female writer of fiction then working in English. The women's movement was in full swing and among many of the more literarily inclined, Lessing occupied a position of respect second only to Virginia Woolf. And she was contemporary in a way Woolf, thirty and more years dead, couldn't be. *The Golden Notebook* (1962), which met with some puzzlement when first published, had become increasingly cited and talked about (if not always read through) by those aspiring toward being what, in the core section of the book, Lessing titled "Free Women." She had also completed the five-volume series *Children of Violence* (more familiarly the "Martha Quest" novels) in which a woman who shared much of Lessing's biography was tracked, in her quest, from her days as a young woman in Southern Rhodesia, through marriages, pregnancies, divorces, to her eventual death in London. By 1973, Lessing had also published—in addition to many volumes of short fiction, a novel (her first) of Africa, *The Grass Is Singing*, two autobiographical prose works, and *Briefing for a Descent to Hell*, a dark, dystopian vision of the future. In *The Summer before the Dark*, a woman approaching middle age, married and with children, embarks on an affair with a man significantly younger than herself. The novel was given

Under My Skin, by Doris Lessing. New York: HarperCollins, 1994.

a front-page review by Elizabeth Hardwick in the *New York Times Book Review*, and in the course of her interesting account of it Hardwick identified the "rather flat, puzzling, aching anguish" that she found characteristic of Lessing's fiction, including her latest. "Enormous sadness and depression" was the particular tone Hardwick heard, and she thought it not wholly to the advantage of *The Summer before the Dark* as a novel.

At present, Lessing's work is a good deal further away from the central concerns of most serious readers of fiction. Nothing in the writing she has published in the last two decades comes even close to challenging these readers, whether female or male, the way *The Golden Notebook* and the Martha Quest novels—especially the concluding, most disturbing one, *The Four-Gated City*—challenged them. She has become a respected and respectable figure to be surveyed in accounts of post–second-war novelists, viewed dispassionately along with Iris Murdoch and Margaret Drabble. So it is a good time for her to weigh in with this enlivening and substantial first volume of autobiography, taking her from childhood up to her move from Africa to London in 1949. Lessing says early in the book that she admires certain people who have chosen to keep their mouths shut; but with rumors of five American biographers at work—in one way or another—on her life, the motive of self-defense came to the fore. Few people are left who can be hurt by what she has to say, at least in writing about the first thirty years of her life. She can tell the truth, as she sees it, "without snags and blocks of conscience." Thus she prepares us for the leisurely, extremely detailed narrative that unfolds in the effort to tell us exactly what it is she's "got" under her skin.

The easiest answer, and the one Lessing more than hints at in the book, is her mother, Emily Maude McVeagh, a nurse who cared for Lessing's father, Alfred Taylor, in London's Royal Free Hospital where he was suffering from shell-shock, depression, and an amputated leg. After the First World War the Taylors went out to Kermanshah, in Persia, where Alfred worked in the Imperial Bank and where Doris and her brother were born; later, after a sojourn in England, the family settled on a farm in Southern Rhodesia, the country in which Lessing spent her young life. She tells us that she now sees her mother as a "tragic figure, living out her disappointing years with courage and with dignity," but there's not much of this sympathetic figure in the book. Rather we're given the woman who, conforming to the procedures back then, refused to feed the infant Doris when she cried; the woman who toilet trained her, who was "a vibrating column of efficiency and ruthless energy," who while Doris leaned against her father's knee (the real one, not the metal-and-wood replacement) went on and on to some visitor about how her children were sapping her strength, how her talents were withering, "how the little girl in particular (she was so difficult, so naughty!) made her life a total misery." When the family traveled home to England from Persia in 1924, Lessing's mother decided they should go via Moscow so as not to expose the children to the heat of the Red Sea. The horrendous journey that ensued, across the Caspian Sea in an oil tanker full of lice and on a foodless train to Moscow where they subsisted on hard-boiled eggs and some bread—bought by the mother at stations from peasant women (with typhoid and typhus everywhere, swarms of beggars and homeless children)—all this formed the substance of stories her mother would tell in future years. Lessing says she doesn't remember these events, nor does she remember how, at the Russian frontier, her mother browbeat a Russian official to let them in even though their passports were imperfectly stamped. Since Doris was only five at the time, one can't blame her for not remembering things other than what her mother emphasized afterwards. But the "nervous flight" from her mother Lessing says she was engaged in as far back as she could remember, may have been in play here; at any rate by age fourteen she was "obdurately against" everything that Emily Taylor represented.

This "state of accusation" Lessing identifies is painful to read about, since next to blaming the father, blaming the mother is always something a daughter can indulge in. Of course Lessing doesn't want to indulge herself—she's too severely moral for that—and at certain moments in the book she speaks of herself as marked out for trouble in a way more powerful than can be blamed on her luckless mother or father. For example, when she decides to abandon not only her first husband, Frank Wisdom, but also the two children she bore him, the autobiographer has a delicate moment to handle. Lessing rationalizes a bit, saying the children would be looked after by loving people who would do the job more efficiently than she. She knew this, not that she hadn't up to that point performed the task just like the other women she saw around her, "but because of this secret doom that was inside me—and which had brought my parents to their pitiful condition." Near the end of the book she speaks of still not understanding, when she settled in London, the fact that she had been "conditioned for tears." These

phrases seem to me attempts at naming what is finally beyond understanding, and what no talk about one's father or mother will explain; namely, the
demon that drove this intensely gifted, perennially dissatisfied—sometimes
to the point of despair and breakdown—young and older woman. "I've got
you under my skin / I've got you deep in the heart of me": Cole Porter's
lines furnish the book's title and act as one of its epigraphs. But we're asked
to ignore the jaunty tone of the song and perhaps not to think of its
concluding advice: "Use your mentality, Wake up to reality," the sort of
advice you take only when you've determined that you "never can win"—
advice Lessing has never been about to take to heart.[1]

It must be said that the young, extremely attractive girl featured in the
excellent photographs in this book seems unaware that her "secret doom"
has already conditioned her to tears. Aware of this odd disparity, Lessing
names this healthy resilient animal, proud of her body, able to make others
laugh—"Tigger," and the nickname survived through two marriages. (When
she became a Communist she was called "Comrade Tigger.") It's Tigger who
has pillow fights with her mother or undergoes her father's tickling so as to
play the game. It's Tigger, the "healthy bouncing beast," who manages to
survive the four years in a convent school to which she was sent. It's Tigger
who marries Frank Wisdom, a young civil servant, who drinks and dances
with the other young marrieds, has children without disaster, says at one
point that she could have made a good veterinarian, or a doctor, or a ma-
tron, or a farmer. The vitality of Lessing's prose, especially in the first half of
the book, testifies to Tigger's claim. What a wonderful place to grow up, her
writing convinces us, as she and her brother sit under the telephone lines
stretching from the Mandor Mine across a grass field to the Taylor's farm:

> Our ears to the metal pole we listened to the thrumming, drum-
> ming, deep-singing of the wind in the wires where we watched, as

1. For someone who, in the autobiography, makes as much of popular lyrics in the
twenties and thirties, Lessing time and again gets their words wrong. She does okay
with Porter's "Under My Skin," but messes up "Night and Day" ("Night and day / I
think of you"). "It's a Sin to Tell a Lie" doesn't begin "I love you, yes I do, I love you,"
and "Swinging on a Star" doesn't say "Do you want to be better off than you are /
Carry moonbeams home in a jar. . . ." Yeats's little poem "The Scholars" does not end
"O God, what would they say, if their Catullus came their way." This probably doesn't
matter, but if she likes them enough to quote them, why not get the words right?

we listened, the birds, hundreds of birds, alighting, balancing, taking off again, big birds and little birds and plain birds and birds coloured like rainbows or sunsets, the most glamorous of them, the rollers, mauve and grey and pink, like large kingfishers.

As with *The Grass Is Singing*, this writing has some of the delicate sensuous life of early D. H. Lawrence. Speaking at one point to the "intense physicality" of Lawrence's prose, she admits that he "must have influenced me." No doubt about it: a memorable Lawrentian passage describes her looking after a brood of hatching chicks when her mother has taken her father to the hospital in Salisbury. As Doris sits up in a cold room and watches the eggs there appears in one of them a "little rough place that meant" birth was imminent:

> I held the egg to my ear, and heard the tap tap tap of the hidden chick, and wept with excitement and relief. Out flopped that hideous chick, dried at once into adorableness, out flopped another . . . soon all over the cracking eggs lay and sprawled the wet monstrous creatures, and between the eggs trembled the pretty dried-out chicks. I ran out, found the oldest and most experienced hen, and put her into a pen where the nest box was already lined with straw and feathers, and when I brought out a couple of dozen little chicks and put them one by one into the nest she seemed not to know her own mind. Then, her brain switched gear, she clucked, and delicately trod her way among them and became their mother.

This is beyond praise, an example of moments when her writing gets under the alert reader's skin.

In fact I found myself appreciating and admiring passages where the grim spirit in the heart of Lessing isn't wholly allowed to upstage superficial Tigger. Something like an older version of the latter can be heard when, from time to time in the book, Lessing addresses contemporary women out of the wisdom of age seventy-five. Gynecologically speaking she compares herself to the fabled peasant woman who never had anything wrong with her—no "pre-menstrual tension," three normal births, easy periods which ended in her early forties, no unpleasant menopause. So she wants to hold out some hope for young women who are prepared only for "womb troubles":

> When I—my generation—looked forward to our lives as females, we were not full of fear and foreboding. We felt confident, we felt in

control. We were not bombarded with bleak information from television, radio, newspapers, women's magazines. If girls were told, from very young, that they can expect bad times of every sort from pre-menstrual tension to menopausal miseries, is it not possible they are attracting bad times?

"I became a Communist because of the spirit of the times, because of the *Zeitgeist*"—so Lessing explains her being recruited into the dissident "progressive" band of believers she discovered in Rhodesia. She makes the decision feel less like a moral act than an accession to the inevitable, just as (she tries to persuade herself and her readers) would be the leaving of husband and abandoning of children. The latter stages of this autobiography, filled with the names of a great many people we have never heard of and are given no reason to have interest in, are rather heavy going. Never one to have second thoughts about a paragraph or a page she's written, Lessing exercises little stylistic shaping of her outpouring of anecdote, character, and situation. Her hope may be that it's enough merely for her to recount them, but this seems to me very much not the case. Certainly she's right to give a reason for writing the book as that she was part of "an extraordinary time, the end of the British Empire in Africa." It may take a more than ordinary care with sentences and paragraphs to make that time come strongly alive to us.

CRITICAL accounts of Lessing's contribution and stature as a writer of fiction mainly bypass her style by acting as if she didn't have one, or at least that it is of not much account, since the substance of what she says is so important. I do not think she would be pleased by this form of condescension, and there is no reason to avoid the question of what difference style makes in her work, since *The Grass Is Singing* and the early "African" stories are written in a direct, unadorned, intelligently observant prose to be admired. D. H. Lawrence's presence is felt, but in a less fevered and rhetorical way. It's with the Martha Quest novels that questions of style and compositional procedure arise. The first four novels of *Children of Violence,* three of which were published before *The Golden Notebook,* are written in the leisurely, extremely conventional novelese Lessing inherited from her realist predecessors; the narrative terms are basically the same as say, Arnold Bennett worked within in *The Old Wives' Tale* and the Clayhanger trilogy. It is expected that we will care about the "story" of this young woman as she deals with her parents, and her marriages, and though it's easy enough to caution that Martha Quest is not Doris Lessing, I would guess nobody reads these books without having some interest in Lessing's biography and how it felt to be acting out one's life in the late days of the British Empire in Africa. Yet readers with an appetite for interesting happenings in fiction may be slightly disappointed as they move through the many pages of these novels. Reviewing the second of them, the ironically titled *A Proper Marriage*, Kingsley Amis—whom one wouldn't suspect of being a devoted reader of Lessing—praised various excellent things in it and confided that "Mrs. Lessing is a whole network of streets ahead of the 'average' novelist." But in trying to summarize the story he apologized for implying that almost nothing happens, "especially when, as here, almost nothing happens." Amis doesn't point out what seems to me the case, that these novels also lack a density of psychological speculation that might fill in for the absence of "action." Lessing pretty much stays inside her heroine—unlike, say, the George Eliot of *Middlemarch*—and takes on a neutral tone of presentation that can, cumulatively, provoke exasperation.[2]

As for *The Golden Notebook* the consensus seems to be that after writing the first three Martha Quest novels, Lessing felt dissatisfied with her conventional narrative and proceeded to deconstruct, interrogate and elaborately play around with the novel form. Ten years after *Notebook* was published she wrote a rather tendentious preface to a revised edition, claiming that most of the criticism the novel received on its appearance has been "too silly to be true." Perhaps so (I haven't made a comparative study) but Irving Howe's review of it in *The New Republic* was anything but silly. He called it "a work of high seriousness," "the most absorbing and exciting piece of new fiction I have read in a decade." Howe, back there thirty-four years ago, was bowled over by the fact that the center of the novel's action was concerned with Anna Wulf, "a mature intellectual woman." This, Howe said, was a rarity in modern fiction, as was Lessing's ability to insist upon connections between the mind of her heroine and the larger social and political events of the 1950s. But there were of course other attractions of the book, especially to those women who made and still make up the bulk of its readership

2. As it evidently did in a reader who scrawled in the margin of our library's copy of *A Proper Marriage*, apropos of Martha Quest's troubles, "Bitch, bitch, bitch. Why doesn't she *do* something? I don't feel sorry for her."

(900,000 hardcover copies sold). Here was a book in which a man is described as looking at every woman by "imagining her as she would be when he had fucked her into insensibility." A novel in which a character goes to bat for the vaginal ("real") as opposed to the clitoral orgasm and in which the "free women," Molly and Anna, ruthlessly satirize Molly's ex-husband, the successful businessman Richard. All strong stuff for 1962, though it seems doubtful whether the book can now be read by either sex with the fresh excitement it once provoked. At any rate it's canonized, the subject of many articles, dissertations, published books, and it's certainly the most highly structured of Lessing's books, probably for better than for worse.

But as the sixties wore on and the world in general became (even) more violent, fragmented and unhappy, so did Lessing's fiction. Her engagement with the irrational, with drugs, with the Sufi mystics and the unsavory psychology of R. D. Laing made the monstrously overlong novel that concludes *Children of Violence* (*The Four-Gated City*, 1969) a book that at least for this reader provided no pleasure, to put it mildly. And things did not improve with the toneless solemn inner journeys in *Briefing for a Descent to Hell* (1971) and *Memoirs of a Survivor* (1974). Even the more available, previously mentioned *Summer before the Dark* turns at its end into a tale of woe, unrelieved by any humor or irony. As for *Canopus in Argos,* the four-volume science-fiction series that followed (1979–82), there must be those who read it with some interest, though no one who is known to me.

After this prolonged stretch of disenchantment with the novel as "bright book of life" (D. H. Lawrence), Lessing published, under the name of Jane Somers, two novels about a woman writer: written in diary form, easy to read, unencumbered by much "thought," they were published pseudonymously, so Lessing said afterwards, to see whether the public that would buy books signed Doris Lessing would do the same for Jane Somers. (They sold only modestly, and were later republished under Lessing's name.) What exactly this little experiment demonstrated I don't really see. Maybe the public and the critics were right not to rave about these books, even though they were "really" authentic products. Maybe the real test would have been, as Jonathan Yardley astutely suggested, for Lessing to have kept on publishing novels under the pseudonym—that would have been a bold experiment. But Lessing didn't, and followed them instead in 1985 with *The Good Terrorist* (1985) about a group of young people in a London "squat," the animating figure of whom is Alice, the "good" girl of the title. Reviewing it, Alison

Lurie unfathomably called it the most interesting political novel since Conrad's *The Secret Agent*. In fact *The Good Terrorist* (unlike Conrad) is shapeless, to the extent of having no chapter breaks in its nearly four hundred pages. In *Under My Skin* Lessing refers to her monomaniacal heroine as "quite mad," but evidently still thought it worthwhile to trace her and her dismal companions' fortunes in a detached voice of narrative reportage. Finally, more or less winding up the eighties, appeared *The Fifth Child*, a short and shocking account of what happens to a family when a mother's fifth child turns out to be a "wild" child, more incorrigible animal than human.

I would trade the last twenty years worth of Lessing's novels for the stories and sketches she published three years ago—in an appropriately named book—*The Real Thing*. The focus here is no more, no less than London, from restaurants, to Regent's Park and Hampstead Heath, to (in an especially attractive sketch) the London Underground as observed by the author riding on the Jubilee Line:

> Charing Cross and everyone gets out. At the exit machine a girl appears running up from the deeper levels, and she is chirping like a fire alarm. Now she has drawn our attention to it, in fact a steady bleeping is going on, and for all we know, it is a fire alarm. These days there are so many electronic bleeps, cheeps, buzzes, blurps, that we don't hear them. The girl is a fey creature, blonde locks flying around a flushed face. She is laughing dizzily, and racing a flight or flock of young things coming into the West End for an evening's adventure, all of them already crazed with pleasure, and in another dimension of speed and lightness, like sparks speeding up and out.

Who knows, maybe one of these girls was nicknamed Tigger. At any rate Lessing's prose has the kind of relaxed power and delicacy, making it all look easy and casual, that is evident in many of the pages from *Under My Skin* and that has been so absent from the anguished, hard-driving, monumentally solemn world of her longer fictions. Cole Porter would not have wanted to live there, but he might have found a spot just under the skin of a writer discovering new things about herself and the world as she moves through her eighth decade.

Hudson Review 48, no. 2 (Summer 1995)

Mailer in Retrospect

❦

SIX WEEKS AGO one of the larger pieces of mail ever received turned up at my front door in the form of a dauntingly wrapped copy of *Harlot's Ghost*, all four pounds of it. It was mid-semester break, my sinuses were full of misery, and I settled in, if somewhat warily, to ingest Mailer's longest book. Somewhat warily since a trusted friend, having read it in proof, termed it a disaster; and since *Newsweek*'s Peter Prescott, a pretty good reviewer of fiction, had just called it "a dry and dusty thing . . . for nearly all of its incredibly long way." Would *Harlot* pass Wyndham Lewis's "Taxi-Cab Driver Test for 'Fiction' "? The test may be administered, with or without a cab driver, by opening any novel at its first page and seeing whether it looks like "fiction"—with all that word connotes about the diverting, the agreeably "made-up," the "interesting" story line—or something rather different, namely art. Here is a little more than the first page of *Harlot's Ghost*:

> On a late-winter evening in 1983, while driving through fog along the Maine coast, recollections of old campfires began to drift into the March mist, and I thought of the Abnaki Indians of the Algonquin tribe who dwelt near Bangor a thousand years ago.
>
> In the spring, after the planting of corn, the younger braves and squaws would leave the aged to watch over the crops and the chil-

Harlot's Ghost, by Norman Mailer. New York: Random House, 1991.

dren, and would take their birchbark canoes south for the summer. Down the Penobscot River they would travel to Blue Hill Bay on the western side of Mount Desert where my family's house, built in part by my great-great-grandfather, Doane Hadlock Hubbard, still stands. It is called the Keep, and I do not know of all else it keeps, but some Indians came ashore to build lean-tos each summer, and a few of their graves are among us, although I do not believe they came to our island to die. Lazing in the rare joys of northern warmth, they must have shucked clams on the flats at low tide and fought and fornicated among the spruce and hemlock when the water was up. What they got drunk on I do not know, unless it was the musk of each other, but many a rocky beach in the first hollow behind the shore sports mounds of ancient clamshells, ground to powder by the centuries, a beach behind the beach to speak of ancient summer frolics. The ghosts of these Indians may no longer pass through our woods but something of their old sorrows and pleasures joins the air. Mount Desert is more luminous than the rest of Maine.

Given the present state of things American, I suppose one may give a momentary thought to George Walker Bush and his trailing clouds of ancestral glory. But the ghosts of more formidable American predecessors haunt the passage (I hear Thoreau, Melville, Hemingway and Fitzgerald in it) and hold out for the reader a promise that is the promise of art—one not to be easily satisfied by any mere novel.

In one sense, as reviewers have pointed out, the promise is unfulfilled insofar as the novel's art fails to resolve certain issues raised early on. *Harlot's Ghost* consists of two disproportionately related sections. The first, titled "Omega" (the last shall be first, evidently), is just over a hundred pages and located on a day in 1983 when the novel's protagonist Herrick Hubbard (mostly though not always called Harry) is driving back from a liaison in Bath with his mistress, Chloe, to his wife, Kittredge, and their island keep off Mt. Desert. The second section, titled "Alpha," consumes the book's remaining twelve hundred pages and is an account of Harry's life and times, from private school days and a Yale degree up through his enlistment, training and service in the CIA between 1955 and 1965. Both sections, we are to understand, are manuscripts written by Harry, the second of which ends

almost twenty years short of where the first begins. In an italicized concluding note to the reader dated "Moscow, 1984" (Harry has gone there to look
for his godfather, Hugh Tremont Montague—the "Harlot" of the title—who
may either be dead or have defected to the Soviets), Harry admits that he
might never finish "the book of Harry Hubbard and his years in Saigon, nor
the stretch of service in the White House when one lived through Water-
gate, no, nor the commencement of my love affair with Kittredge." (Kittredge was married to Hugh Montague but left him for Harry after her and
Hugh's son was killed in a rock-climbing accident from which the father
survived, but in a wheelchair.) So there are lots of loose ends, and the book
concludes with the tease, or the promise, "To be continued."

Behind and not very far behind Harry is of course Norman Mailer who
weighs in on page 1,284 with an Author's Note in which he tells us that the
book was written "with the part of my mind that has lived in the CIA for
forty years." He calls his novel "the product of a veteran imagination that
has pondered the ambiguous and fascinating moral presence of the Agency
in our national life for the last four decades." This mention of four decades
takes us back to the beginning of veteran Mailer's literary career, to the
publication in 1948 of *The Naked and the Dead*, and to the ensuing books
that make up so unusual and controversial a road taken.

In considering the sheer bulk of *Harlot's Ghost*, we remind ourselves that
gigantism has always been the keynote of Mailer's imaginative plans for
himself. In a preface to his first (unpublished until a 1977 facsimile edition
of it) novel, *A Transit to Narcissus*, he notes that even before *The Naked and
the Dead* he must have written a million or so words in stories and various
drafts of *Transit*. In *Advertisements for Myself* (1959), itself an outrageous
and mainly fascinating display of a novelistic ego's demands, his "advertise-
ment" for "The Man Who Studied Yoga" divulged plans for the eight-part
novel to which "Yoga" was prologue. The prologue's hero, Sam Slovoda,
would dream eight stages in the travels of a mythical hero, Sergius O'Shaugnessy, "through many worlds, through pleasure, business, communism,
church, working class, crime, homosexuality and mysticism." "Not a modest novel," he went on to admit—and not one that was going to get written.
Mailer tells us that he abandoned the scheme after finishing a draft of *The
Deer Park;* but in the very next paragraph he directs us to fragments later in
Advertisements which are said to be "from that long novel which has come

into my mind again, a descendant of *Moby Dick*" (what else?). One of the fragments referred to is "The Time of Her Time" in which Sergius, settled in his Village loft, gives instruction in bullfighting and—in his avocation as self-styled sex saint—initiates Denise Gondelman into the mysteries of the orgasm. The big book of which "Time" was to be a part, confided Mailer, would take at least ten years and be, by the standards of 1959, probably unpublishable.

In all their superficial contradictions and inconsistencies, these early extravagant claims are worth noting for the way they bring out a deeper consistency in Mailer's vision of himself and his projection of that self onto a reader. In other words, it was not just in the recent *Ancient Evenings* or in *The Executioner's Song* that Mailer went too far: excess, from the beginning, was of the essence of the scene. But what marks "The Man Who Studied Yoga" and even more "The Time of Her Time" as important expansive moments in Mailer's literary career is that each of them in its different way is entertaining. To apply one of Frost's formulations about his own poetry, it feels as though the writer were entertaining ideas (or scenarios or characters) to see if they entertained him. This was a feeling one did not get from Mailer's writing in The *Naked and the Dead* or *Barbary Shore*. For one thing there is more comedy in the shorter pieces: like the story (from "Yoga") about how Cassius O'Shaugnessy unscrewed his navel and the disastrous event it led to (his ass fell off); or like New York City's garbage wars as observed by Sergius (in "Time") when he heads into the Lower East Side to look for help in cleaning up his apartment and encounters a gang of kids at play:

> They were charming, these six-year-olds as I told my uptown friends, and they used to topple the overloaded garbage cans, strew them through the street, have summer snowball fights with orange peel, coffee grounds, soup bones, slop, they threw the discus by sailing the raw tin rounds from the tops of cans, their pillow fights were with loaded socks of scum, and a debauch was for two of them to scrub a third around the inside of a twenty-gallon pail still warm with the heat of its emptied treasures.

There is an ease and confidence about these supple observings which would animate some of the best writing—fictional or non—Mailer produced in his great decade, the 1960s.

When fiction pays attention to what people eat or what happens to their garbage, human relationships are anchored in homely rather than ethereal circumstances. So food plays a lively role in *Harlot's Ghost* as a handy indicator of character and social milieu. Over the course of the book Harry has a number of good meals at the likes of Harvey's Restaurant and Sans Souci, but occasionally partakes of more humble fare. During his weeks of testing at the CIA's I-J-K-L complex in Washington (before the agency's move to Langley, Virginia, in 1961), he takes a course in World Communism from a Commie hater named Raymond James ("Ray Jim") Burns:

> On our last night, Bullseye Burns threw a party for our class in his small apartment in a newly built four-story complex of middle-cost housing in the outskirts of Alexandria, Virginia. He had three kids, all boys, all towheads, and I learned on this night that he and his wife were high school sweethearts from Indiana. Mrs. Burns, plain-faced, slab-shaped, served us the casserole dish of cheese and tuna and hot dog relish that had been her party fare for twenty years. (Or, as she called it, her "main-eventer.") It was obvious that she and Ray Jim barely bothered to speak to each other any-more. . . . I concluded that people like Jim Ray did not quit their marriages until they were feeling inclined to take an ax to their mate.

That casserole has the right slablike ingredients and harmonizes nicely with the narrator's genial reversing of Ray Jim into Jim Ray. A second passage of cookery is rather more spicy: Harry, now posted to his first assignment in Berlin under the novel's most colorful character (and a historical personage to boot), William King ("King Bill") Harvey, prepares to leave a nightclub called *Die Hintertür* with his German mistress-to-be, Ingrid:

> Ingrid was also eating an enormous "Grilled American" of West-phalian ham, tomatoes, and Muenster cheese. I sat down beside her in twitchy detumescence while she slogged down a vast mug of beer, thereby communicating to me in twenty minutes how pro-foundly one might, over twenty years, come to dislike the eating habits of a mate. Poor Ingrid. The Back Door, as she put it to me with a toothsome grin, never allowed their help enough of food and drink to produce more than a goat turd for the other back

door. On this night therefore, in which my own sphincter had almost played a prominent role, insight came over me at last: I was in the presence of German Humor. *Die Hintertür.* I got it. A night-club for assholes.

I quote these passages not because they contain anything of special significance to the story and its thematic preoccupations—although Harry's allusion to his sphincter in the second exhibit refers to a proposition rejected earlier that evening from his unscrupulous rogue colleague (and another of the book's best-drawn characters) Dix Butler. They illustrate rather a level of writing frequent in the book that in its breezily informal conduct appears to be unashamedly enjoying itself. One thinks again (I do) of Frost asking rhetorically in an interview "What do I want to communicate but what a hell of a good time I had writing it?" Mailer often seems to be having a good time constructing the sentences and paragraphs in *Harlot's Ghost,* and this spirit can be infectious. Despite all the fuss generated by his harping on the largeness of his ambitions—to get into the ring with Tolstoy, write the longest novel or the successor to *Moby Dick*—much of his page-to-page invention takes place with an idiom and material no more elevated than the ones just quoted. Quite simply, they are where most of the action is.

At least two prominent reviews of *Harlot's Ghost* would have us believe that action to be of little consequence. John Simon rehearsed step by step the plot (an old gambit of his) under the assumption that readers would perceive the inherent ludicrousness of Mailer's enterprise. (Plots can be made to look pretty silly when extracted from the novel's prose and displayed to readers who have not yet read the book.) And Louis Menand, always a sharp-minded critic, behaved in *The New Yorker* as if the whole thing were totally misconceived. In Menand's view, Mailer was trying to do ten things at once and had succeeded in finishing none of them. Compared with 1960s Mailer—the writer whom people of Menand's generation read (said he) for an "aggressive and great-souled refusal to cater to sanctimony whether it was the establishment or the establishment's enemies"—*Harlot's Ghost* was much too easy on the CIA and American foreign policy over the past decades. Mailer's unwillingness to challenge and provoke thus produced a flaccid novel. Menand also complained about the large amount of "Alpha" devoted to letters between Harry—from his various outposts in Berlin, Uruguay (where he works under E. Howard Hunt), and Florida (Bay of Pigs time)—and Kittredge who herself works for the agency, in exactly what capacity it is not fully clear. "The most disembodied fictional love affair outside *Clarissa*," Menard calls it.

Nobody ever wished *Clarissa* longer, but one does keep turning its pages as the warfares and stratagems between men and men, men and women, women and women, unfold. If Mailer can be compared to Richardson, it could just possibly be as a master of narrative, and so much the better for Mailer. (It is also true that, as with *Clarissa*, not all the letters in *Harlot's Ghost* are of equal interest and vitality.) As for Mailer's unwillingness to challenge and provoke, it may have to do with the fact that as he moves toward seventy he finds it harder to take on the loudly aggressive calling-to-court of America's politicians that excited Louis Menand (and others of us) three decades ago. Recall the end of his contribution to a *Partisan Review* statement about Vietnam in which, shockingly, he put forth the possibility that Vietnam was a "happening" staged by Lyndon Johnson because he could not control things at home:

> Cause if it is Daddy Warbucks, couldn't we have the happening just with the Marines and skip all that indiscriminate roast tit and naked lunch, all these bombed-out ovaries, Mr. J., Mr. L.B.J., Boss Man of Show Biz—I salute you in your White House Oval; I mean America will shoot all over the shithouse wall if this jazz goes on, Jim.

"Jim" indeed! In *Harlot's Ghost* this vivid idiom, put in the service of a rather different politics, characterizes King Bill Harvey: "That's why we go into every skirmish with the KGB under a handicap. That's why we even have to classify the toilet paper in the crap house. We must keep reminding ourselves to enclave the poop." The other figure who talks this way and makes a single, memorable appearance in the book is Lenny Bruce who addresses a nightclub audience of which Harlot, Kittredge, and Harry are part: "That first show was terrific, in fact, if I say so myself, it was so good that I came . . . Yes I came and now I feel out of it. Ah fellows, I have to get it up for the second time." Kittredge and her husband are appalled; Harry tells us that he has never heard such laughter in a nightclub before: "Laughs slithered out of people like snakes, tore out of them, barked forth, wheezed forth, screamed out."

We presume Harry is not laughing that way, since typically he is detached and contemplative in his response to excessiveness. His own language and idiom are unhipsterish, an exception being some hopped-up language in "Omega" where he describes lovemaking with his mistress in Time-of-her-time Maileresque: "With Chloe it was get ready for rush, get ready for the sale, whoo-e, gushers we'd hit oil together. Recuperating he felt low-down and slimy and rich as the earth. You could grow flowers out of your ass." Throughout "Alpha," by contrast, he is the nice (though Wasp) Jewish boy that has always been one of the parts of Mailer's identity. There is a strategy here: Harry needs to be relatively sane, fearful, prudent, sometimes uncertain, in order to set off in all its weird craziness CIA doings in Berlin, Uruguay (a particularly pointless far-out bunch of "doings"), and Cuba. Louis Menand points out rightly that the agency is Mailer's Circumlocution Office, and surely Dickens may be invoked in connection with this too-long book. After all, how lumbering, badly plotted, and sometimes inertly written is *Little Dorrit* in its modest 968 pages. How John Simon might have wished about *Dorrit* that Dickens, like Thomas Wolfe, had had a great editor; how awkwardly Menand would find its different sections to stand in their relationship to one another.

In Carl Rollyson's new and nicely discriminating biography of Mailer, he makes the claim about him that no American writer, not even Hemingway, has "so fused the invention of a literary style with the creation of a writer's identity."[1] The claim is made during a discussion of *Advertisements,* especially "The White Negro" and "The Time of Her Time," and it makes sense with respect to those aggressively challenging, sexually and racially combative efforts. But with *Harlot's Ghost* it is impossible to identify *a* literary style discernible on every page and ascribable to the novel as a whole; or rather let us say that the very inclusiveness of Mailer's narrative voice is such as to accommodate perceptions ranging from the sublime to the ridiculous. To make things further complicated, that voice refuses to provide guidance on how to tell one level from the other. Early in "Omega," Harry's car, on its way back to Mt. Desert, goes into a severe skid just at the moment when its driver remembers how he and Kittredge pledged there would be honesty between them. Fortunately for Harry, it is a three-hundred-sixty degree skid that leaves him still headed for home and "beyond fear":

1. Carl Rollyson, *The Lives of Norman Mailer: A Biography* (New York: Paragon House, 1991).

I felt as if I had fallen out of a ten-story window, landed in a fireman's net, and was now strolling around in a glow and a daze. *"Millions of creatures,"* I said aloud to the empty car—actually said it aloud!—*"walk the earth unseen, both when we wake and when we sleep,"* after which, trundling along at thirty miles an hour, too weak and exhilarated to stop, I added in salute to the lines just recited, "Milton, *Paradise Lost,"* and thought of how Chloe and I had gotten up from bed in her trailer on the outskirts of Bath a couple of hours ago and had gone for a farewell drink to a cocktail lounge with holes in the stuffing of the red leatherette booths.

From unfallen Adam's voice in Book 4 of Milton's poem to the holes in those red leatherette booths is only as far as from the beginning of a sentence to its end, a distance negotiated with no particular fuss by the narrative voice. Unlike the tense polemical thrusts of early Mailer (the writer as bullfighter or boxer or cocksman), this relaxed, expansive voice (all too expansive, detractors would say) can entertain widely different perspectives and not be overwhelmed by them. Like the style of early Mailer, this one is explorative, but in a less threatened and threatening way. You might almost call it mellow. The inclusiveness of range in this latest Mailer means that while Harry can rise to heights of spiritual self-definition—as when, a newly recruited CIA man, he thinks that "Happiness was the resonance one knows in the heart when the ends of oneself come to concordance in the morning air"—he stays enough in touch with earthly things to produce, when the occasion demands it, a good joke:

> "Why won't Baptists," I asked her, "make love standing up?"
> "Why won't they?"
> "Because people might think they were dancing."

In perhaps the most perceptive review the book has received, Thomas R. Edwards shrewdly suggests that *Harlot's Ghost* invites itself to be thought of as something like religious epic, "Mailer's *Paradise Lost,* as it were, in which the cold war could figure as the War in Heaven, the Creation, and the Fall." He goes on to note the fusion of sacred and secular levels in various characters from the novel. It should be clear from my own focus that what seems to me the book's major mode of performance is religious epic gone askew, the way CIA operations do; in other words—and since, as Kenneth Burke

reminds us, comedy is the literary form which sees human beings as necessarily *mistaken*—this religious epic is a comic one. Edwards concludes his
review by quoting Samuel Johnson on *Paradise Lost* in a passage I wish I had
found myself but will shamelessly appropriate nonetheless:

> To paint things as they are requires a minute attention, and em-
> ploys the memory rather than the fancy. Milton's delight was to
> sport in the wide regions of possibility; reality was a scene too
> narrow for his mind. He sent his fancies out upon discovery, into
> worlds where only imagination can travel, and delighted to form
> new modes of existence, and furnish sentiment and action to supe-
> rior beings, to trace the councils of hell, or accompany the choirs of
> heaven.

Edwards notes that these terms have something to do with spying; they also
bring out the overweeningness of Milton's and Mailer's imaginations. For
both imaginations, reality is a scene too narrow. It is even possible that
having Harry remember the Milton line with the word "spiritual" left out
(Adam tells Eve in the poem that "Millions of spiritual creatures walk the
earth / Unseen, both when we wake and when we sleep") is Mailer's way of
despiritualizing his religious epic and playing up the comic-grotesque possibilities of spying gone over the edge. In Milton's line, the spiritual creatures behold God's work "with ceaseless praise" both day and night; Mailer's creatures are more equivocal, even just plain strange, and perhaps of the
devil's party without knowing it.

   Maybe, after all, any modern epic has to be comic and satiric, less like
Paradise Lost than like Byron's "Vision of Judgement":

> The angels all were singing out of tune
>   And hoarse with having little else to do,
> Excepting to wind up the sun and moon
>   Or curb a runaway young star or two . . .
>
> The guardian seraphs had retired on high,
>   Finding their charges past all care below.

At the end of *Harlot's Ghost* Harry acknowledges that he has not, like
Milton, quite risen to the height of his great argument: "Unlike God, I have
not been able to present all of my creation." For too many years we have

observed the critics lamenting Mailer's failure to live up to this or that, his immense talent wasted on various misconceived enterprises, his preoccupation with X when clearly he should have been occupied with Y. My own attitude is closer to Dryden's on Chaucer: if Mailer the novelist fails to live up to God, he still has given us God's plenty.

Terry Southern: R.I.P.

≼§≽

Terry Southern, whose novel-writing days were behind him, had completed a book about Virgin Records and was on his way to teach a course in screenwriting at Columbia University when he collapsed and subsequently died of respiratory failure. His obituary in the *New York Times* called him a screenwriter and emphasized, as his notable achievements, the scripts of *Dr. Strangelove* and *Easy Rider*. The former of these, as directed by Stanley Kubrick, is truly a marvelous piece of work that may be seen with delight again and again; the latter—except for the scenes in which Jack Nicholson appears—is dismal stuff. But before Southern's Hollywood phase, he produced three short novels all of which have been unavailable for years. *Flash and Filigree* (1958) and *The Magic Christian* (1959) were published here and in England, under Southern's own name; *Candy*—which for a time enjoyed notoriety—was first brought out in 1958 by Maurice Girodias's Olympia Press, publishers of *Lolita,* and less distinguished "dirty" books. Presumably written by one "Maxwell Kenton," *Candy* was in fact the product of a collaboration between Southern and an Olympia Press hopeful named Mason Hoffenberg. It was eventually published commercially in this country in 1964, the *Lady Chatterley* trial having opened the gates. Southern also produced a collection of short fiction and essays, *Red-Dirt Marijuana and Other Tastes,* a novel about the making of a pornographic film *Blue Movie,* 1970, then after a couple of decades a final novel, *Texas Summer,* an extension of a story he wrote earlier. There are good things in each of these works, but I'll concentrate here on early Southern, the "send-up" novels where his originality is most evident.

Southern was sending up, in these books, the American 1950s, that decade whose most significant icon was The Communist Menace, against which American Good in its varied forms—religion, family, true married love, and good grooming—were massed. In the second half of the decade, true, the Beats had come into their own—Kerouac's *On the Road* and Ginsberg's *Howl* were the principal documents of Beat rebellion against stifling convention—but those writers were "sincere," let it all hang out, and wrote swollen rivers of prose-poetry. By contrast Southern was hip, arch, campy without being inclined toward the homosexual. He had a gift for fixing on midcult media favorites like the popular TV quiz show "What's My Line," watched by all good American families before they went to bed on Sunday night. In this extremely popular entertainment, a panel of celebrities — Bennett Cerf, Dorothy Kilgallen, Arlene Francis, Steve Allen, and other forgotten names— interviewed (blindfolded) a Mystery Guest, who after "signing in" answered the panelists' various questions about his or her identity. In *Flash and Filigree* the show became "What's My Disease," in which the contestant is wheeled in shrouded in a cage and is questioned by panel on where the disease is located ("Is it—your face?" "Are these manifestations . . . above, or below, the waistline?" "Is it of the limbs?") until eventually one of them asks, triumphantly, "Is it elephantiasis"? Whereupon the following:

> The moderator took up the triumph quickly and with grand good humor. "Yes, it *is* elephantiasis!" and at that moment, as the shroud was dropped and the contestant revealed to them all, the audience took in its breath as one in a great audible gasp of astonished horror, and then burst into applause for the Professor, the contestant, the moderator, and the whole panel. . . .

Nothing in *Flash and Filigree* has much to do with anything else: we move from a dubious character named Treevly, who treats a persistent lesion by packing it with a cancer culture and covering it with a Band-Aid; to Dr. Fred Eichner of the Hauptmann Clinic, who has a major passion for running stoplights at excessive speed; to a protracted seduction scene between "Babs" Mintner, a nurse at the clinic, and her young admirer Ralph. The sex scene (all preliminary of course) runs for pages and has dialogue like this to fuel it:

> "No, Ralph, not any more, please, not now, Ralph, please listen, Ralph, not here, please, let's wait, really, Ralph, darling, please, no really please, oh Ralph I love you please don't, really don't please Ralph I can't darling I love you please, oh Ralph, please, I can't Ralph. . .

and on and on.

Candy takes the all-American girl—of whom Babs Mintner is a fine specimen—into rather more disastrous experiences for which seduction is scarcely the word. Her "experiences" with, among others, Professor Mephesto, her uncle Jack, and Dr. Irving Krankheit culminate in a quite tasteless scene where she befriends a hunchback, feeds him dinner at her apartment, then can't deny his slobbering importunings: the fellow keeps pointing to his hump and accusing Candy of denying him her favors because of "it," and the poor girl is so embarrassed that she eventually accedes to him. After a quite travestied consummation, the hunchback leaves and wakes Candy from her nap, "cross as a pickle" (an expression occurring more than once in Southern): "'*Darn* it!' she said aloud, and with real feeling for she had forgotten to have them exchange names." Later she decides, with much sentiment, that she will think of him as "Derek."

By the time *Candy* was finally published in this country, Lenny Bruce was fully on the scene, and Southern's outrageousness seemed less eye-opening. But in 1958, after the American public had been entertained with novels like *The Caine Mutiny, Marjorie Morningstar, The Man in the Grey Flannel Suit,* and other corporate enterprises, it was quite something to be introduced to Candy Christian's Aunt Livia whom Candy thinks of as a "lovely and sophisticated" woman. As Uncle Jack Christian picks Livia up to have a drink with him and his niece, Livia notes a pregnant woman on the corner— "She's going to have that baby before the light changes! Good God, did you ever see anything like that? If I look another moment I shall vomit all over us." She then turns to Candy, asking "*You* aren't pregnant, I hope?" to which the girl replies, in one of her favorite comebacks, "N-O spells *no.*" After Livia compliments Candy on how lovely she's looking, the girl flushes deeply as Livia proceeds:

"Have any of the boys gotten into those little white pants of yours yet?" Aunt Livia asked, as though she were speaking about the weather.

"*Really* Liv," said Uncle Jack, coughing. "This hardly seems the appro—"

"But, isn't she *lovely*?" his wife persisted, turning to Jack Christian, "a ripe little piece she's getting to be, I'd say. It seems to me that's the first question that would occur to anyone."

There's a wonderfully "naive" matter-of-factness to much of Southern's narrative in which the unspeakable is spoken as if, well, anyone in his right mind would say it.

But *Candy* goes on for too long and exhausts its one joke. Southern's most original and permanently rereadable book is *The Magic Christian*, a slim volume of 150 pages about the exploits of billionaire Guy Grand ("Grand Guy Grand") who spends his life and much of his inexhaustible fortune setting up monstrously embarrassing situations, or—as he puts it— "making it hot for people." In the first of these, from the perch of his day coach stopped at the train station in a small New England town, he calls out the window to the hot-dog vendor for a red-hot, then as the train begins to move and the vendor passes the hot dog to Grand, "Guy Grand leaned out and handed him a five-hundred dollar bill. 'Break this?' he asked tersely." The resulting action may be imagined. Grand's other exploits include constructing an enormous vat, on a street corner in Chicago's Loop, filled with quantities of manure, urine and gallons of blood (purchased from the stockyards) into which he drops 10,000 hundred dollar bills, then stirs them in with a large wooden paddle. Burners are lit, the pot boils and morning finds a "large moronic scrawl" (FREE $ HERE) on the vat. Again, he has made it hot for people. In other episodes Grand fixes a prize fight, bribing the champ and the contender to behave in the most effete, mincingly effeminate way until one of them finally lies down in the ring, kicking his heels and weeping in childish pique. He buys a movie theater and proceeds to mess with the clips of famous forties films, like *Mrs. Miniver* and *The Best Years of Our Lives.* In the former, he inserts a few seconds at the point when kindly Walter Pidgeon, thinking idealistic thoughts of Mrs. Miniver (whom he has just met), is idly playing with a paper knife while he sits at his desk. Grand cuts to the knife, holding the camera on it just long enough to be too long, and confusing the audience with the irrelevant thought of violence to come. After the show he stalks about the lobby, muttering "What was that part about the *knife*? . . . I thought he was going to try and *kill* her! Christ, I don't *get* it!" In the *Best Years of Our Lives*, as the World War II amputee courts his small-town sweetheart on the family porch swing one summer evening, Grand inserts a cut to "below the girl's waist where the hooks were seen to hover for an instant and then disappear, grappling urgently beneath her skirt." This is of course supremely tasteless and cruel, but (for some of us) made more than palatable by the perfect diction of "grappling urgently."

Norman Mailer, in *Cannibals and Christians*, said the most interesting thing about *The Magic Christian*, and by extension Terry Southern as well, when he called the book a "classic" in which the aristocratic impulse turns upon itself:

> Never had distaste for the habits of a mass mob reached such precision, never did wit falter in its natural assumption that the idiocies of the mass were attached breath and kiss to the hypocrisies, the weltering grandeurs, and the low stupidities of the rich, the American rich.

For Mailer, *The Magic Christian* marked the end of this aristocratic impulse; it was a classic of Camp. For Southern, it was also, virtually, the end of his run as a novelist: Hollywood, along with plenty of drugs and alcohol, did its work. His "slender, unwholesome talent," as John Simon once put it, may be for an age—the extravagant 1960's—rather than for all time. But he had a thing to say, said it, and never apologized, never explained.

Sewanee Review 104, no. 3 (Summer 1996)

Robert Penn Warren's Late Poems

᠊᠍ᡣᠥᡣᠥ᠊

C ALVIN BEDIENT'S NEW BOOK on Robert Penn Warren's poetry is
rhapsodic in its overall tone and posture, and it should be said that
such an impulse is wholly admirable—the impulse, that is, to make the
strongest possible case for the achievement of a still living writer. Since
attaining the age of eighty years, Warren is especially prone to having himself be named the King of American Poets. We have no laureates, but Robert
Lowell died in 1977 and if one looks around—as king-makers look around—
for a sufficiently venerable and also very good poet, then Warren really has
no competition, neither Richard Eberhart nor Stanley Kunitz nor Karl
Shapiro, nor somewhat younger American poets, interesting as they may
be. Bedient puts the case for Warren's preeminence at the end of his first
chapter ("His Last Grand Phase") by asking rhetorically, "Who mirrored
with passion the world's body? Where was the poet as weighty as these others [he has mentioned Lowell, John Ashbery, and James Merrill] but their
coarse and necessary complement, the poet writing with brains, bones,
heart, sex and courting in the American landscape original moments of
being?" The conclusion to his introductory chapter is as unqualifiedly eloquent a plea for a contemporary writer as one has met with recently:

In the Heart's Last Kingdom: Robert Penn Warren's Major Poetry, by Calvin Bedient.
Cambridge: Harvard University Press, 1984. *New and Selected Poems, 1923–1985,* by
Robert Penn Warren. New York: Random House, 1985.

With his great question concerning the adequacy of existence for the total reverence of the heart, he has made determined casts into memory, the slipstream of the now, dream, the heart, Truth, to find whatever joy, fate, blessedness, or nightmare awaits him. His fears have been great, but his capacity for admitting and confronting them has been quickening, and his yearning has never abated. Here is a poet who has found the right relation . . . between struggle and submission, glory and truth, nobility and self-knowledge, joy and pain, quest and common sense, art and experience: a relation of strong and poignant accord.

I quote at length from Bedient because he goes on at length—and at the beginning of his book—in an effort to make the highest claims for Warren's uniqueness: "that very unusual thing, a poet of tragic joy [the phrase is Yeats's in "Lapis Lazuli"]—indeed the first such among American poets."

In support of his high claim for Warren, Calvin Bedient is eclectic, even promiscuous, in the cast of names summoned up for this support, as in the page following the "tragic joy" claim, where first Katherine Mansfield in her journal, then Kafka ("Writing . . . is a form of prayer"), then Ibsen, briefly ("But can he who has been seen by God continue to live?"), and, finally, Emily Dickinson all show up for a pithy quotation or so. At other points he invokes Nietzsche, Heidegger, Ricoeur, Cioran, Lacan, and Buber, among others, in ways that for me didn't make his case for Warren's greatness any more powerful. Yet when Bedient is at his best—as a practical critic of Warren's performance in verse, line by line—he needs none of these supports. To pick out a couple of examples from many more or less at random, here he addresses himself to an aspect of Warren's grammatical and rhetorical inclinations:

Warren's omission of articles can make one appreciate what thresholds, linchpins, and cushions they usually are. Song, a soft subject in itself, becomes Platonically severe in "Song is lost / In the blue depth of sky" (and the sky no less severe), where the song is, after all, that of a particular lark in a particular location ("over meadows of Brittany"). Not for mortal ears, this song, nor for mortal transit, that sky. The elided articles help hold them off from us.

Or he tackles the question of Warren's frequent use of compounds and their artistic justification:

> Warren's most brilliant use of compounds may be the daring string of clichés at the end of "Acquaintance with Time in Early Autumn." The heart, the poet says, has "picked today as payday, the payment / In life's dime-thin, thumb-worn, two-sided, two-faced coin." Weary alike in their familiarity and profusion, not to mention their aural peas-in-a-pod similarity, these compounds yet hint, in series, of a clatter and a sum, as of several coins spilling out of a slot-machine at once—several, not one; something, not nothing. The compounds are, to be sure, ironically "two-sided": divided yet single, as desire is, desire that wants life, wants death.

Observations such as these, even when they don't convince fully, are vigorous examples of how hard Bedient works at speaking back to the poetry. At one moment he quotes from an interview in which Warren says that criticism is a matter of "redoing" the work—"You repaint the picture, rewrite the book, recompose the music, by going inside, if you are really experiencing it properly." This "very difficult creative act" is what Bedient is always attempting, to the extent that after two hundred pages (and perhaps sooner than that) the often admiring reader feels he has had a workout, and may have just had enough.

I don't mean to imply that the book is all practical criticism without a larger argument, since Bedient has very much of one, namely that the watershed in Robert Penn Warren's poetry is *Audubon: A Vision* (1969). Until then his poetic career was "a long partial failure" which Bedient describes in his own "creative" manner thus:

> Dreamily piecing together a quilt of terms and rhythms from Marvell, Yeats, T. S. Eliot, Auden, Ransom and others, the young, and later not so young, Warren pulled it up over his jutting country-boy knees, presenting himself as an invalid of virtue, a casualty of the collapse of the sublime. He had yet to see that a certain raw-boned vigor (both of attitude and word) was to be his salvation.

Rising above his previous volumes "like a curiously abrupt, grand escarpment," *Audubon* signaled the accession to a new freedom and power, and though none of Warren's subsequent volumes is its equal (and though,

Bedient admits, many of the poems from them are failures), they earn him the title, through their many successes, of the sublime American poet of tragic joy.

This dramatic but too neatly schematic view of Warren's literary career depends upon one's being able (as I am not able) to see *Audubon* as a great poem. I read it rather as an interesting experiment in writing the long poem, but perhaps too committed to the "sublime" mode (which Bloom and other academic critics have been touting recently), a mode Warren doesn't resist as much as he might. Another way of putting it would be to acknowledge, as may not have been acknowledged enough, that Warren is an often humorless poet—though when his humor does appear it invariably enriches the poem. But his tendency over the years to indulge too quickly and often in large questions about Time is one which—if my own experience is shared by others—can be a wearying one, especially when the poetry is taken in large doses.

Bedient recognizes this tendency by saying, wittily, that "Warren has three bagfuls of words"—the first bag of which, composed of "*Truth, Time fate, No-Time,* and so on" has "caused some readers to sneeze, or feel fleeced." They are sneezing at the "philosopher" in Warren, judging that his poetry suffers as that philosopher performs. (This is, of course, the sort of criticism made of Melville and Faulkner, so Warren is in distinguished company.) For that reason and because of the amount of repetition and overinsistence in his writing, it seems wise that during the past thirty years, since the great flood of poems began with *Promises,* Warren has acted as a stern critic of his own work in the three "new and selected" volumes of poems published in 1965, 1975, and 1985. Unfortunately for the effectiveness of Bedient's criticism, his book wasn't able to take account of the most recent of these, published last spring when Warren turned eighty. Sixty-two years of poems: there has been nothing like it (with the exception of John Hall Wheelock) since Hardy, whose "Neutral Tones" bears the date 1867 and whose final volume, *Winter Words,* was published the year of his death in 1928. (In case you're counting, "Hap" and a number of other early Hardy poems bear the date 1866, which gives him, like Warren, sixty-two years of poems. Warren is likely soon to break the record.)

By preceding *New and Selected Poems* in the publication of his own book, Bedient was unable to consider the forty-eight new poems with which Warren opens his collection and that assume a place at the cost of radical surgery to previous books. (For example, *You, Emperors and Others* has been trimmed to three poems; *Incarnations* consists of but five; while even a quite recent volume, *Being Here* [1977–80], preserves just ten of its originally fifty poems.) But I will now gradually move away from Bedient and take the risk of sounding overenthusiastic about an eighty-year-old poet's most recent work. These forty-eight new poems seem to me to include some of the best ones Warren has ever written; moreover, a number of them—including "Mortal Limit," "After the Dinner Party," "Covered Bridge," "Seasons," "Little Girl Wakes Early," and "History During Nocturnal Snowfall"—are written in rhymed quatrains ("Mortal Limit" is, of all things, a sonnet!) whose presence makes hash out of Bedient's critical point about Warren's poetry— that "he had first to reject not only rhyme but the trivializing idea of the poem as a longish decorative bead-chain of identically carved stanzas." If at some point in Warren's career he "had" to do this by way of coming into "his mature manner" (the title of Bedient's second chapter) he has come back to it with a vengeance in these latest poems. The case is rather, I think, that Bedient's overvaluation of the unrhymed *Audubon* causes him to downplay and blame rhyme as something Warren needed only to be liberated from. Granted, rhyme is not as centrally present to him as it was to Hardy; but when Warren rhymes, it is with a doggedness that reminds of no one so much as Hardy.

In one of his interviews, Warren noted that he wrote two kinds of poems, speculative ones and nostalgic ones; yet many of the new ones really don't fall into either category. In fact the following poem, quoted in full, seems to me one that could not have been predicted by anyone familiar with the poet's earlier work:

After the Dinner Party

You two sit at the table late, each, now and then,
Twirling a near-empty wine glass to watch the last red
Liquid climb up the crystalline spin to the last moment when
Centrifugality fails: with nothing now said.

What is left to say when the last logs sag and wink?
The dark outside is streaked with the casual snowflake
Of winter's demise, all guests long gone home, and you think
Of others who never again can come to partake

Of food, wine, laughter, and philosophy—
Though tonight one guest has quoted a killing phrase we owe
To a lost one whose grin, in eternal atrophy,
Now in dark celebrates some last unworded jest none can know.

Now a chair scrapes, sudden, on tiles, and one of you
Moves soundless, as in hypnotic certainty,
The length of table. Stands there a moment or two,
Then sits, reaches out a hand, open and empty.

How long it seems till a hand finds that hand there laid,
While ash, still glowing, crumbles, and silence is such
That the crumbling of ash is audible. Now naught's left unsaid
Of the old heart-concerns, the last, tonight, which

Had been of the absent children, whose bright gaze
Over-arches the future's horizon, in the mist of your prayers.
The last log is black, while ash beneath displays
No last glow. You snuff candles. Soon the old stairs

Will creak with your grave and synchronized tread as each mounts
To a briefness of light, then true weight of darkness, and then
That heart-dimness in which neither joy nor sorrow counts.
Even so, one hand gropes out for another, again.

This beautifully realized work gives the impression of amplitude and leisure, both in the development of its seven stanzas and in the deliberately
extended pausings within its individual lines. Although there is the occasional compound ("heart-concerns" and "heart-dimness"), the overall
pitch is confident and relaxed, rather than strained—as is sometimes the
case with Warren's compounding. The rhyming is mainly strong, but the
enjambed lines (sometimes over the stanza break) make for continuity in
the speaking voice, help create a Frostian or Hardyesque "sound of sense."
More significant than any of these technical matters is the presence of an
additional person here, the "You two" with whom the speaker eventually
becomes united in a concord of need. Compared with some of Warren's
more heavy, oh-so-knowingly "dark" utterances from earlier poems (the
featuring of blood and guts, Time and Death), I find more significant
wisdom, a more ample and satisfying view of life, in the little "story" which

unfolds in "After the Dinner Party" and in a number of other poems from the new "Altitudes and Extensions" section of *New and Selected Poems.*

I do not mean to sound as if I were saluting the proverbial "mellowing" of an octogenarian poet; at any rate the label will not do for a poem that is both as explorative and as secure, as bold and as reserved, as "After the Dinner Party." But in thinking about Warren's career as a poet and his "views" on life as expressed in-and-outside his poems, we may be helped by the following analysis put forth by his brightest student ever, Randall Jarrell, in a letter written in 1944 to a young woman (Amy Breyer deBlasio) both Jarrell and Warren were fond of:

> I've just seen Red's *Selected Poems* and that's the only real thing wrong with the good ones: the world and everything in it, in them, is so purely Original Sin, horror, loathing, morbidness, final evil, that to somebody who knows Red it's plain he manages his life by pushing all the evil in it out into the poems and novels. All his theory says is that the world is nothing but evil, whereas the practice he lives by says exactly the opposite. . . . In other words, if Red were bad to people or Cenina [Warren's first wife], and lost his temper and made unkind remarks about his friends, his poetry would get to be considerably more cheerful.

Jarrell went on to say that this practice is "therapeutic" (pushing life's evil into the poems you write, while being nice to people) but "the best poetry there is isn't that." As far as I know, Warren has not come—in the forty years since Jarrell made the remark—to be known for losing his temper and being bad to people, and it's also not right to say, flatly, that his poetry has become "considerably more cheerful." But take the ending of another recent poem, a meditation titled "Far West Once" about an aged man remembering how, years previously while tramping up a gorge, he had thought that someday he would repeat the climb in memory only. This is a familiar theme of Warren's: in the words of "Rattlesnake Country"—on which Bedient has some salient commentary—"The compulsion to try to convert what now is *was* / Back into what was *is.*" "Far West Once" ends like this:

> How long ago! But in years since,
> On other trails, in the shadow of
> What other cliffs, in lands with names
> Crank on the tongue, I have felt my boots

Crush gravel, or press the soundlessness
Of detritus of pine or fir, and heard
Movement of water, far, how far—

Or waking under nameless stars,
Have heard such redemptive music, from
Distance to distance threading starlight,
Able yet, as long ago,
Despite scum of wastage and scab of years,
To touch again the heart, as though at a dawn
Of dew-bright Edenic promise, with,
Far off, far off, in verdurous shade, first birdsong.

The "scum of wastage and scab of years" that has figured so largely in Warren's earlier poetry as the bodily and spiritual burden of living in the world, now is prefaced by "Despite"; for the claim is that the heart can still be touched, the "Edenic promise" still glimpsed—the music heard, a "redemptive" music. Such a claim would be empty, merely a wishful lunge at Positive Thinking (the aged poet deciding to affirm) were it not for the exquisite cadence there at the poem's end which proves on the pulses of its own song that something important is being heard:

To touch again the heart, as though at a dawn
Of dew-bright Edenic promise, with,
Far off, far off, in verdurous shade, first birdsong.

Those prolonged hesitancies of the comma and the repeated "Far off" are instrumental in making this poetry an experience to the ear as well as the eye, maybe even in making it like something "more cheerful" in overall effect than the kind Warren wrote in earlier days.

By dwelling on his most recent work and hazarding the judgment that a good portion of it will last as long or longer than anything he has produced, I risk slighting the earlier narratives, poems whose virtues as "story" are more important than their compositional line-by-line rhythms. These narratives also contain Warren's most authentic brand of humor. "Folly on Royal Street before the Raw Face of God" (which Bedient writes well about) begins, after its enjoyable folly of a title, with "Drunk, drunk, drunk, amid the haze of noon" as Warren and his two companions head down Royal Street in New Orleans of a spring Sunday, "irrevocably drunk" and presently regarded by The Law:

<pre>
                         A cop,
      Of brachycephalic head and garlic breath,
      Toothpick from side of mouth and pants ass-bagged and
           holster low,

      From eyes the color of old coffee grounds,
      Regarded with imperfect sympathy
      La condition humaine—
      Which was sure-God what we were.
</pre>

"Ass-bagged" jostles with *"La condition humaine"* delightfully, and "sure-God" is the perfect idiom with which to sum it up. Or there is a memorable confrontation in the most outrageously titled "Old Nigger on One-Mule Cart Encountered Late at Night When Driving Home from Party in the Back Country," as the post-partygoer takes a sharp right turn too fast and "There it is: death-trap. / Oh the fool-nigger— ass-hole wrong side of / The road, naturally." That the poem moves on from race-condescension to a moment when Warren in imagination addresses the black man as "Brother, Rebuker / my Philosopher past all/ Casuistry" is a moving and convincing evoking of the Other who is himself. Here is a spaciousness of feeling often thought to be unavailable to Warren's tight-lipped, tortured view of things.

Such poems as "American Portrait: Old Style" and "Amazing Grace in the Back Country" (from *Now and Then: Poems 1976–1978*) are similarly unconstricted, notable for the way they explore a society and history larger and perhaps more interesting than the Self. Finally there is Warren the balladeer, some of whose productions seem to me—like the poems mentioned so far—destined to survive. There is "English Cocker: Old and Blind," or "What Voice at Moth Hour," or "Vermont Ballad: Change of Season" (all from *Rumor Verified: 1979–1980*) which last poem may close out this attempt—under the stimulus of Calvin Bedient's book—to appreciate Warren's largeness and variety as a poet. "Vermont Ballad: Change of Season" is Hardyesque, even down to its diction and situation, as it begins

<pre>
      All day the fitful rain
      Has wrought new traceries,
      New quirks, new love-knots, down the pane.

      And what do I see beyond
      The fluctuating gray
      But a world that seems to be God-abandoned—
</pre>

Last leaf, rain-soaked, from my high
Birch falling, the spruce wrapped in thought,
And the mountain dissolving rain-gray to gray sky.

The flux in its "brilliantly flashing red / Through all flesh, in vein and artery webbed" has now turned "viscous and gray" and the poet asks, dispiritedly, "But who is master here? / The turn of the season, or I? / What lies in the turn of the season to fear?" The answer comes in the poem's final tercets, which effect an imaginative "turn" that is made, as in Hardy's lovely "A Light Snow-Fall after Frost," through the advent of another person, somebody out there who simply won't be swallowed up into omnivorous subjectivity of the sort contemplated but rejected by the first of the tercets:

If I set muzzle to forehead
And pull the trigger, I'll see
The world in a last flood of vital red—

Not gray—that cataracts down.
No, I go to the windowpane
That rain's blurring tracery claims as her own,

And stare up the mountain track
Till I see in the rain-dusk, trudging
With solid stride, his bundle on back,

A man with no name, in the gloom,
On an errand I cannot guess.
No sportsman—no! Just a man in his doom.
In this section such a man is not an uncommon sight.
In rain or snow, you pass, and he says: "Kinda rough tonight."

Such a not uncommon sight, and such an unmemorable thing to say (almost as bad as Wordsworth's Leech-gatherer) about the weather at a "change of season" that had sunk the poet into such gloom, is as welcome to the reader as to Warren himself. His achievement in poetry has been to pay attention memorably to no more than "Just a man in his doom."

Salmagundi, no. 72 (Fall 1986)

Donald Hall's Poetry

❧

"MIRROR, MIRROR, ON THE WALL, / Who is Donald Andrew Hall?" begins an early, short poem by the subject in question. There is an easy answer: Donald Hall has been for four decades one of the most thorough literary professionals in America. Author of many books of poems (*Old and New Poems,* published in 1990, collects the shorter ones that he wishes to keep), he has also written a number of elegantly shaped prose reflections of which *Life Work* is the latest. Children's books, a poetry textbook, a volume of short stories, and a richly anecdotal and shrewd consideration of some poets from this century (*Their Ancient Glittering Eyes,* which appeared in 1991) are further items in the steady work of forty years. He has won prizes and traveled to China, Japan, and India giving readings with his wife, the poet Jane Kenyon.

The career surely appears to be a highly successful one. Yet somehow Hall doesn't very often show up in the anthologies. Born in 1928, he is part of an impressive list of American poets who greeted the world in the years 1926–1929, a list that includes Snodgrass, Ammons, Merrill, Creeley, Ginsberg, Wagoner, O'Hara, Bly, Kinnell, Ashbery, Merwin, Wright, Levine, Sexton, Rich, Howard, and Hollander, all of whom, with the exception of Hall, are

The Museum of Clear Ideas, by Donald Hall. New York: Ticknor & Fields, 1993. *Life Work,* by Donald Hall. Boston: Beacon Press, 1993.

represented in *The Norton Anthology of Modern Poetry.* Nor does he figure in *The Norton Anthology of American Literature,* nor in Helen Vendler's *Harvard Book of Contemporary American* Poetry. (He has not refrained from taking the occasional lively swipe at both Norton and Vendler.)

The result of this exclusion, perhaps the assumption behind it, is that here in the 1990s Hall is still thought of as essentially a fifties poet who edited (with Robert Pack and Louis Simpson) an influential anthology, *New Poets of England and America* (1957) that was taken as celebrating what Randall Jarrell called the era of "The Poet in the Gray Flannel Suit." In the anthology Hall represented himself by foursquare poems in rhyme and stanza such as "My Son My Executioner" and "The Body Politic" ("I shot my friend to save my country's life"), which ended rather heavily in portentous wisdom. When Jarrell reviewed Hall's first book, *Exiles and Marriages,* in 1956, he called the poems "commonplace"; and somehow that notion of Hall's work has stuck around. Whatever poetry colleagues like Ammons and Creeley, Ashbery and Rich are, they aren't commonplace, and I suspect that the contrast did Hall's reputation no good. Yet the first entry under "commonplace" in the *Oxford English Dictionary* is "a passage of general application." In this sense I would say that Hall's books over the years, especially his most recent ones, bear out such a charge by illustrating what it means to be human.

The Museum of Clear Ideas consists mainly of "Baseball," a long poem divided into innings and extra innings, and a sequence of short poems titled "The Museum of Clear Ideas," subtitled "Or Say: Horsecollar's Odes." *Life Work* is short, consisting of two equal sections of prose, the first of which gives us various thoughts on the subject of work and, in economical but telling detail, sketches out Hall's daily labor as a writer. The second section begins, shockingly, with his discovery, having written a chunk of the new book, that he has metastasized cancer of the liver and will need to have it removed if he hopes to survive. *Life Work* ends with Hall, after the operation, telling us that from now on he will undertake only short-term projects since, in the book's final and very moving sentence, "There is only one long-term project."

It is interesting to note that William Arrowsmith, in a review of Hall's first book of poems, called it entertaining, "a handsome first book," but was also hard on it, asserting that most of its poems sounded "as though Mr.

Hall were an old man, in deep control of dead experience, and nowhere capable of surprise." That was a harsh but pertinent thing to say about a manner that the young poet had taken on too quickly. In an interview many years later, Hall himself admitted that he no longer knew the person who wrote, for example, "My Son My Executioner" (first called "Epigenethlion") with its "meter, rhyme, paradox, irony, abstraction." But, he said, he can still recognize and hear himself in the poems "associated with Surrealism" that he began to write in the late 1950s. And he mentions Robert Bly and James Wright as poet-friends who were also at that time moving beyond iambics and irony into free verse and fantasy—as in "The Long River," the first such poem Hall wrote in this mode:

> The musk ox smells
> in his long head
> my boat coming. When
> I feel him there,
> intent, heavy,
>
> the oars make wings
> in the white night,
> and deep woods are close
> on either side
> where trees darken.
>
> I rowed past towns
> in their black sleep
> to come here. I passed
> the northern grass
> and cold mountains.
>
> The musk ox moves
> when the boat stops,
> in hard thickets. Now
> the wood is dark
> with old pleasures.

What part of himself did Hall still hear in this little poem? Surely the syllabics that have been—and, in the new volume of poems, still are—an important part of his technique, making the free verse decidedly not slack.

Perhaps he also heard a sensibility (if you can "hear" sensibility) less rigid, less abstract and tightly controlled than the early poems manifested.

HERE one's personal taste comes to the fore, and I confess that I don't find much sustenance in these poems of the surreal, deep-image variety that Hall wrote in the 1960s. Their deliberate sacrifice of tonal range and variety in the interest of something less personal, more "universal" or psychologically profound seems to me a bad trade-off, even though writing them enabled Hall to move beyond the Yvor Winters-like cast of certain early poems. (Hall has a fine memoir of Winters, with whom he studied at Stanford, in *Their Ancient Glittering Eyes.*) At any rate there is a consensus, correct I think, that Hall's emergence as a truly interesting, humanly satisfying poet coincided with his abandoning an academic career at the University of Michigan and moving to his grandparents' house in New Hampshire.

The title poem from *Kicking the Leaves,* published not long after that move, has a leisured spaciousness to it. There is a deepened, elegiac sense of life looked back on (Hall was about to turn fifty), but also a spirit of acceptance and celebration, as in the poem's final section:

> Face down, I swim into the leaves, feathery,
> breathing the acrid odor of maple, swooping
> in long glide, to the bottom of October—
> where the farm lies curled against winter, and soup steams
> its breath of onion and carrot
> onto damp curtains and windows; and past the windows
> I see the tall bare maple trunks and branches, the oak
> with its few brown weathery remnant leaves,
> and the spruce trees, holding their green.

The long lines manage to incorporate a sweep of sound that feels supple and ongoing. A number of poems from *Kicking the Leaves* and its successor volume, *The Happy Man* (1986)—"Names of Horses," "Stone Walls," "Traffic," "Twelve Seasons," and "The Day I Was Older"—were the best ones that Hall had written. Undergirded by their rhythms and their sonorities, they also exhibit an effective prose sense, vindicating Pound's insistence that poetry should be at least as well written as good prose. Hall had already produced such prose in his memoir of his New Hampshire grandparents on the farm (*String Too Short to Be Saved,* 1961), and he would go on to write more of it in *Seasons at Eagle Pond* (1986), an admirably poised account of his and Jane Kenyon's life there. The poems that he was writing were now continuous with his reflections in prose, and the only notably adverse criticism of the poems or the prose was directed at their picturesque rural nostalgia. Yet nostalgia and rural picturesqueness helped make Hall's poems attractively what they are.

The charge that Hall is, on occasion, too soft and too sweet cannot be brought against his long poem in three parts, *The One Day* (1989), which some have thought the height of his achievement. I'm not convinced that those three parts have the feel of a truly inevitable sequence, but what's noteworthy about *The One Day* is its bite, a sardonic humor that from time to time surfaces into bitterness, as in these lines from its third section ("To Build a House") about corrupt housebuilding in latter-day New England:

> Buy fifty acres of pasture from the widower:
> Survey, cut a road, subdivide: bulldoze the unpainted
> barn, selling eighteenth-century beams with bark
> still on them: bulldoze foundation granite that oxen sledded:
> bulldoze stone walls set with lost skill; bulldoze the Cape
> the widower lived in: . . .
> Build weekend houses
> for skiers and swimmers; build Slope 'n' Shore; name the new
>
> road Blueberry Muffin Lane, build Hideaway Homes
> for executives retired from pricefixing for General Electric
> and migrated north out of Greenwich to play bridge
> with neighbors migrated north out of Darien. Build huge
> centrally heated Colonial ranches—brick, stone and wood
> confounded together—on pasture slopes that were white
> with clover, to block public view of Blue Mountain.

Heretofore Hall mainly had kept his "deep" feelings separate from his ironic-satirical ones, but they are together now and give his tone a darker, more fantastic coloring than it previously showed. It sounds a bit like a New England version of Ginsberg's *Howl*.

THE combining of feelings in an irony that goes deep is even more satisfyingly present in *The Museum of Clear Ideas*, especially in the title poem, which consists of thirty-eight odes written by one Horsecollar (Horace Horsecollar was a minor Walt Disney character). Lacking Latin, Hall informs us in a note, Horsecollar undertakes to follow the original Horace visually by reproducing the number and shape of stanzas in Horace's first book of odes. The resultant poems don't just look like their Horatian counterparts, they are written in syllabics as well. It is an amazing tour de force. Hall, who wrote a profile of Marianne Moore, herself a mistress of syllabic verse, succeeds here in writing quantitative verse in English that is not only correct but extremely readable.

The poems are further related to their classical predecessors at the level of subject and content. Horsecollar's fifteenth ode, for example, models itself on Horace's "Pastor cum traheret per freta navibus," in which Paris, speeding back to Troy with Helen, is suddenly held up for instruction as Nereus checks the winds and prophesies what will come of their adultery. Horsecollar's ode is titled "When the Young Husband" and gives us this man picking up "his friend's pretty wife" for lunch and a first afternoon of passion in a hotel room. As the car, like Paris's ship, stops in traffic, "Prophecy" speaks: "The misery you undertake this afternoon / will accompany you to the ends of your lives." After proceeding to unravel the scene to come ("the first / kiss with open mouths, nakedness, swoon, thrust-and-catch; / endorphins followed by endearments"), "Prophecy" provides a longer vista of events:

> Then, by turn: tears, treachery, anger, betrayal;
>   marriages and houses destroyed;
>
> small children abandoned and inconsolable,
>   their foursquare estates disestablished forever.

It is an arresting poem, made more so by a strategy that Hall practices in many of the odes, that of having Horsecollar's poem come to a seeming end, only to be followed, after a break, by a further reach of words (no Horatian equivalent for these) that contradict or present an alternate perspective to the one just stated. In "When the Young Husband" the answering voice begins

> Or say: Why this whining? You liked
> your nooky well enough, back when
> you had your teeth. . . .

and proceeds to insist on how much the "You" enjoyed his adulteries—how much the energy of his middle years was devoted to "security measures: / maildrops, codes and safehouses." It concludes with a nasty but telling question:

> Do you croon guilt's anthem now
> —after twenty years of diligence
> and a gold watch—because your bald
> agent retires from the company?

THE long poem "Baseball" is a more relaxed and genial venture than either *The One Day*, or the Horsecollar odes. It is built on the conceit of the poet explaining the game to an outsider, specifically Kurt Schwitters, the Dadaist collagist. Each of the nine "innings" into which the poem is divided contains nine stanzas of nine lines, every line with nine syllables. This quite extraordinary prosodic feat is all the greater for its being unobtrusive; the poem moves swiftly, yet seems to be taking its time:

> All winter aged ballplayers try
> rehearsing their young manhood, running
> and throwing in Florida's sunshine:
> they remain old. In my sixtieth
> year I wake fretting over some new
> failure. . . .

The trick is to talk about baseball in terms of life and vice versa. The trick, in other words, is metaphor, saying one thing while meaning another:

> The bodies of major league baseball
> players are young. We age past the field
> so quickly; we diminish, watching
> over decades, observing the young
> as they dodder. . . .

The poem's speaker is called "K. C." (as in At The Bat) and sounds like Donald Hall; he has a wife, Jennifer (Jane Kenyon, scarcely in disguise) and lives in rural New Hampshire. There is no attempt to effect a separation between the man who suffers and enjoys, and the mind that creates. Yet the cool, humorous but genuinely exploratory way in which Hall treats his material serves as a check against sentimentality and mawkish self-revelation. It is a matter of taste and judgment, both qualities on ample display here as sometimes they are in baseball.

After the nine innings conclude, we have the astringent interruption of Horsecollar's odes, and then, in an excellent stroke of judgment, the book ends with three "Extra Innings." As the game lengthens, so does Hall's poetic line, from ten- to eleven- to the twelve-syllable line of the final inning. The analogy between games of baseball and games of poetry is established through lore appropriate to each; but if you don't pick up on all that lore, you're not condemned to exclusion from the reading experience. That is, you may not know anything about the Red Sox or Dwight Evans ("Kurt, last night Dwight Evans put it all / together") and you may recognize precious little about syllabic verse. Still, I think the main rhythms and tones and sense of "Baseball" come through.

The twelfth and final inning, ending the book, coincides in time with the fall of 1991, and the poem's tone deepens beyond the chatty, sharp wit of earlier innings or the asperities of the Horsecollar odes. Inning twelve is elegiac, and, though Hall from his early days as a poet has been prone to elegy, he has now earned the right to it:

> Today as the leaves fall
> red and amber, our town's yellow schoolbus returns
> up the gravel road in a mild September rain
> for the waiting child who wears his yellow slicker
> and carries last year's beat-up Big Bird lunchbox, first
> day of school. Chill nights at Fenway bring April back
> with annual ironies of remembered dreams
> and retrospective foresight—as gardens go down
> behind the house, under the hill. Here Jennifer
> last spring raised a wild dazzlement of daffodils,
> and under the high sun of July prodigious
> peonies of privacy; whiter than winter:
> where buttercups flourished by a stony wellhead,
> now dry stalks wither. . . .

As Hurricane Bob shuts down Fenway Park two days in a row,

K. C. monitors a possible recurrence
by checking the level of his blood's CEA
each quarter, raising anxiety to lose it
for three months more of Jennifer's shorts, poetry,
and baseball. My father is thirty-five years dead,
buried on Christmas Eve. . . .

Coleridge once exclaimed, "All the images rose up before me as life," and something like this occurs at moments in reading Hall—the illusion that we're dealing not with words on the page, artfully arranged, but with life itself, the very thing. The poem has reference.

The end of *The Museum of Clear Ideas* leads us directly to *Life Work,* about which not much needs to be said except that, as the author remarks near its close, "This book ends otherwise than it started." So do all books, yet it may be that this one is shorter than originally conceived because of the cancer surgery in which Hall loses "two-thirds of my liver and nine-tenths of my complacency." Shorter or not, it is "otherwise," in that halfway into the book, with its hero under the knife, the reading and writing stakes seem to have been raised. "Keep your health and woik, woik, woik," said his Connecticut grandfather Hall. With health not exactly kept—though the operation is successful—the life work of writing takes on an even greater burden of urgent necessity, so that when we read once more about grandfather Wesley Wells's day on the farm, or of the "women's work" done by his wife, Kate, we see also that writing about this is the only alternative to weeping. You can't watch the Red Sox day and night.

WHAT makes *Life Work* invigorating, a book on the side of life rather than the other thing, is a saving, tough humor that reminds us of Horsecollar's Odes, though it is less programmatic. While Hall waits to be admitted to the hospital for the operation, his wife bumps into an acquaintance "who is possibly (in the argot of Carlton Fisk) 'dumb as a stick.'" The acquaintance asks her about their health, and after she tells him her husband's situation, the man mumbles to her—"with a musing, faraway look in his eyes—'I never did get to know Don, the way I wanted to.'" Hall's apt comment on the whole thing is, "Oh, it's a burden for us *morituri*, the way we frighten everybody." At another moment, taking the dog for a walk, he is annoyed to find himself still working, forming sentences like "leaves that mark the dirt underneath with their bright signatures." He tells himself to shut up and stop the writing for a while. Doubtless salutary advice, so long as he stops it only for a while. Near the beginning of the book Hall expresses the hope that he is doing his "Best Work—although I understand that it is unlikely at sixty-three and a half." Unlikely it may be, but in *The Museum of Clear Ideas* and *Life Work* this is exactly what Donald Hall has done, and we are the beneficiaries.

New Republic, February 14, 1994

Donald Davie as Critic of Modern Poets

❦

I BEGAN TO READ Donald Davie's criticism a little more than thirty years ago, as a graduate student with a special interest in modern American and British poetry. I had confidence in my own ear for rhythm and was inclined to complain about poets who seemed to lack it—the ear, the rhythm; but my assumptions about who mattered most in the modern scene were the result of valuations inherited mainly from the current marketplace, as shaped by some powerful critics. In my case those valuations derived from reading (and rereading) F. R. Leavis, R. P. Blackmur, and Randall Jarrell. From Leavis—and from Cleanth Brooks as well—there were the authoritative arguments made, so they seemed, for the central achievements of Eliot and Yeats, writers who were further elucidated and complicated by Blackmur's essays on them. (Blackmur also made the case for Pound's importance—Leavis seemed interested only in "Mauberley.") Both Blackmur and Jarrell had written engagingly and convincingly about Wallace Stevens and Marianne Moore; while Jarrell—alone of the three, and with what in the early 1950s was still a minority opinion—provided strong appreciations of Frost and of William Carlos Williams. I knew Frost, Eliot, and Yeats well; Stevens and Williams less so; Pound and Moore not very well at all. But I believed in cultivating a catholic taste, and when I soon began to teach courses in modern poetry these poets (joined by Hardy, Hart Crane, and Auden) figured in various combinations and juxtapositions. During the years when I began to ply my critical wares, first in the classroom and later in print, it was Davie's voice as I encountered it in books, essays, and reviews that presented me with the liveliest, most challenging invitations to reconsider my assumptions and opinions about these poets. Or at least—which is of course not "least" at all—to try to emulate his example of, in Eliot's words about Aristotle from *The Sacred Wood*, "intelligence itself swiftly operating the analysis of sensation to the point of principle and definition."

A way of pointing to the salience of Eliot's phrase in regard to Davie's criticism is to note how rarely he has practiced that criticism for its own sake; that is, he seldom composes a piece of practical criticism of a modern poem, or of a poet's oeuvre, in which he is content merely to be appreciative—simply to render what it felt like to read the poet or the poem. "The point of principle and definition" has been something ever present to his mind, and even when he seems to be concerned with interpreting a text—as in the essay on Stevens's long poem "The Auroras of Autumn"—a defined principle emerges from the analysis. In the case of "Auroras," Davie discovered that it was not the "assured masterpiece" he at first thought it to be; that all its parts were not equally fine, and that "specious concreteness and facile alliteration" coexisted along with passages of undeniable splendor. The "principle" here was that, contrary to the reverent assumption accorded Stevens by many critics or acolytes, every part of a long (or a shorter) poem was not invariably "great," even when composed by Stevens.

Another way of noting this inclination to move off from appreciation toward "principle and definition" is to identify the air of tendentiousness, at least of vigorous argumentativeness, in Davie's prose style. One of his favorite ways to begin a sentence is with the strong conjunction "For," as may be exemplified in the early pages of *Purity of Diction in English Verse* where sentences like the following occur: "For the greater part of any language consists of so-called 'dead' metaphors"; "For just as law is consistent, inflexible and determinate . . . so language is fixed and determinate"; "For such poetry, by exploiting 'rhythm, sound, music' . . . may revivify metaphors gone dead"; "For if the poet who coins new metaphors *enlarges* the language, the poet who enlivens dead metaphors can be said to *purify* the language." In later writings he modified this habitual opening gambit, but it serves as indication of the brisk assertiveness he brought to deal with both his subject and his readers.

Davie's style—the way he puts things—shapes what gets said in his criticism. Although he was not averse to criticizing the Leavis from whom he learned so much (see particularly his "Second Thoughts: F. R. Leavis's 'How to Teach Reading'"), he has also spoken memorably about what makes it exciting to read the man—not just, Davie says, as a critic but as an *author*. Reviewing Leavis's *Anna Karenina and Other Essays* he wrote that "even if these essays were as heterogeneous as they seem at first glance, the very idiosyncratic style would make a unity of them." And pointing to the thorough colloquialism of Leavis's writing, he noted:

> It is the colloquialism which makes the writing as a whole, and especially the syntax, difficult. And it is the difficulty, the corrugation of the style, which gives the writing substance and savour. The author wrestles—with his subjects certainly, but no less, and by that very token, with himself. The voice (for this is English as spoken) is utterly distinctive. And that is why it is utterly right for us to wrestle also; we wrestle with the man, not just with what the man has said.

Nothing could be further from the donnish dismissal of Leavis as one who didn't know how to write English. Davie's statement is a wonderfully just perception to have had about Leavis's style; and though the wrestling figure is not the right one to characterize our relation to a voice as urbane and usually as good-humored as Davie's (though it, too, is "English as spoken"), still that voice actively engages us, invites and challenges us to assent to its arguments as it briskly marshals and conducts them along.

Urbane and good-humored as he so often is, Davie can be devastatingly abrupt toward work he finds shabby. At such moments he feels no necessity to cite chapter and verse to prove his case, but simply quotes lines for us to read, then assumes the case is proven. In a review of Williams's last volume, *Pictures from Brueghel,* Davie identifies what he calls "a poetics of ad-libbing" through which various "figures" are named by way of approaching, circuitously, a subject. In Williams those figures are often flowers, the more cherished as they are fetched from unpoetical places ("the waste lot, the rubbish heap, the suburban bypass"). But Davie goes on to point out: "In these later pieces we are more often disconcerted by figures such as flowers which by our standards are very poetical indeed. Not only asphodel but daisies, mustard-flowers, jonquils and violets, even, and indeed especially, roses—flowers, or rather the names of flowers, are all over the place. The device is at its lamest in 'The Pink Locust'":

> The poet himself,
>   what does he think of himself
>   facing his world?
> It will not do to say,
>   as he is inclined to say:
>   Not much. The poem
> would be in that betrayed.
>   He might as well answer—
>   "a rose is a rose
> is a rose" and let it go at that.
>   A rose *is* a rose
>   and the poem equals it
> if it be well made.

About this passage he comments: "This is something worth saying. But the way of saying it! From whatever standpoint this is surely wretched writing, ad-libbing at its most poverty-stricken." The persuasiveness of the comment comes importantly from our sense that not just a critic but a poet—a writer of poems himself—has thrown up his hands in words like *lament* and *wretched* that he has no choice but to use. As with the urbane and good-humored presence encountered elsewhere, Davie's terse dismay or disgust, no less than his urbane good humor, emerges through a speaking voice—though with a different accent from Leavis's contorted, contracted one—that is unmistakable. The voice is sometimes capable of speaking with a fine contempt, as in a parenthetical reference to Richard Howard's pretentious *Alone with America*, "wherein America, a whore with a full engagement-book, gets to have forty-one living poets alone with her, one after another." This is about as memorably sharp as he allows himself to become, and for that reason is all the more to be treasured.

As a critic of major British and American poets who wrote before World War II, some of them on into the 1960s, Davie evidences even-handedness in the way he seasons any praise of a writer's achievement by pointing out what that achievement excludes or cannot give us. Here I want to bring together, since they are widely scattered, his commentaries on six of these poets—Hardy, Pound, Yeats, Eliot, Stevens, and Williams. Frost and Hart Crane seem never to have engaged him, and except for an excellent short essay on Robert Graves and some comments on D. H. Lawrence, British poets from the 1920s and 1930s are also absent from his purview—for example there is scarcely a word about Auden. It should first be said that because Davie is a poet-critic, his critical approach to the whole matter of "technique" is slanted toward the needs and inclinations of the reader who is also a poet, rather than one who is solely a critic (most likely an academic). At one point he declared himself on this matter by writing a rejoinder to Leavis's essay "How to Teach Reading," itself a rejoinder to Pound's "How to Read." Davie took issue with Leavis (and stood firm with Pound) on two basic issues, the second of which concerned the matter of "frequenting" (Leavis's word) other literatures and how large a part translations of those literatures should play in literary education. Davie maintains with Pound that if we don't—and we usually don't—have the requisite language to read a text, we should actively seek out whatever good translations of that text exist. But the first point of divergence from Leavis was more complicated. Leavis had maintained that literary technique should be studied and judged only "in terms of the sensibility it expresses"; thus he rejects Pound's conception of a technique that could be studied in this or that book: in Pound's words, "not . . . the books that have poured something into the general consciousness, but . . . books that show *how* the pouring is done, or display the implements, newly discovered, by which one can pour."

As a poet who himself learned much from Pound's tips about writing and writers, Davie draws the line against Leavis, the poet against the critic, when he says about the latter's notion of "technique" that "if we take it literally, it must mean that no poet, for instance, can learn any more, or any differently, from a previous poet, than a reader can learn. And surely, this is clearly untrue." By the end of the essay, he admits that Pound's title was misleading, since "How to Read" was really a guide for writers, not readers; and he concludes with this interesting question and its consequences: "Must we, in order to be good readers of the poetry of the past, put ourselves in the position of a poet of the present? . . . if this is what is required of the reader, he must adopt a high-handed and predatory attitude to the past intolerably presumptuous in anyone else. . . . I doubt very much whether in fact any person who is not a poet (professionally, I mean, with all seriousness) can put himself imaginatively in the situation of one who is." He does not end the essay by declaring unequivocally that yes, we must put ourselves in such a position and can do so only if we are professional poets; yet if I read the passage correctly, the force of its rhetoric is such as to suppress the conditional "if" and make us admire, even as we fail to measure up to, the strong-reader-as-poet.

As far as I can judge, however, Davie's trenchant criticisms of the moderns cannot be understood—and to that extent discounted—as the attitudes of a poet-critic partial to certain habits of verse writing and averse to others on the basis of whether they confirm or deny his own practice as a poet. We don't, that is—or don't except upon reflection and abstraction—shake our heads knowingly at one of Davie's particular critical judgments, having anticipated it because of something we knew the poet in him is already committed to. Rather, those who cannot (as I cannot) put themselves in the situation of the professional poet can nonetheless entertain and test the specific judgments about specific poets and poems without feeling at all excluded. Davie's are not high-toned pronouncements by one poet upon another, but just the opposite; in his critical style he is always aware that there is a reader to be addressed and, if possible, persuaded. I can think of no other critic in whom the social dimension of criticism comes so much to the fore.

Let us test these assertions by looking at what he has had to say about Wallace Stevens, one of the modern poets who might seem relatively peripheral to his interests. The occasion for his first writing about Stevens—altogether he wrote only a few short pieces about him—was Faber's publication in England of *Selected Poems* in 1953. Davie begins then by assuring English readers, many of whom he presumes will not know Stevens's work well or at all, that this is a poet to be mentioned in the same breath with Eliot and Yeats and Pound. A large claim to make for Stevens at that time, even in America, yet after making it he does not proceed, as might be expected in a more conventional critic, to attempt a statement of Stevens's value by showing how it is illustrated in the poems from the selection. Instead he quotes, in its entirety, the second stanza of "Le Monocle de Mon Oncle," and—following a remark of Yvor Winters about the line "Shall I uncrumple this much-crumpled thing"—points to some of its felicities. After this brief example of Stevens's density as a rhetorician, Davie quotes, again in its entirety, the eleventh, penultimate stanza:

> If sex were all, then every trembling hand
> Could make us squeak, like dolls, the wished-for words.
> But note the unconscionable treachery of fate,

That makes us weep, laugh, grunt and groan, and shout
Doleful heroics, pinching gestures forth
From madness or delight, without regard
To that first, foremost law. Anguishing hour!
Last night, we sat beside a pool of pink,
Clippered with lilies scudding the bright chromes,
Keen to the point of starting, while a frog
Boomed from his very belly odious chords.

About this Davie writes: "This is thoroughly late-Victorian, poor Browning or poor Meredith. Activity masquerades as agility; violence as energy; it is hectic and monotonous. Refusal to use abstractions brings about locutions neither abstract nor concrete, but fussy blunt gestures. . . . And the point is that this stanza differs from the stanza about the red bird, only in degree. The stuff is the same, and in the later stanza it has been worn threadbare, that's all." Surely at this point Davie's English reader (or any reader for that matter) might feel confused: how can such a writer be mentioned in company with Yeats, Eliot, and Pound?

The question, or rather the doubt, is not removed when Davie later speaks of "Le Monocle"'s "precious title" and says that for all the poem's "jazzy superficialities" it is nonetheless old-fashioned. Contrasted with the organization in work by Eliot or Pound, that of Stevens is discursive, moving from point to point while the reader tries to keep hold of the thread, to follow along. Further, and in the main, for Stevens "the poetry and the meaning do not coincide. To get at the meaning, you have to go *behind* the poetry, whereas if you go behind Eliot's poetry you have gone beyond the meaning too." Unlike *The Waste Land* or "Mauberley" or "Byzantium" you can write a prose paraphrase of "Le Monocle." In an account that—like earlier remarks about the "If sex were all" stanza—sounds adversely critical of Stevens's method, Davie claims that "the gorgeousness, we cannot help but feel, was laid on afterwards, the flesh upon the skeleton, the clothes on top of that." It recalls, he says, at its best, Keats in his odes; at its worst, some "uninspired Victorian imitating the Keatsian manner"—at which point he quotes, without further comment, a famous moment from "Sunday Morning": "Death is the mother of beauty; hence from her, / Alone, shall come fulfilment to our dreams / And our desires." Presumably Davie had in mind some "uninspired" mythical Victorian poet ringing the changes on Keats's line from "Ode on Melancholy"—"She dwells with Beauty—Beauty that must die."

I am not concerned to defend or argue with these judgments, nor with the essay's main point that Stevens's poetry is "a poetry of excess, among other things of rhetoric in excess of meaning, rhetoric for its own sake, for its 'essential gaudiness.'" (To make this less of an accusation, Davie reminds us that we might also say this, sometimes, about Shakespeare, especially the Shakespeare of the sonnets.) What is challenging and perhaps also a bit perverse about such an approach to Stevens is that Davie ends the essay insisting that he is "profoundly grateful" for the beauty this poet "so generously provides": "Only if that point is taken, can I go on to admit that, for my own part, I think the very greatest poetry is more chaste, less florid than this. It would seem to follow that I prefer an ethic more austere, a heroism less confounded with 'panache.' That inference, too, I do not refuse. Yet it is Stevens's achievement that whenever we pick up his poems, he makes such reservations seem graceless and niggling. He is a great poet indeed." That adjective ("great") he would use again later when he reviewed the *Collected Poems,* even as he claimed that they also manifested "the absence of any sheerly rhythmical interest."

Purity of Diction in English Verse, Davie's first book of criticism, was published the same year as the essay on Stevens's "essential gaudiness"; thus we understand the use of "chaste" as a term of praise. At the same time he was writing the unflorid poems that would soon be published in *Brides of Reason* and *A Winter Talent*—so the professional poet's voice can be heard in these strictures on Stevens. But at the end of the essay Davie does something similar to what Matthew Arnold praised in Edmund Burke: "the return . . . upon himself," in which the mind counters its own principled truth with another truth momentarily even more powerful—in light of which truth previous reservations seem "graceless and niggling." Yet Davie's usefulness as a critic—in this instance as a critic of Stevens—doesn't really lie in his admission or concession that, yes, after all the niggling is said and done, he is still a great poet; rather it lies in the way the niggling shakes up our received ideas. Given the adulation with which Stevens is commonly regarded in the academy today, in America if not in England; and given the refusal of so many books about him to discriminate among his poems (let alone among the different parts of a single poem, as Davie did with "The Auroras of Autumn"), Davie's doubts about Stevens are tonic indeed. And tonic too is the following sentence from a review of the *Collected Poems*, which collection had for him the effect of ironing out Stevens's variety (as Davie found it in *Harmonium*) into "one idiosyncratic, inimitable manner." At the very end of the review comes this: "At the very end of the volume, the unexpected and beautiful recent poem, 'To an Old Philosopher in Rome,' only brings into relief and justifies our weariness with poems purged of all human action and passion, always in a major key, and with only one subject—themselves and the nature of their own operations." This might be the common reader's complaint—if there were such a reader—against Stevens, although made by a very uncommon reader indeed, especially as seen in the light of today's received opinion.

Much of Davie's provocative liveliness as a critic comes from his willingness, even his eagerness, to put the case *against* a poet in order to see what can be determined about the limitations and liabilities of a particular style. If, as is the case with Stevens, the poet is one for whom major claims are made, then the critic may be all the more obliged to test those claims by measuring individual poems against them. But when he writes about a poet for whom such claims are not being made and whose work may be relatively neglected—an Ed Dorn, a George Oppen, a Roy Fisher, a Basil Bunting— then Davie becomes quite benign (and less interesting, since frequently I don't share his high admiration for them). At his combative best, a little like Yvor Winters—whom Davie often quotes, often approvingly—and Randall Jarrell, he can strike through the mask of received ideas about a poet or poem, forcing us to take another look.

There is a nice example of this in a review of the first volume of W. C. Williams's *Collected Poems*. Davie has grave reservations about them, calling Williams "the most embarrassing poet in the language. . . . He doesn't get under our skin; he makes it crawl." Not only does he say what some of us have been saying to our students about "The Red Wheelbarrow" ("which by now has surely bored everyone to tears"); he handles with irreverence comparably sacred items in the Williams oeuvre "This Is Just to Say":

> I have eaten
> the plums
> that were in
> the icebox

and which
you were probably
saving
for breakfast

Forgive me
they were delicious
so sweet
and so cold.

He comments:

> The word for this, the only word for this, is "cute." Technically, if
> we must break a butterfly on a wheel, this little squib is much like
> that other squib "The Red Wheelbarrow": in each case, the ex-
> panses of white page around the printed word enforce . . . a hushed
> portentousness that the words in themselves, whatever the tricksi-
> ness of spacing and lineation, do nothing to earn. This apparently
> (and really) trivial item must have significance, else why is the
> statement of it framed with so much white paper. . . . And of course
> significance is claimed not just for the goodness of plums but for
> the ritual of raiding the icebox, and for the wrist-slapping, smiling
> low tension between modestly affluent man and wife. No wonder
> we all feel cozy with it—until we remember that such coziness is
> hardly the effect aimed at or attained by poets of the past whom
> Williams on occasion measures himself against.

Perhaps to a generation of television watchers, attuned to the lovely woman
who confessedly ate *all* the Frusen-Glädjé and would do it again, Williams's
poem is less of a much-admired novelty than it was to those who have
treated it as close to profound. At any rate, Davie's paragraph appears to me
much more enlivening than the moral appreciation commonly bestowed
upon the poem. And this doesn't mean we must dismiss the "little squib"—
only that we are challenged to say why "squib" isn't the right word for it; or
why "cozy" is the wrong way to describe how we feel about its atmosphere;
or why "hushed portentousness" does not accurately characterize the effect
of those white spaces. The hostile criticism may spark us to defend what we
would otherwise be unlikely to formulate.

To bend a phrase of Harold Bloom's, Davie is a "strong critic" insofar as he does not follow his predecessors, but strikes out instead on lines that swerve from or subvert their ways. Yet he is not "strong" the way, say, Hugh Kenner is, or Bloom himself, each of whom chooses certain modern poets as essential to The Pound Era or The Age of Stevens, while treating others as peripheral or inferior (Pound, Eliot, and Williams figure as such for Bloom; Stevens and Crane for Kenner). Even the moderns Davie is most involved with and most indebted to he approaches with circumspection, as can be seen in the full-length books on Hardy and Pound. Both books struck me on first reading, and still on rereading, as warily circling their subjects rather than—as with Bloom on Stevens, Kenner on Pound or Eliot—making an unambiguous case for an achievement and its centrality. In *Thomas Hardy and British Poetry* Davie argues that Hardy—not Pound or Eliot or Yeats—is the most important presence in contemporary British poetry; and he discusses such contemporaries as Philip Larkin and Kingsley Amis, Jeremy Prynne and Roy Fisher, by way of example. But the book lacks a convincing effort to demonstrate Hardy's greatness as a poet, making the case by the best poems, as a more traditionally evaluative critic like Arnold or Leavis would do. Instead in the opening chapters Davie points out the limitations of Hardy's "engineering" mode of putting poems together, to such an extent that he pays insufficient attention to other poems by Hardy that transcend or reject that mode. (He later pays such attention to the "Poems of 1912–13" in his fine essay "Hardy's Virgilian Purples.") And so the "Hardy" at the center of the book doesn't quite seem to be there as an indispensable poet, rather as one who has just somehow hung on. In *Ezra Pound: Poet as Sculptor,* since we come to Davie's treatment of him in the wake of Hugh Kenner's advocacy, there is similarly no banging of the drums. A case is made for, but also against, the early poems: "Mauberley"— which he has written about more than once—brings out no settled line of judgment but shows the critic changing his mind about how good and what sort of a poem it is; large stretches of the *Cantos* are rejected as impossible to admire. One reads Davie on these poets with the sense that he is discovering something about his subject as he writes—the mood, in Leavis's old phrase, really feels "exploratory-creative." And we cannot read him without participating in the process, bringing to bear our own sense of, or our uncertainties about, various poems.

Davie has written about Pound on so many different occasions that I shall make no attempt here to organize his changes of mind and emphases into a pattern or sequence. (In "Davie and Pound" Bernard Bergonzi has done something on that order.) In fact the primary "pattern" may be an ongoing, often troubled and eloquent expression of the very mixed feelings one should rightly have about Pound's worth. With Yeats, however, in two substantial essays Davie concentrates on discovering a vocabulary with which to describe and praise Yeats's achievement in his "middle" volumes, particularly *The Wild Swans at Coole* and *Michael Robartes and the Dancer*— an achievement that greatly involves their being what Davie calls "models of poetic diction." Again, speaking as the poet-critic, he finds that such models may be useful for contemporary practitioners, even as the later Yeats who wrote "greater" poems like "Among School Children" and the Byzantium ones may conversely lead poets astray. Davie's writing about Yeats is instructive and cool-headed, but it is his response to Eliot's work that I should like to single out and conclude with as demonstration of the enlivening combination of idiosyncrasy and sanity that he brings to the modern poets.

His criticism of Eliot is brief, consisting of an essay on *Four Quartets* ("T. S. Eliot: The End of an Era"), a review of the *Collected Poems 1909–1962* ("Mr. Eliot"), an extended comparison with Pound, which is perhaps his single best essay ("Pound and Eliot: A Distinction"), and a discussion of Eliot as Englishman, with special reference to *Four Quartets* ("Anglican Eliot"). Aside from calling the *Collected Poems* a "fantastic achievement" and pointing out that Eliot had published between hard covers "not a single poem which he now needs to blush about reprinting," Davie is unconcerned with ranking the poems or engaging in a critical survey of Eliot's progress from *Prufrock* to the *Quartets*. Davie's single focus of concern is with the "symbolist" or postsymbolist nature of Eliot's poetry, a commitment—he argues convincingly—much less remote than Yeats's and demonstrating an attitude toward language fundamentally different from Pound's: "Eliot presents himself as pre-eminently a rhetorician, a man who serves language, who waits for language to present him with its revelations; Pound by contrast would master language; instead of serving language he would make it serve—it must serve the shining and sounding world."

Eliot serves language by having it talk "about nothing but itself, continually gnawing its own vitals." As illustration of this process, Davie provides a brilliant reading of the passage from "Burnt Norton" that begins "My words echo / Thus, in your mind": " 'Thus'! Thus? How? What is the connection, the resemblance, thus confidently asserted? Words spoken one by one are like footsteps—well yes; . . . But it turns out that the footsteps never happened, for they are footsteps in a direction which was never taken. So it appears that the poet's words dropping into the silence are like, not any actual footsteps, but only his thoughts of those footsteps." He demonstrates just how assiduously Eliot's language gnaws its own vitals, just how far away from a "real world" of things and events is its verbal remove.

In Davie's terms the "musical" rather than "logical" structure of Eliot's postsymbolist poetry means that on occasion—as in much of "The Dry Salvages"—what seems to him and other readers to be "woolly and incoherent language" (Max Eastman once called a passage from "Ash-Wednesday" "an oily puddle of emotional noises") may be serving larger ends, may be parodic—a moment in a "procedure in which the true key is never sounded," so that all the voices in the poem are somehow "off-key." In "The End of an Era" Davie argues that the *Quartets* represent a state of postsymbolist intricacy and subtlety beyond which it was impossible, indeed undesirable, to go. Looking around him, with himself and other younger poets in mind (it was 1953), he hoped for "something quite different in the offing." Twenty years later he seemed more inclined to dwell with satisfaction on what in the *Quartets* Eliot had given us by combining symbolist music with the most prosaic statement and reiteration. Yet his acceptance of Eliot typically is made with important qualifications, as if to guard against unequivocally thrusting the poem upon us to be swallowed whole: "It is small wonder if the product of such extreme tension is a poem remarkably uneven in tone if not in quality; a poem which has to make a formal virtue out of its own disparities, by inviting us to think that it switches tone only as Beethoven does when he completes a slow movement and embarks upon a scherzo."

Davie closes this account of Anglican Eliot and the *Quartets* on a truly urbane and momentous note by asking how a poet could ever have gotten himself into such a situation, "creating such a tension and attempting to resolve it": "I conceive that this might come about if a poet, compelled by temperament as well as history to school himself in the ironic reticences of Henry James on the one hand and Jules Laforgue on the other, should find himself wanting to speak to and for a nation which conceives of itself as cornered into a situation that is wholly unironical because not in the least ambiguous. For such a poet (who may be wholly imaginary) I should feel affection as well as esteem."

No one has spoken more gracefully and wisely than this about the Eliot of *Four Quartets*. Criticism is among other things a social act, and Davie's criticism of the great modern poets, for all its stringency, is also generously hospitable.

The Last Man of Letters: Julian Symons

❧

I N A 1991 AFTERWORD to *The Rise and Fall of the Man of Letters*, John Gross admits that the title is an exaggeration: "Rise yes—but Fall? Men and women of letters were still with us when this book was first published; they are still with us today." Nonetheless the professionalization of literary studies in the university, the ubiquity of literary theory, and the various "cultural studies" alternatives to literature currently available have indeed issued in what Gross calls, cautiously, "a diminished role" for the species of reader-critic his book catalogues. More incautiously, the Man of Letters might be termed a dying breed, or—as a publican put it about his brethren in a Kingsley Amis novel, "We're a dime breed. Dine out like the dinosaurs." The breed of men of letters suffered a notable and much regretted diminishment in late 1994 when Julian Symons, a shining example of that way of living and writing, died at eighty-two. Novelist, biographer, cultural historian, poet, and indefatigable reviewer of every sort of book, he was, as his friend George Orwell described them in "Why I Write," one of the "minority of gifted, willful people who are determined to live their own lives to the end"—and who do this preeminently through writing.

In my judgment the three foremost English men of letters whose lives more or less spanned this century are Geoffrey Grigson, V. S. Pritchett, and Symons. Grigson died in 1985; Pritchett (now Sir Victor and about to be ninety-five) ceased to publish some years back. But Julian Symons, who began his career writing poems and criticism in the late 1930s, sustained a heavy schedule of literary production to the very end, even after he was diagnosed as terminally ill with cancer. Like Pritchett, he never attended university. Son of an English mother and an emigrant Russian Jewish father whose feckless character included a vagueness as to just exactly what his name was ("Symons" was an adopted Englishy one), Julian was the youngest of four children who grew up in a large house in Clapham, South London. In his memoir, *Notes from Another Country*, he wrote about the stammer which afflicted him as a child, causing him eventually to be sent off for a time to a school for backward children. In fact, his significant "schooling" was really the tutelage of his brother A. J. A. Symons, a truly fabulous character, author of *The Quest for Corvo*, connoisseur and promulgator of rare editions and fine wines, dead at forty-one and the subject of his youngest brother's first and most original biography (*A. J. A. Symons: His Life and Speculations*, 1950). With A.J.'s encouragement and suggestions, Julian read widely and promiscuously, the fruits of which reading may be seen in the calm authority that came to inform his critical writings.

But as a young man of twenty-four, when he brought out the first issue of his little magazine *Twentieth Century Verse*—it ran for two years until the war put paid to such ventures—he struck a rather different tone from the calmly dispassionate one:

> We do not stand on any platform, do not believe that poetry is in some odd way a tributary of politics, or music, or machinery. . . . We are not publishing for Sunday School teachers, nor, on the other hand, are we much interested in such already outworn acrobatic parlour tricks as those of Mr. E. E. Cummings.

A request for subscriptions, sent out to one thousand prospective readers, was responded to by a grand total of nine who were willing to put their four shillings on the line. Symons was undeterred: "We are not a political magazine and do not admit that poetry need be concerned with politics," he wrote in the second issue: "Our object is to print good poems preferably by young poets." As an editor, his model was Grigson, whose magazine *New Verse*, a bi-monthly, had been running since 1933. *New Verse* was still going strong, mainly as a vehicle for publishing the Auden Group and for Grigson to use the "billhook" (as he later called it) on various poetasters and the overpraised undeserving. While *Twentieth Century Verse* was by no means unfriendly to Auden and poets associated with him (there is a good appreciation of Louis MacNeice by Symons in one of the issues), "young poets" like Roy Fuller, D. S. Savage, Ruthven Todd, Gavin Ewart, Kenneth Allott, and Symons himself were given space to display their wares. The magazine was especially interesting, however, for its attention—not uncritical, but sympathetic—to American poetry, as seen in Symons's essay "How Wide Is the Atlantic" and his running of an American poets issue that included Wallace Stevens, Yvor Winters, John Berryman, Theodore Roethke, Conrad Aiken, and others. In 1940 Symons would write one of the first intelligent English appreciations of Stevens, also a balanced piece on Hart Crane as a "failed genius."

But *Twentieth Century Verse*, like Grigson's magazine, is fun to read largely because of the provocative, even cheeky tone in which bad poets were dismissed, as in this bit from a Symons review of three slim volumes by poets now forgotten. "Here are three ways of not writing poems," the notice begins, proceeds to quote examples from each writer, then concludes:

> Mr. Peacock's words are pedantically dull, Miss Stanley-Wrench's words naively dull, Mr. Ford's words sophisticatedly dull. Mr. Pea-cock has been printed by *Scrutiny*, Miss Stanley-Wrench won the Newdigate, Mr. Ford's poems are introduced by W. C. Williams; and there is nothing in their books to balance these serious disadvantages.

How did a young man in his mid-twenties become so assured in the bravura way he laid down pronouncements about what his magazine was for or against and which poets were worthy and which not? Such bravura, which allows no doubt or ambiguity to color the critic's judgments, undoubtedly had to do with Symons's early apprenticeship to the figure he called—in an issue of *Twentieth Century Verse* dedicated to him—"the most valuable and interesting writer of our century." This was Wyndham Lewis, whose "width of vision" Symons particularly admired and whom he saw from time to time during the late thirties. "Meeting Wyndham Lewis," a short memoir he wrote twenty years later, amusingly describes what it was like to have "lunch" with Lewis at the latter's studio in Notting Hill: four hard-boiled eggs, bread, butter, and a bottle of whisky, accompanied by intense conver-sation about ideas, books, and writers. Over the course of his life, Symons wrote on Lewis often, reviewed books by and about him, and noted in an eightieth-birthday interview that the two major influences on him as a young man were Nietzsche and Lewis: "What a pair, some will say—no wonder he came to no good." The nice piece of wit, as it holds one's younger self in humorous perspective, is typical of the benign irony permeating all Symons's writing and distinguishing it from the fierce, sometimes humorless "genius" of Lewis, not to say Nietzsche.

It was through the spirit of Wyndham Lewis that I moved into Julian Symons's orbit. While writing a book on Lewis, I had looked up the issue of *Twentieth Century Verse* devoted to him, and in the course of so doing became interested in Symons as well. When I landed in London in 1968 for a sabbatical year, I sent him a copy of the book with no high expectations of his liking or even reading it. To my great delight he responded almost immediately, saying not only that he liked it very much but would set about to review it, if possible in the *Times Literary Supplement*. He further suggested that we have lunch together and named as our place of meeting The Salisbury, a pub with much ornate glass in St. Martin's Lane, where he and Lewis used to meet. No fear that I should be unable to identify him, he said, just look for "the oldest graybeard in the place." I found him, we had a drink, then went on to a Chinese restaurant where he had booked a table. He showed himself to be both a good trencherman and a companionable drinker, and he picked up the tab. I was exhilarated at what felt like an entrance to literary London, as well as charmed by a combination of intelligence, wit, and human kindness that never diminished in the twenty-six years of friendship to follow.

At this point in his literary career Symons was fifty-six and had turned out an impressive number of books of various sorts. His series of crime novels began in 1945 with the publication of a manuscript his wife, Kathleen, found in a drawer. *The Immaterial Murder Case*, really a sendup of the detective stories, was followed by thirteen others, the latest of which—*The Man Who Killed Himself* (1967)—showed him at the top of his form. These novels were accompanied by a number of nonfiction works. There were biographies of his brother A.J. and of Thomas Carlyle (still an excellent introduction to Carlyle's life and works), and of the now-forgotten journalist and rogue-financier, Horatio Bottomley. There were historical studies of the expedition to relieve General Gordon at Khartoum; of Sir Redvers Buller's campaign in the Boer War; and of the General Strike of 1926. A collection of essays, *Critical Occasions* (1966), contained notable reminiscences of friendships with Lewis and with George Orwell, who had helped set Symons on his journalistic career by recommending him as his replacement for a book column in the *Manchester Evening News*. After two early volumes of verse Symons had ceased to publish poems, though later on he would bring out two small pamphlets of them.

As I began to acquaint myself with his fiction it was with the sense that, rather than reading a bona fide novel—as, say, by Orwell or Graham Greene—I was instead reading a "crime novel," which by the addition of that qualifying adjective made it something less than serious to be engaging in, an activity one might treat oneself to perhaps before dozing off. Symons himself, never one for self-promotion, was offhand and self-deprecating about his contributions as a fictionist. After all, "thrillers," detective fiction, crime stories were lumped together, reviewed separately from "real" novels and usually reviewed by another crime novelist. There was an air of quaintness and indulgence about the whole operation. At any rate, he never suggested to me that I would be missing much if I neglected to read the novels he'd written so far—and there he misled me.

In *Bloody Murder*, Symons's history of the genre ("From the Detective Story to the Crime Novel" is its subtitle), he drew a distinction between "serious novelists" and "entertainers." The former are emotionally involved in their work, offering personal feelings about the world and society; the latter think always and only of what will amuse their audience, thereby eschewing any truck with ideas. But this must be too simple a distinction, since in most good novelists "ideas" and "entertainment" are bound up together in their art. Robert Frost liked to say that he entertained ideas to see if they entertained him. With a few exceptions, Symons's novels, early and later, are consistently entertaining, moving along briskly with executive skill, showing us character through well-registered individual voices that are presided over by a narrator not averse to making mischief. Consider the opening paragraph of *The Man Who Killed Himself*:

> In the end Arthur Brownjohn killed himself, but in the beginning he made up his mind to murder his wife. He did so on the day that Major Easonby Mellon met Patricia Parker. Others might have come to such a decision earlier, but Arthur Brownjohn was a patient and, as all those who knew him agreed, a timid and long-suffering man. When people say that a man is long-suffering they mean that they see no reason why he should not suffer forever.

That final sentence is not only entertaining but offers an idea I'd never entertained before.

Brownjohn, a henpecked husband living with his wife, Clare, in a London suburb, doubles half the week as Major Easonby Mellon, a shady operator who runs a Matrimonial Assistance office in the city. While Brownjohn is supposedly traveling for his electrics firm, he in fact assumes his other life, while pretending to Joan—the woman with whom he lives part of the week in London—that he's in government secret service. Brownjohn is repressed, the slave of Clare; Major Mellon is indulged, sexually and otherwise, by Joan. So it stands until the plot begins to thicken as the attractive Patricia Parker pays a visit to the major in his office, initiating a train of events: "There could be no doubt that two women and two lives presented a problem, especially when a man was really interested in a third." So Brownjohn decides Clare must cease to exist: "A life without Clare! The prospect was almost too heady to contemplate. Contemplating it, he fell asleep." In Symons's best novels, such as this one, the comic perspective is never absent for long. It's partly a matter of narrative tone, partly the incidental but real satisfactions of encountering pleasing expressions and bits of slang that at least this American reader hadn't previously encountered. Someone wondering whether a couple is happy asks if it's all "tickety-boo" with them; cockneyisms have a way of cropping up, like "on your Franchot Tone" (being on your own) or "a bit Harry Groggers" (being tired). There is enlivening energy in the novelist's individual sentences.

After early experiments with the donnish detective story (*Bland Beginning,* 1949), Eric Ambleresque international intrigue (*The Broken Penny,* 1953), and first-person tough-guy narrative à la Raymond Chandler (*The Narrowing Circle,* 1954), Symons settled down to write mainly third-person omniscient narrative with a built-in playful doubleness of tone informing character and atmosphere. For all his modesty to me about how seriously to take his fiction, he insisted later in the interview mentioned above that the best crime fictions were indeed "good novels" that should be reviewed alongside other novels. And he adduced Hammett's *The Glass Key,* Symons's favorite crime story, as comparable to what "serious" novelists like Hemingway and Faulkner were producing at the same time. The point can be made contemporaneously by mentioning Ruth Rendell—whose work Symons admires—as a novelist no less serious and often a good deal more interesting than compatriots like A. S. Byatt or Margaret Drabble or Beryl

Bainbridge. His old friend, the Canadian writer George Woodcock, put the case succinctly in a biographical entry Woodcock once wrote about Symons the novelist:

> He is concerned with the decay of a society, with cultural pretenses, with politics as a corrupting element, with the manners of a world he has made his own: the Bohemian borderland where failed artists and hack writers, advertisement men and broadcasters, and their lesser hangers on, come together to create a setting whose very alienation from moral stability tends to encourage the emergence of crime.

He has learned his lesson from Wyndham Lewis, added Woodcock, perhaps thinking of such alienations from moral stability as Lewis explored in novels like *The Revenge for Love* or *The Vulgar Streak*.

By the 1970s Symons had established himself as an all-purpose reviewer on both sides of the Atlantic, even as his productivity on different fronts, if anything, increased. In 1972, for example, he published his darkest crime novel, *The Players and the Game*, with its acknowledged reference to the Moors Murders. That same year appeared the first edition—there would eventually be three—of *Bloody Murder* (*Mortal Consequences* in this country). Finally, less well known but to my taste thoroughly indispensable, is the too-short memoir, *Notes from Another Country*. The memoir takes a look back at such matters as his adolescence in South London, the days of *Twentieth Century Verse*, his employment at Victoria Lighting and Dynamo company where he worked until, despite his best efforts to avoid it, he was drafted. The brief, unbrilliant career of his army service—cut short because of a botched operation on one arm, after which he was discharged—provides some of the best comic writing in the book. At the end of *Notes from Another Country*, he writes of being sixty and of how much more he looks forward to experiencing and understanding ("postpone that coronary or street accident for another few years if you please"), then concludes with the kind of measured sense of things that informs his work generally. On the whole, he says, he adheres to Montaigne who wrote, "The finest lives are, in my opinion, those which conform to the common and human model in an orderly way, with no marvels and no extravagances." Symons adds, "I have moods in which I do not think this is true: but most of the time I believe it, and then it is a powerful consolation for the fact that I shall never again inhabit the other country about which these notes are written." So when, in the same book, he confesses uncharacteristically that "the thing I regret most in my life is the lack of deep and high creative talent as a writer," it is the exceptional yearning to be marvelous and extravagant that proves the daily orderly rule of writing from 9 AM to 1 PM and produces the steady work accumulating from such a procedure.

ONE evening in the winter of 1974, when I was spending another sabbatical year in London, attempting to lead the Literary Life by getting published in the weeklies, I had dinner with Julian and in a moment of expansiveness suggested he might like to serve a year as Visiting Writer at Amherst College. I was about to become chairman of the English department and thought I could use my power in such a way as to benefit us all. Julian, who had never taught a class in his life, was enthusiastic about the idea, which eventually came to pass—though not without some obstreperous opposition from younger members of the department who didn't agree, evidently, that this elder Brit crime writer was the proper person to inspire young creative writers. Nevertheless it worked out very much for the best. The Symonses came to Amherst in mid-August, spent their first few nights in the momentarily vacant Emily Dickinson house (discovering a dead mouse under the bed on their first morning), and stayed on through the academic year. During it Julian wrote most of his biography of Poe and was also a huge success as a teacher not only of poetry and fiction writing, but of crime fiction. He participated as well in our introductory staff course where, overambitiously, we read everything from Virgil to Matthew Arnold to Flannery O'Connor. In the weekly meetings he was a source of literary knowledge and also provided, from time to time, the needed deflationary comment on overenthusiastic professorial enthusiasms. In an engaging essay written after the fact ("A Year in Academe," in *Critical Observations*, 1981) he poked some fun at our habits but also came away impressed, he wrote, "by a sort of fervour, a sense of dedication to scholarly ideals in the faculty." There was also, to be sure, "a hint of self-conscious superiority" that went with this. But, as one student put it, Amherst was indeed "Camelot" and Julian agreed: "Camelot, given stability and severity by quite a bit of New England highmindedness." This seemed to him, on the whole, "a good recipe for a liberal education."

The Amherst students who took his classes that year were fortunate in their exposure to a working critic, untouched by any academic system or vocabulary, willing to say in response to various undergraduate judgments

and assertions, "Yes, but . . ." This was the true teacher's and critic's principled role and more than once had been recommended as exemplary by
F. R. Leavis. The trouble with Leavis was that his "Yes, but" turned more and
more into "No," as the only response to anyone who saw things differently
from him. By contrast Symons, while giving us nothing like Leavis's re-
valuative essays on major figures in English poetry, fiction, and criticism,
managed to remain flexible and diverse in his critical operations after the
manner recommended by Matthew Arnold. His "A Word on Late Leavis,"
reviewing *Anna Karenina and Other Essays*, was firm in praising the critic
on Tolstoy and Samuel Johnson, but equally firm in deploring his "narrow
dogmatism," "lack of charity," and "failures of imagination and sympathy."
These faults are demonstrated, irrefutably to my mind, in the course of
showing why what was once "passion" in Leavis had turned into "prejudice." A similar narrowing and hardening was precisely what did *not* happen in Symons's own critical work, most of it done in the form of reviews
that will doubtless never see hard covers. As for the English nonacademic
reviewer-critics mentioned earlier, Symons was less flamboyant, violent,
and vindictive than Geoffrey Grigson; but he stayed equally away from the
mildness that informed V. S. Pritchett's refusal to say anything about a
writer unless it was something on the nice side.

The poet in Symons never died out and resurfaced memorably in the two
years that followed the sudden death of his daughter Sarah: the poems that
ensued, privately printed, were a testimony of love and pain, made just bear-
able by being given formal shape. Some years after that, my wife and I traveled for a few days with Julian and Kathleen in the West Country of England,
especially Shropshire. One day as we meandered through a park and paused
to look down at the landscape with the river winding through it, one or the
other of us brought up Housman and Julian began to quote from Housman's
loveliest, most heartbreaking poem, "Tell me not here, it needs not saying":

> Possess, as I possessed a season,
>   The countries I resign,
> Where over elmy plains the highway
>   Would mount the hills and shine,
> And full of shade the pillared forest
>   Would murmur and be mine.

As a writer he never resigned anything, and the last fifteen years of his life
yielded ten works of fiction, among the best of which are *The Blackheath*

Poisonings (1978), *The Criminal Comedy of the Contented Couple* (1985), and *Death's Darkest Face* (1990), his most complex if not most satisfactory thriller. *Playing Happy Families*, which appeared last year, revealed not the least loss of energy or technical inventiveness. Besides these, he brought out among other works of nonfiction, short biographies of Hammett and Conan Doyle, a highly readable and idiosyncratic account of modernism (*Makers of the New*, 1987), and an anthology of Wyndham Lewis's writings with interspersed commentary (*The Essential Wyndham Lewis*, 1989), in which he had his last say about the old Enemy who was his precursor. All manner of awards were bestowed on him as the grandmaster of crime novelists; he traveled extensively (and enthusiastically) to address interested audiences in Sweden, Spain, Hungary, and America.

One of the ways in which he was a true man of letters was by being a splendid correspondent, writing pages filled with everything from gossip and personal disclosures to large literary judgments. A letter to me from 1981 contains a first paragraph thanking for the "hilarious" letter I had written, saying that he and Kathleen laughed not just with me but *at* my attempt to follow a low-sodium diet (it didn't last long) and to save a doomed soap opera, *Search for Tomorrow*, from cancellation. Further down came an account of a Faber publishing party at which both Larkin and Amis were encountered:

> K annoyed with Amis because she said "Hallo" and he replied "Hallo" and nothing more. A failure of recognition? Not possible? Anyway while talking enthusiastically to Lark and Am, I gestured too wildly with a glass of wine and slopped some over Lark's totally white suit—he was wearing white suit and tie, had been to Lords for Test Match. He moved away—quickly without look of pleasure—but actually wrote me polite letter a day or two later saying sorry for abrupt departure.

A paragraph later brought this bit of experience with a physician:

> At several sessions he has taken to expelling my warts with frozen nitrogen which he sprays at me, having first poured it from a large thermos flask into the spraying device, spilling lots of it on the floor where it smokes and sizzles. Spraying away, stop watch in hand to see he doesn't burn my skin away completely, he talks of spondees and dactyls and the benefits of a classical education. A

classy lot, our English specialists. The results are good but not perfect. What's perfect however?

In the last few years he endured a couple of operations, one of them a successful one for colon cancer, and except for some angina and a hearing loss seemed unimpaired when we visited him in England in the fall of 1993. But the following March brought bad news of an inoperable pancreatic malignancy. He said that a book of his crime essays was slated to appear but that he would probably abandon the novel he was halfway through. Then, having given me the bad news, he began a new paragraph by referring to a review of mine I'd sent him: "Not but what it's just about time for me to leave a world in which Pritchard—*Pritchard*—is praising Nicholson Baker and comparing him to Proust and Nabokov." He went on, vigorously, to point out that Baker's art, compared to the two masters, was "of a very different kind, a very inferior kind." Never have I been so satisfactorily chastened, nor moved by a spirit which, in the face of a grim verdict, could still play around with his shocked reader.

About that time, as an octogenarian he had been asked by a London magazine to answer some questions about death, such as what was his "ideal way to go." He answered, "Where should a writer die but at his desk? Ideally, after writing 'the end' to his best book with a pen—no word processor in sight." One was thus pleased to hear that the novel he'd planned to leave half-finished had been completed earlier in the fall. But the end was in sight: in a letter to a young Canadian writer who'd gotten to know and admire him, he wrote:

> This will be in the way of a signing-off letter. . . . I'm now seeing the sign marked EXIT rather distinctly. . . . I live as my brother A.J. said when on the way out, from week to weak. I don't mind about dying, perhaps I have lived long enough. . . . If my health takes an upturn of course you'll hear from me again. If not, look out for the obituaries.

The following day he died suddenly of a heart attack, saved by that from the more drawn-out rigor of death by cancer. As far as I can make out, no person-of-letters is following in his footsteps. Who would be so rash as to try?

American Scholar 65 (1996)

Name Index

❧§❧